Eiléan Ní Chuilleanáin's Female Figures

Eiléan Ní Chuilleanáin's Female Figures

Patricia Boyle Haberstroh

First published in 2013 by
Cork University Press
Youngline Industrial Estate
Pouladuff Road, Togher
Cork, Ireland

British Library Cataloguing in Publication Data
A CIP catalogue record for this book is available from the British Library

ISBN 978–1–85918–498–1

Typeset by Carrigboy Typesetting Services
Printed in Spain by Grafo
www.corkuniversitypress.com

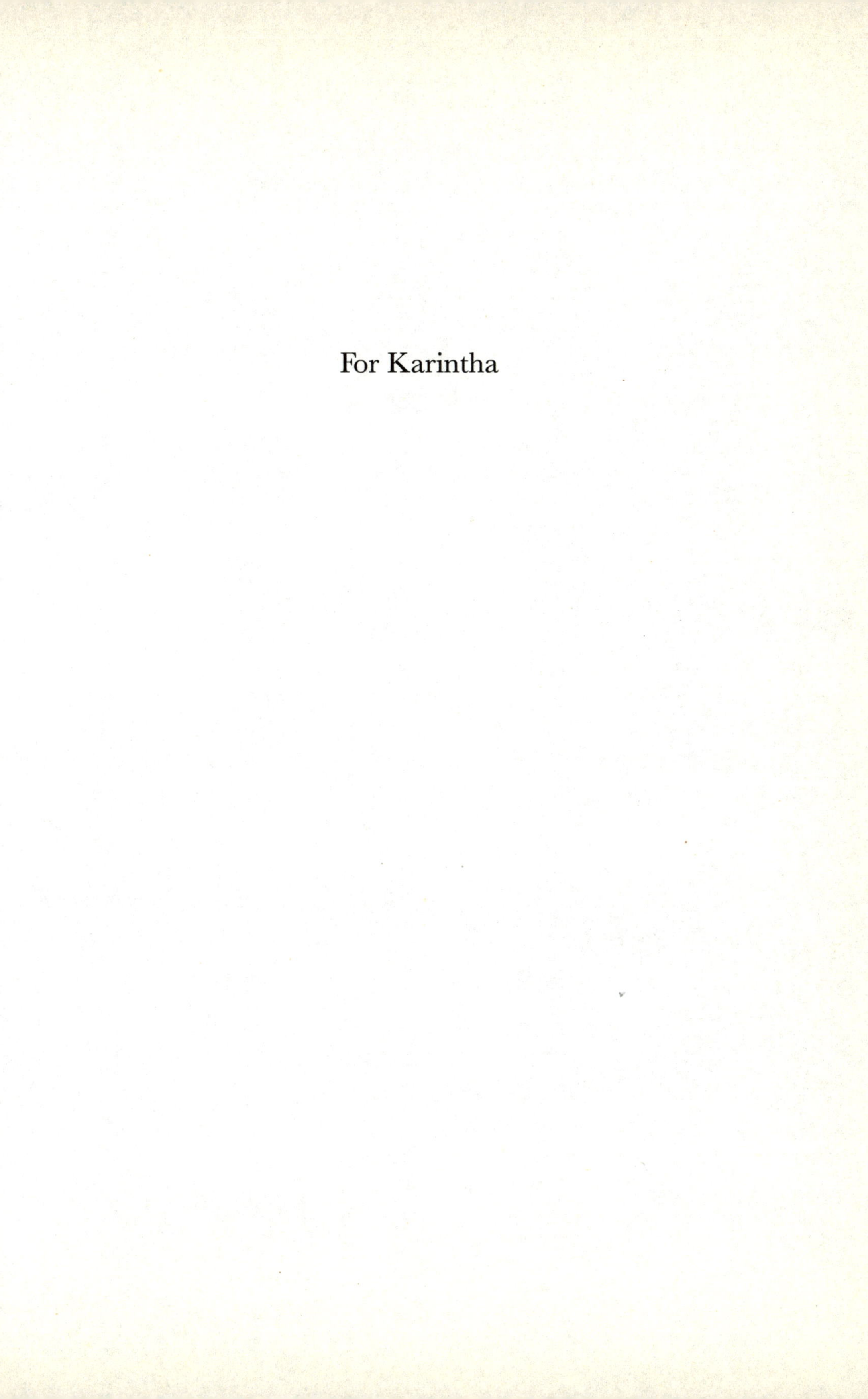

For Karintha

Contents

Acknowledgements

I wish to thank La Salle University in Philadelphia for grants and release from teaching which allowed me to work on this book, and the Fulbright Foundation for a fellowship to begin this work. The Institute of Irish Studies at Boston College Dublin graciously provided me with a fellowship and space for research and writing in Ireland. I wish also to acknowledge the work and help provided by Maria O'Donovan and Aonghus Meaney of Cork University Press. The poems of Eiléan Ní Chuilleanáin are first published by The Gallery Press, Loughcrew, Oldcastle, County Meath, Ireland and are reproduced with kind permission. Eileán Ní Chuilleanáin has been most gracious in talking with me about her poetry. Finally, Charles Haberstroh has provided the encouragement and understanding any partner needs to complete a book.

I suppose that by writing about female figures in what seem to me to be positions of power, strength and control, and also the lack of control, makes me a political writer in that I see these as political issues.

Eiléan Ní Chuilleanáin in an interview
with J. Watson Doering

CHAPTER 1

Beginnings

I know how things begin to happen
But never expect an end
'Early Recollections' (*SP* 24)[1]

Eiléan Ní Chuilleanáin once explained: 'What attracts me is that which I do not know'.[2] Sometimes stepping over boundaries into unknown territory brings enlightenment; however, often Ní Chuilleanáin's subjects and speakers are suspended in liminal states, in what an early poem described as 'waters between' (*RG* 32). Nevertheless, learning the limits of what you can know is valuable knowledge which has its own reward, and the journey is worth the effort. In one of the distinguishing characteristics of Ní Chuilleanáin's work, the re-visioning of the female figure, the impetus comes often from what she does not know, her sense that the lives of women have often been blocked – overlooked or, in history, unrecorded – and that a woman poet is in the unique position of addressing that issue, especially when much about women's lives has been lost. Moreover, the gap between women's lives and the representation of those lives in history or literature leads to her imagining many types of figures, a way of getting beyond some images she found limiting. Her imaginative creation of historical or religious females, her deconstruction and reconstruction of women from folklore and myth, her portrayal of female members of her own family, her dramatisation of the ordinary lives of women and of experiences from her own life led to a collection of female figures who live in an imaginative space but clearly challenge some established attitudes towards women in Ireland. In a world of continual change, her imagery illustrates the possibility of renewal and revision.

However, Ní Chuilleanáin's intention is not to write only for and about women, nor to present any unvarying truth about women's lives. Arguing for 'the psychological importance of images', this poet believes that 'a woman artist may also aspire towards creating an image of herself and her sex from a feminine point of view, and by a logical progression she arrives at an outlook on the whole of human experience which, by that originality of perspective, is able to explore what has been missed by the male vision'.[3] A statement like this suggests that Ní Chuilleanáin sees her work as creating images which give a complex view of women's lives and achievements and, by extension, a more comprehensive view on the 'whole of human experience'. Her poems are full of speculation and unanswered questions, inviting the reader to continue to explore new angles on human experience; as the speaker in 'The Flood' (*S* 26) proclaims: 'I'm out again, straying / Earnest as ever I quested / In search of the neutral ground'.

Before one can appreciate the significance of such a statement, and of Ní Chuilleanáin's revising efforts, of her foregrounding women as subjects and speakers in many of her poems, it is important to understand the historical situation that gave rise to it. The lack of recognition of the achievements of Irish women, as well as problems with one-dimensional representations of women in many popular Irish historical and cultural narratives, was early on an important factor in this regard. As she says in her introduction to the 1985 collection of essays *Irish Women: Image and Achievement*, 'the study of the Irish woman's image through history is also the study of the gap, most easily appreciated for the last couple of centuries, between that image and what many Irish women have actually experienced.'[4] In the introduction to their collection *Women Surviving: Studies in Irish Women's History in the 19th and 20th Centuries*, Maria Luddy and Cliona Murphy likewise argued that 'traditional interpretations of historical events are cast in universal terms and would seem to include women', but in examining many of the events in Irish history with which people are most familiar, they maintained that the significance of these events for women, or women's part in them, had not been sufficiently investigated. Raising 're-vision questions', according to Luddy and Murphy, 'questions the whole basis of traditional historical enquiry … [and] requires a radical re-conceptualizing of what is considered historically important'.[5]

Much has been accomplished since the 1980s both in re-conceptualising women's roles in Irish culture and in uncovering the achievements of Irish women by scholars like Mary Cullen, Catriona Clear, Margaret

MacCurtain, Margaret Ward, Linda Connolly and Carol Coulter, among others, but it is a long-term undertaking to fill the many gaps between what Ní Chuilleanáin described as 'image and achievement'. The Irish poet Eavan Boland, suggesting that Irish women remained 'outside history', has also discussed this: 'when it came to construct the version of its history which would address those realities [oppression, colonisation, liberation] what emerged, perhaps inevitably, was a relentless narrative of heroes.' Boland, noting the exclusion this construct of history involves, and the difference between the past and history, claims that 'in certain circumstances a version of history can actually suppress what is really happening', 'by what is not said, rather than what is'.[6] Ní Chuilleanáin, as we shall see, defines the situation of women in Irish culture in a slightly different way from Boland, as a 'spiral progression' in which women disappear and have to be constantly 'recuperated' into history,[7] but both poets identified a problem with the recognition of women, and with the image of the female within Ireland's culture and its recorded narratives. Creating new images of women, alternatives to a 'relentless narrative' of male heroes, became a mission both poets undertook.

If, as is often the case, a nation's literature reflects its public values and mores, and parallels its historical record as it were, a more inclusive analysis of Irish history would suggest that a similar re-vision of the predominant view of Irish literature, as well as its images of women, was needed, and this has indeed been taking place. Continuing debates in Ireland illustrate that the literary suffered the same fate as the historical record. The first three volumes of the ambitious *Field Day Anthology of Irish Writing*, published in 1992, provoked such controversy over the few women writers included that it led to a serious and very public debate over the acknowledgment of the achievements of women writers.[8] As a consequence, Field Day commissioned another volume, covering women writers; that project led to the 2002 publication of two volumes, IV and V, to fill the gap left by the first three volumes.

This project in itself became somewhat controversial, in that it marginalised women writers in their own volumes ('in the annex' was a popular metaphor), though correcting the omissions in the first three volumes made this decision seem inevitable. Volumes IV and V of the Field Day anthology, *Irish Women's Writing and Traditions*, an enormous ten-year undertaking by several women writers and scholars, ended up as an excellent resource introducing a reading public to writers they might not otherwise have read, interrogating traditional categories and genres of writing and providing primary sources for a much more inclusive view of Ireland's literary heritage.[9] These volumes, along with such projects as the Munster Women Writers Project at University College Cork, under the leadership of Patricia Coughlan and Éibhear Walshe, and Maria Luddy's and Gerardine Meaney's *A Database of Irish Women's Writing 1800–2005* increased the visibility of Irish women writers. For poetry, Anne Colman's *Dictionary of Nineteenth-Century Women Poets* (1996), Joan McBreen's anthology *The White Page/An Bhileog Bhán: Twentieth Century Irish Women Poets*, published by Salmon in 1999, and Peggy O'Brien's *The Wake Forest Book Of Irish Women's Poetry: 1967–2000* (1999; 2011) help to publicise work by women and challenge assumptions and presumptions about the nature, themes, genres and forms of Irish literature.[10] In her 2010 volume *Gender, Ireland, and Cultural Change*, Gerardine Meaney emphasises the significance of this 'feminist recovery' of work by Irish women in redefining Irish literature:

> The volume of writing by Irish women would indicate that neither the construction of the myth of the writer as spokesman for his tribe, nor the configuration of the canon in national and masculine terms, … were in any way disabling for the production of work in a very diverse set of genres and media by a very large number of women. The Women in Modern Irish Culture Database had by 2008 identified work by 9,334 women … between 1800 and 2005 … Their silence has been a construct of literary criticism and history of a very narrowly defined canon, not a historical reality.[11]

No matter what argument one makes for the lack of recognition of Irish women writers (and there are many made), the statistics in Ireland speak for themselves, the case of poets providing a clear example of the problem. For a good part of the twentieth century, the most visible poets in Ireland published, reviewed and promoted were male. Ní Chuilleanáin explains the situation: 'When I seriously began to publish in the 60s, there was still a very strong feeling that poetry was for males … if you look for women poets writing in English in the middle of the century in Ireland, there are very few.'[12] At the beginning of the twentieth century, however, this was not necessarily the case, as a number of women poets were more visible in the literary worlds, though again not receiving as much recognition as their male colleagues. In 'The Other Irish Renaissance: The Maunsel Poets', David Gardiner explains the role that women played in the success of the Maunsel Press, which prospered during the Irish Literary Revival in the early years of the century:

> The eldest and most established of the Maunsel poets were women. Katharine Tynan (1861–1931), Dora Sigerson Shorter (1866–1918), Alice Milligan (1866–1953), Susan Mitchell (1866–1926), Ella Young (1867–1956) and Eva Gore-Booth (1870–1926) formed the core of the early Maunsel list and contributed to what financial security Maunsel had before the press's compensation from the British government after the Rising ... From the North and South of Ireland, these poets engaged in mythological 'Celtic poetry', but did not limit themselves to the topics of the cultural nationalists, writing frequently of domestic concerns, everyday topics, and themes far removed from Ireland.[13]

Though read at the time, these poets soon disappeared from the more popular histories and anthologies of Irish poetry.

Ní Chuilleanáin has written that, while a male succession had been established from the nineteenth-century poets James Clarence Mangan and Samuel Ferguson to Yeats, women were confronted with a break that suggested that no similar female tradition existed. She argues, however, that one can see a line, for example, from Lady Jane Wilde, who wrote under the name Speranza, in the nineteenth century to Katharine Tynan in the twentieth. In her introduction to *The Wilde Legacy*, Ní Chuilleanáin noted that, after 1922, 'there is a silence'.[14] Explaining that she was unaware as a teenager of female poets, she describes how she later came upon the work of Lady Wilde, whom she identifies as 'an ancestor for a woman poet'. Though she does not claim Lady Wilde as a major poet (closer to Thomas Davis than to Samuel Ferguson, she feels), Ní Chuilleanáin sees her as someone who illustrated that women's views of their own lives were important. For Ní Chuilleanáin personally, Lady Wilde's interest in folklore also demonstrated a 'way of contacting the feminine past', a vision Ní Chuilleanáin herself shared.

Although there were women poets writing in the middle years of the twentieth century in Ireland, few were recognised. Noting that the two best-known female poets at mid-century were Eithne Strong and Máire Mhac an tSaoi, who writes in Irish, Ní Chuilleanáin addressed some of the reasons for this in her essay, 'The Borderlands of Irish Poetry':

> It was not by chance that a generation of women writers, of whom I am one, emerged in the 1960s, when pressures to allow women to have a profession, to control their lives, their finances and their fertility were mounting, eventually to bring about the legislative changes of the 1970s. The politicising of women's issues in Ireland coincided with their poeticising, and they became poetic subjects in both Gaelic and English. ... The poetry-reading, that unquantifiable late-twentieth-century phenomenon, revealed to numbers of women poets that they had a special, female audience as well as the more general one which they had probably begun by going in search of.[15]

For much of the twentieth century, however, from the point of view of a wider reading public, the visible Irish poet was generally thought to be male, and the poetic speaker was often assumed to be a male voice considered to be 'universal'. The images in this better-known poetry likewise often focused on male subjects, figures and speakers. As women poets gained more recognition, it became obvious they had some different stories to tell, informed by their own experiences. Ní Chuilleanáin herself has suggested that we might consider that the modern Irish poet need not be 'a man in the foreground, silhouetted against a place', but rather, harking back to Gaelic bards, the poet can 'be male or female, nomadic without losing tribal identity'.[16]

In some ways, Ní Chuilleanáin was in a unique position as a woman poet in Ireland, as she was one of the few women who was published early in her life and also appeared in the original Field Day volumes. Her inclusion probably resulted from the visibility gained from her winning an *Irish Times* poetry competition while she was still a graduate student at Oxford, her early and continued publication by Gallery and Wake Forest University Press, and her academic position at Trinity, which she has held since she left graduate work at Oxford. Despite this, however, and despite several collections of poetry, her work did not gain as much critical attention as it should have; it was not until 2007 that a collection of essays focused on her work was published by the *Irish University Review*, under the editorship of Anne Fogarty.[17] Her *Selected Poems* followed in 2008, as well as Irene Gilsenan Nordin's book *Reading Eiléan Ní Chuilleanáin, A Contemporary Poet*,[18] nearly forty years after the early recognition she received for her work. Her tenth collection, *The Sun-fish* (2009), won the Griffin Prize for poetry, earned a Poetry Society recommendation and was shortlisted for both the T.S. Eliot Award and *The Irish Times* Poetry Now Award. In the intervening years, Ní Chuilleanáin continued to read in Ireland and beyond, and to publish new collections, creating a body of poetry and prose notable for its originality and for its highlighting the importance of a woman poet's voice in Irish literature.

The narrative of Ní Chuilleanáin's life illustrates the many ways in which she and her family have been part of the literary and political culture of Ireland. She came of age in the 1960s at a point when many of the issues mentioned above, including the images and roles of women, were being raised. However, she was prepared as a young woman to understand and assimilate much of the change that was coming. The history and activities of her family no doubt had an influence on this, and her mother's career as a writer introduced her early to a life in which a woman had both a career and a family. From her early education through her academic work at Trinity, Ní Chuilleanáin was in touch with the questions raised about women writers and women's writing.

Ní Chuilleanáin was born in Cork City, the oldest of three children born between 1942 and 1950 to university professor Cormac Ó Cuilleanáin, and writer Eilís Dillon. Dillon, born in 1920, was the daughter of Thomas Dillon and Geraldine Plunkett. Thomas Dillon, born in 1884, was a member of the Irish Republican Brotherhood and of *Sinn Finn*; Geraldine was the sister of Joseph Mary Plunkett, poet and a leader of the Easter Rising executed at Kilmainham Jail. Both of Eilís' parents had been jailed at one time. Geraldine's memoirs, *All in the Blood*, edited by her granddaughter Honor Ó Brolchain and published in 2006, described both national and family affairs including the 1916 Rising and the War of Independence.[19] The Dillons and the Plunketts were involved in republican politics for many years.

In 1940, at age twenty, Eilís married Cormac Ó Cuilleanáin, who as a young man had also been actively involved with the Irish Republican Party; he was interned at the Curragh during the Irish Civil War. After marrying, the couple settled in Cork, where Cormac was a university lecturer in Irish. Eilís cared for their three children, managed a university hostel where Cormac was warden, and began a prolific writing career that before her death produced fifty books, including historical and young adult novels and mysteries. In a memoir, 'In the Honan Hostel', Eilís describes her daily work overseeing students and preparing menus, and then compares it to her own household at the university:

> I applied the same principle to my house, where I had to think of a housekeeper and a children's nurse and three children, including a baby who was born after we went to live in the Warden's House. When all this was in order, after a tour of inspection of the hostel, by half-past ten in the morning, I was sitting at my desk beginning my other life as a professional writer.[20]

Dillon writes that she spent about two and a half hours at this 'other life' before she returned to the hostel to have lunch with the students. Thomas McCarthy maintains that Dillon challenged the secondary role assigned to women in the new Irish Free State, a woman who 'contradicted history, contradicted this convention of lesser being that the Catholic state conferred upon women'.[21] An accomplished cellist who played with the Cork Symphony Orchestra, Eilís was fluent in Irish, a translator with a special interest in Italian, and one of the founding members of the Dante Alighieri Society in Cork. She is also well known for her translation from the Irish of Eibhlin Ní Chonaill's eighteenth-century poem 'The Lament for Art O'Leary'. A model for her daughter and an example of an Irish woman who had both a successful profession and a family life with children, Eilís Dillon is a familiar figure in Ní Chuilleanáin's poems.

Described by Mary Leland, in her book *The Lie of the Land: Journeys through Literary Cork*,[22] as 'a child of the college', Eiléan Ní Chuilleanáin enjoyed a happy and comfortable childhood on the Cork campus. After a few early years at a school run by 'formidable Republican ladies who knew little about education',[23] Ní Chuilleanáin moved to an Ursuline convent school. Part of a close family, she and her siblings absorbed many of their parents' interests and skills. Influenced by Eilís Dillon's musical talent, Ní Chuilleanáin's sister Máire eventually became a principal violinist with the London Philharmonic, and images of, and allusions to, music appear in many of Eiléan Ní Chuilleanáin's poems. Their parents' facility with languages and translation inspired all of the children, including Eiléan's brother Cormac Ó Chuilleanáin, who teaches Italian at Trinity, and, like his mother before him, has also published mystery novels, under the name Cormac Miller. Eiléan Ní Chuilleanáin, fluent in languages from her early years, has translated work from Italian and Romanian; and with poet Medbh McGuckian, she published *The Water Horse* (2001), a translation from Irish of poet Nuala Ní Dhomhnaill's work. Eilís' influence upon her children's reading is described by her son Cormac, who writes in the introduction to her novel *Death at Crane's Court* that their house was full of international fiction, British children's books, Irish writers and 'racy dead foreigners like Maupassant and Apuleius, bought quickly before the Irish censorship board got to them and had them banned'. Cormac also notes that she was 'well versed in folklore and fairy tales; she believed strongly that the bloodiness of traditional stories should not be airbrushed out of children's books',[24] an attitude reflected in Eiléan Ní Chuilleanáin's folklore imagery as well.

In Cork, Ní Chuilleanáin earned a BA in English and History in 1962 and an MA in English in 1964 from University College, after which, encouraged by her family, she moved to Lady Margaret's Hall at Oxford for additional graduate work. Ní Chuilleanáin sees this as an unhappy point in her early life, leaving the relative comfort of Cork at a time when her parents, because of her father's health, also moved to Rome. She finished an MA at Oxford but left in 1966, declining to pursue a doctorate after she was offered a position at Trinity College in Dublin. Her first collection of poems, *Acts and Monuments*, published in 1966 when she was twenty-four, won the Patrick Kavanagh Award. Ní Chuilleanáin was soon active in the Irish poetry scene in Dublin, as well as in academic life, teaching Renaissance literature at Trinity. By 1975 she had published her collection *Site of Ambush* and established, with writers Leland Bardwell, Pearse Hutchinson and Macdara Woods, the literary magazine *Cyphers*, which has become over the years a leading source for new work from Ireland and beyond.

In an essay in *Poetry Ireland* after the launch of the seventieth issue of *Cyphers* in 2010,[25] Ní Chuilleanáin describes her involvement with its birth and evolution. From early poetry readings in Sinnott's pub in South King Street where 'the noise of a hostile regular of the pub and the crash of the cash register combined to make some voices inaudible', the editors saw the need to publish some of this work and launched *Cyphers*. Intent on making the journal a success, Ní Chuilleanáin and the other editors persevered with Arts Council funding and 'the good humour of our printer'. Ní Chuilleanáin performed, and continues to perform, many jobs for the magazine, explaining how this developed: 'More than the six pounds that Patrick Kavanagh's widow could afford to donate to the founding, she taught me to keep accounts properly. It was the beginning of my long career as amateur bookkeeper and administrator.'[26] Ní Chuilleanáin and one of the other editors and a fellow poet, Macdara Woods, eventually married, moved to Ranelagh and adopted a son, Niall, who as an adult follows in the family tradition as a musician.

Ní Chuilleanáin's father Cormac died in 1970 after a long illness and in 1975 her mother married the Irish writer and academic Vivien Mercier. As Mercier spent part of each year teaching at the University of Santa Barbara in California, her mother travelled there with him. Ní Chuilleanáin remained close to both, sharing a house at times with her mother in Italy, where Ní Chuilleanáin and Macdara Woods would eventually establish a residence and spend part of each year. The years 1989–94 were particularly difficult for Ní Chuilleanáin as she dealt with the deaths of her stepfather, sister and mother. Many of the poems in the volumes *The Girl who Married the Reindeer* and *The Brazen Serpent* reflect the experience of grief engendered by these losses.

A key influence upon Ní Chuilleanáin's early life was her father's siblings; Cormac Ó Cuilleanáin was the only male in a family with six females. As a few of her poems illustrate, Cormac, like many males, had a somewhat privileged position in terms of education and a career, while his sisters engaged in traditional domestic chores for women. None of the sisters married and three of them became nuns. The effect of her aunts' lives on Ní Chuilleanáin's sense of women's experiences started early, and several of her poems portray their work and situations. Ní Chuilleanáin describes her respect for these women, two of whom lived abroad as nuns in the 1940s:

> My six aunts, born between 1898 and 1907, aged between twenty-four and fifteen when the Irish Free State was born, belonged to the first cohort of women entering an independent Ireland, and their lives form a commentary on one aspect of the new political and ecclesiastical world that came into existence then … The fact that three of the six went into convents is perhaps less surprising,

> appears less a break with the world they knew, when their lives – active, troubled, but also sheltered and companionable – are compared to the equally protected, religious, and ritualized lives of the other three who remained in what was called the world.[27]

Ní Chuilleanáin speaks of how these women influenced her life, as she often visited them in the convents where they lived. She believes that as a young woman her aunts would have liked her to become a nun, but her father, who 'had barely escaped his family's tidal pull towards celibacy',[28] did not encourage this. Her respect for the lives and work of nuns, which Ní Chuilleanáin sees as suggesting much about the history of women, persisted as it found its way into her work in poems ranging from 'J'ai Mal à nos Dents' in the 1989 collection *The Magdalene Sermon*, to 'The Real Thing' in *The Brazen Serpent* in 1994, 'Anchoress' in *The Girl who Married the Reindeer* (2001) and 'The Sister' in her 2010 collection *The Sun-fish*.

Over the years, Ní Chuilleanáin's long academic life at Trinity, which began in 1966, has focused on Renaissance poetry and culture and she remains, 'despite many distractions', a scholar of the European Renaissance and English Reformation. She has a particular interest in the relationship between religion and literature and has written essays on Thomas More, Donne and Sidney. Other interests and publications include women writers such as the novelist Maria Edgeworth and the poet Speranza. A prolific and diverse array of scholarly publications, including many on translation, has appeared from the 1980s onwards. Ní Chuilleanáin has also served in several administrative posts at Trinity, including Head of the Department of English, Dean of the Arts Faculty, and Coordinator of the M. Phil in Medieval Language, Literature and Culture.

However, it is her life as a poet for which Ní Chuilleanáin has become best known. Influenced by her mother's writing, Ní Chuilleanáin says she chose poetry because her mother wrote prose and she wanted to be different. As Ní Chuilleanáin herself has noted, when she began to publish, women poets were clearly not as acknowledged as their male counterparts. As they began to become more visible, many were caught in the middle of a developing feminism and a subsequent backlash against its various terms, definitions and judgments. They were accused by some of politicising their work if they spoke out or wrote about women's lives and women writers in Ireland, or were expected by others, in Ní Chuilleanáin's words, 'to write about feminism'.[29] Charges that feminists were by definition separatists hung in the air, and the natural evolution of defining and refining what feminism represented provided problems for emerging poets who wanted to avoid easy classifications, and yet write from the point of view of a woman. In this atmosphere, the category 'woman poet' could be seen as reductive, and a woman poet's work dismissed as reflecting a narrow and specifically female 'political' view of the world.

The biggest obstacle for women writers was often that their work was defined only in terms of these definitions of women's writing and not seen as also having a broader, human dimension, even though in most cases it did. With the development of the various stages of feminism, some of these problems were lessened, but Ní Chuilleanáin, like many other women writers, tried to stay above the 'issues' fray, aware as a writer of a potential clash between politics and poetics. Nevertheless, in image, subject, setting, theme and language, Ní Chuilleanáin's feminism is both clear and forceful. Ní Chuilleanáin has said that she does not want to be seen as writing only about 'women's issues',[30] and her insistence that poetry by and about women ultimately reflects human experience is a very significant hallmark of her work. The female figures she creates reflect a myriad of subjects and broad themes that run the gamut from spiritual quest to dealing with the 'amplified hiss / Of time passing, like nothing … / But singular grief' ('The Flood' *S* 26).

We cannot maintain, therefore, nor would Ní Chuilleanáin, that all male poets automatically misrepresent the lives and feelings of women, nor that women writers are automatically presumed to be more accurately portraying the diversity of women's lives, as some early feminist critics claimed. As feminist approaches to literature evolved, an acknowledgement of the variety and diversity of male and female sex and gender experiences and the ways in which such factors as class, religion or politics result in different, rather than shared, values among women and women poets was soon clear. Ní Chuilleanáin's poetry reflects this broader approach, as she gradually developed ways to reflect the diverse spiritual, political and cultural landscapes within which she lived.

When we consider how few Irish women poets found their way into print during the twentieth century, however, we have to ask, as Ní

Chuilleanáin did, whether the predominance of male voices excluded many perspectives that women poets can provide. In an interesting essay contrasting two poems on war memorials, Helen Lojek examines Eavan Boland's poem 'Heroic' and Seamus Heaney's 'In Memoriam Francis Ledwidge', suggesting that while the subject, war memorials, is essentially the same, the focus of Heaney's poem tends to be Irish and historical, and that of Boland's feminist and cultural.[31] Lojek argues that the speaker in Heaney's poem, though not a soldier, can relate male to male with Ledwidge, because on some level they share a similar world. On the other hand, the speaker in Boland's poem does not have the same relationship to such a memorial and, ultimately, Lojek maintains, is asking whether one can recognise in a woman's life different kinds of heroism. As we shall see in the following chapters, these are the types of questions Ní Chuilleanáin also raises, if more obliquely than Boland. Nevertheless, Ní Chuilleanáin would not argue that particular experiences or perspectives are necessarily restricted to women poets; she has said, for example, that there are contemporary male poets writing about 'the modern, non-patriarchal family from a masculine point of view'.[32] At the same time she insists on the need to hear women's voices, and to present some unconventional images and points of view. Of the male subjects in her poems, Ní Chuilleanáin once explained: 'I tend to see male faces in my poems as averted. Perhaps because I want to stress that I AM LOOKING AT THEM as usually the woman is being looked at.'[33]

The Female Figure in Irish Literature

'Looking at them' might also be applied to the ways in which females had often been portrayed in Irish culture and literature, one of the motivations for women poets to create their own female figures. As Irish women poets, including Ní Chuilleanáin, Medbh McGuckian, Nuala Ní Dhomhnaill and Eavan Boland, became more visible in the last quarter of the twentieth century, diverse and multidimensional images of the female began to appear as well. Traditionally, Ireland's cultural and religious values often promulgated images of women which celebrated the puritanical morally good girl, where acknowledgment of female sexuality often focused on sin or repression. Allied to this image was that of the silent mother willing to sacrifice herself for nation or family, what Nuala O'Faoláin once described as 'the saintly Irish mother'.[34] The work of women scholars and the introduction of Women's Studies programmes have resulted in much research on these cultural stereotypes, and a process of revision and reconstruction highlighting the accomplishments of women throughout Irish history is ongoing. Likewise, in literature, poets like Paula Meehan, Mary O'Malley, Sinéad Morrissey, Vona Groarke, Caitriona O'Reilly, Leanne O'Sullivan and a host of others have been actively involved in creating alternatives to these images in their own poetry. One advantage of the increased visibility of such women poets is their challenge to the symbolic and iconic roles that the female figure has played in Irish history and culture, many of which found their way into poetry. From the political exploitation of Mother Ireland, which imagined the nation as a passive woman continually victimised, to the sentimentalising of the literary and mythic Dark Rosaleen and Cathleen Ní Houlihan, these figures could be used as gendered constructs to reinforce social stereotypes about women and serve the needs of political and religious movements.

Complicating these images was the trope of Ireland as female. This identification and representation has a long history; we can see it in the early Gaelic bardic tradition connecting woman with the land. Such images eventually merged with those derived from invasions and colonisation so important in Ireland's history. Ní Chuilleanáin feels that in the Gaelic-speaking world, there is some identification of the female with the sovereignty of the land, which goes back a long way. However, she also maintains that in that world, 'there is a place for the woman's voice which has been memorably shown in a succession of writers and works'. While she says that there were not many women poets at any stage, there has been a tradition of women poets which one can trace back to the eighteenth century and before.[35] The complicated history of Ireland, however, and the fact that few Irish people know Gaelic literary tradition well leave most readers without access to their work.

In Irish literature in English, there are several female figures identified with Ireland, many of them drawn from Gaelic sources but translated into political symbols as Ireland struggled to be free from colonial rule. These figures – the *aisling*, the *Speirbean* (Sky-woman), *Roisin Dubh* (Dark Rosaleen), the *Sean Bhean Bhocht* (Shan Van Vocht), and Cathleen Ní Houlihan – are represented as either beautiful young maidens or old women sometimes transformed into young maidens in the course of a narrative. The eighteenth-century *aisling* figure developed from the dream vision genre of Gaelic love poetry into a political figure identified with Ireland. Tom Dunne explains that in Jacobite *aisling* poetry, 'Ireland, personified as a beautiful woman, appears with a message of hope that the Stuarts will return and restore the old order'. Dunne describes the persistence of the form, and the image, even when its literary value was questioned:

> Because in literary terms it rapidly became hackneyed and clichéd after its high point in the luminous baroque creations of Aogán O Rathaille (1670–1729) and Eoghan Rua Ó Súilleabháin (1748–84), and because the long-ailing Stuart cause was finally dead and buried by the close of the Seven Years War (1763), the *aisling* poetry of the later eighteenth century and beyond has been regarded as meaningless in terms of contemporary concerns, and proof of a moribund literary tradition. And yet, whatever the literary judgment, these traditional Jacobite formulae, with their archaic references to Bonny Prince Charlie and the Catholic powers, continued to be adapted to articulate popular grievances about rent, tithe, the new police, or the activities of Bible Societies by songsters dependent on popular support, right up to the Famine.[36]

Though that *aisling* figure may have become a literary cliché, related to that image were popular nineteenth-century female figures associated with a suffering nation, political freedom and, especially at the end of the century, the nationalist cause. James Clarence Mangan's translation of the Gaelic poem 'Roisin Dubh' became one of Ireland's best-known poems, evolving into lyrics for some well-known twentieth-century songs. What had once been a Gaelic love song became, in Patrick Pearse's translation, a prediction of victory for the nationalists, albeit bloody ('the sea shall roll in red waves, and blood be poured out'), in their struggle against the English. The opening lines address a nation personified as a victimised woman who will be saved by friendly and protective male, and Roman Catholic, forces:

> Little Rose, be not sad for all that hath behapped thee:
> The friars are coming across the sea, they march on the main.
> From the Pope shall come thy pardon, and from Rome, from the
> East –
> And stint not Spanish wine to my Little Dark Rose.[37]

Perhaps the best-known of these figures was Cathleen Ní Houlihan, imagined, among other versions, in a play by Yeats and Lady Gregory in which an old woman (a version of the Shan Van Vocht) convinces her son not to marry so he can fight the forces of oppression, promising him immortality if he dies for the cause. The old woman is miraculously transformed into a young woman 'who had the walk of a queen' to become a symbol of how the sacrifices of young men will lead to Ireland's freedom. While Yeats and others later questioned the effect of such images,[38] they no doubt remained in the popular imagination, as David Cairns and Shaun Richards explain:

> Whereas for some writers, 'Cathleen Ní Houlihan' or the 'Shan Van Vocht' was no more than a convenient representational form, there is clear evidence that many others, including among them two of the leaders of the Easter Rising, Patrick Pearse and Joseph Mary Plunkett, believed in 'Mother Ireland' and 'Roisin Dubh' as real personalities ... Thus endorsed, the notion of an Ireland, symbolically represented as 'woman', whose destiny was to be independent and united, passed into the educational and cultural formation of two generations of Irish men and women.[39]

Many see the original sources of these images of passive and victimised women, especially with male domination of the female symbolising England's colonialisation of the Irish, as a consequence of the rise and dominance of the English over the Irish, and of the English over the Irish language. However, Sarah McKibben, in examining Gaelic poetry from the defeat of the Irish at Kinsale, also sees some change after 1607 when the image of the suffering or dying female becomes a metaphor in some Gaelic poetry. McKibben attributes this to attempts to rationalise political events, from the Flight of the Earls to the historic Plantation of Northern Ireland:

> This gendered and increasingly sexualized metaphor of the abandoned and despoiled female Ireland dramatizes the painful consequences of defeat and colonial domination, yet also arguably shifts attention from a more proximate and humiliating cause: the weakness, incapacity, or absence of Irish men, as well as the dishonor of their ongoing accommodation with English power ...

> Stressing their country's victimization allowed them to voice collective suffering while repositioning Irish men as potential, if belated, rescuers.[40]

McKibben goes on to analyse how, in some of this poetry, representation of the female gradually evolves into rape, adultery and prostitution, 'strategically shifting the focus from masculine to feminine dishonor'.[41] Working from this idea, we could also consider how in nineteenth and early twentieth-century nation-building, the images of Mother Ireland, a woman needing protection from defilement and dishonour, becomes again a rationale for armed conflict and bloody sacrifice. Both Gerardine Meaney and Ailbhe Smyth have discussed what Meaney has described as 'the symbolic function of women in nationalism' and what Smyth has called 'the enforced silence of women and their simultaneous importance as a representational category' in cultures where 'gender becomes subaltern to dominant nationalism'.[42]

In her study *Ireland's Art and Ireland's History*, Síghle Bhreathnach-Lynch, former Curator of Irish Art at the National Gallery of Ireland, traces other causes influencing cultural images of Irish womanhood. She sees the female figure in the nineteenth and twentieth centuries as constructed by the English colonialist's representation of the passive peasant companion to the buffoonish male Paddy; by nineteenth-century romanticised ideals of primitive places and peoples; and by nationalist representations of the Gael in the late nineteenth and early twentieth century. Describing the latter, Bhreathnach-Lynch maintains that the new nation's agendas created a kind of hyper-masculinity which affected representations of women:

> While Irish men were encouraged to be strong, virile and active in the affairs of the country, Irish women were encouraged to be, first and foremost, mothers whose duty was to inculcate their children, especially their sons, with love of country, of Gaelic traditions, and of freedom. The central meaning of a woman's existence was through her family, her space confined solely to the domestic sphere.[43]

Like others, Bhreathnach-Lynch also emphasises the various legal rulings in the new nation in the first half of the twentieth century which reinforced this view of women. These included limited access to jobs and professions, the obligation to give up civil service and other positions upon marriage, and laws outlawing divorce, birth control and jury service for women, culminating in the 1937 Constitution where woman's place in the home defined her identity. The effects of these were to last well into the century, and it was not until the 1970s, as Ní Chuilleanáin mentions above, that serious challenges about the rights of women began to influence public views and public policy.

Within the new Irish state, the role of the church, especially Irish Catholicism, played as large a part in creating images of women as did political movements. The Blessed Virgin Mother and other saintly women, especially within Catholic Ireland, were presented as ideal guides for female behaviour and used as warnings to women about expected behaviour. The young maiden, silent mother, shrew, asexual virgin became handy icons to reinforce a repressed sexuality, confirm women's place in the home, or idealise a sentimentalised image of the Irish mother. The close relationship between church and state tended to reinforce these images in the public consciousness as Irish women faced what Claire Connolly has described as 'an ongoing struggle between women's material lives and cultural understandings of woman as metaphor',[44] a variation of Ní Chuilleanáin's distinction between image and achievement. Irish attitudes towards sexuality, which affected both women and men, were influenced strongly by images of women, that owed much to an idealisation of Mary and the saints. Chastity and virginity were stressed above all, and the female body, as well as the material processes of menstruation, intercourse and childbirth, were little discussed, though the unlimited birthing of children was seen as carrying out God's role for women, ultimately tethering many to the domestic realm.

While the Irish nation/landscape was often sexualised so that male penetration of a victimised female could symbolise the fate of an invaded nation, the issue of female sexuality, or the actual realities of the sexual and the erotic, remained taboo at every level. In speaking of her early life, Ní Chuilleanáin remembers a typical Irish response to the body: 'Images of the body … were in our town kept literally under lock and key, the classic nudes in the cupboard in the librarian's office, the cast of athletes from the antique in a shed beside the materials laboratory in the college where my father worked.'[45] Ní Chuilleanáin describes a personal revelation when, at twenty, she walked through a Berlin art gallery and turned a corner after leaving three rooms of Rembrandts: 'There before me was Correggio's Leda and the Swan, full of blue and white narrative space, and perversity. Here was the body at the centre of a story, female and pleased in all its dimensions.'[46] Ní Chuilleanáin's interest in Italian art provided her with a visual representation of female physicality; she speaks, for example, of paintings of Mary Magdalene which emphasise her bodily features, features that appear in her own poems about Magdalene.

The Irish repression of female sexuality also carried into poetry for women writers; this often meant a kind of self-censoring of taboo subjects, an awareness of what would be acceptable to a reading audience. Added to this was the dearth of women's poetry available for the average reader, or even the emerging writer, given the dominance of published poetry by males. The poet Mary Montague in her essay 'The Art of the Body: poem as female self-portrait' says that she was seventeen before she was introduced to any contemporary Irish poets and then 'met no women at all'. Citing the value of women's poetry, she adds:

> Male poets have revered and delighted in women's bodies, but being a woman, inside a woman's body, is complex. We menstruate, we lactate, we give birth. We take in, we give out. The womb is central to our lives and bodies but we never see it, so there is an element of unknowing, even of our own selves … Women *are* different, and it's our very different approach to our bodies, and the sex we have with them, that makes our poetry relevant. Not better, not worse, but good and relevant … for a woman reader it can be really affirming to read poems about sex that are not from a man's point of view.[47]

Montague's statement is an illustration of recent changes in Ireland, where the state and the church have much less influence over the lives of women, and poets have created images of women more in line with real, rather than romanticised, lives. The feminist struggle for women's rights has brought to the forefront gender inequalities that needed to be addressed, including issues of divorce, reproductive rights, sexual freedom and domestic violence. The continuing challenges to the authority of patriarchal churches, the scandals involving sexual abuse by clergy, as well as the large immigration of people into Ireland during the years of the Celtic Tiger have made people aware of the different cultural, racial, religious and class attitudes towards women's lives and roles. The recent need to see Ireland not as a homogeneous but as a heterogeneous society, with the multiplicity of possible views of women's lives and cultures this presents, undercuts any generalisations one might want to make.

One result of these changes is that representations of the female and the female body have been rescued somewhat from a reductive metaphoric association with the land, and their role in promoting models of behavior advanced by religious institutions and beliefs has been weakened. Much of the poetry by contemporary women illustrates this change. Nuala Ní Dhomhnaill, for example, who writes in Irish, resurrects the energy of mythological figures like the tripartite goddess the Morrigan to recreate powerful and vocal female figures; she also challenges Christian images of the iconic Virgin Mary in a poem like 'Annunciations', describing a female figure to whom: 'never was it known / that a man came to you / in the darkness alone, / his feet bare, his teeth white / and roguery swelling in his eyes'.[48]

Leanne O'Sullivan's volume *Cailleach, The Hag of Beara* also humanises a mythic figure of the wise old woman, the *cailleach*, whose petrified body is believed to form a large rock in the landscape of west Cork. Resurrecting the *cailleach*, O'Sullivan stresses the importance of this woman's speaking voice and of her experiences as lover, mother and daughter as she is seen 'drawing out a thing unfinished, moving still in half-light'. Ní Chuilleanáin also uses this figure in her poetry, often placing her in a contemporary context. Eavan Boland's 'Anna Liffey' likewise transforms the female symbol of the River Liffey, a major character in Joyce's *Finnegans Wake*, into a contemporary Dublin woman modelled on her own life, and Galway poet Mary O'Malley's image of the folkloric Seal Woman features a figure who leaves the sea to wander around contemporary Galway City, commenting on what she sees.[49]

Women's bodies as objects are also the focus of many recent poems by women writers. Catherine Phil MacCarthy's 'Sand Goddess' imagines a group of children destroying a female sand figure on a beach as the speaker, alluding to Dark Rosaleen, asks 'Could it be / Duibhne of the black hair / come to restore us to history?' MacCarthy imagines the fate of such a figure, suggesting that she is there 'for the spoiling'. In the poem, the children are portrayed as 'awed by the reality / that a woman is a body / they have never been this close to, / and finally that a woman is a body / even they can dismantle'. In a poem like Paula Meehan's 'Hannah, Grandmother', the role of the priest-confessor is challenged when a granddaughter remembers her grandmother whispering in her ear: '*Tell them priests nothing.* / Was I twelve? Thirteen? / *Filthy minded. / Keep your sins to yourself. / Don't be giving them a thrill. / Dirty oul feckers*'.[50]

As the following chapters will illustrate, Ní Chuilleanáin has been part of this reimagining of the female image, emphasising in her poetry the materiality and sexuality of the female, reaching into folklore and myth to create new versions of older images, refocusing our views of the lives of nuns and saints so we see them in a new light, and recording her own poetic responses to such personal experiences as the deaths of her mother and sister. From her earliest poems, the female figure has been a central image as Ní Chuilleanáin looks to past and present for richer images of women, fulfilling Theo Dorgan's prediction in the introduction to *Irish Poetry Since Kavanagh* (1996) that 'we will be librated into a poetry written as much by vigilant women as by men'.[51]

CHAPTER 2

Female Figures and Poetic Strategies

> I watch for the outline, widening the maritime stare.
> The angles are a scattered puzzle. I will not
>
> Let it take shape yet, trying
> To freeze the dappled light and foam.
>
> 'Their Shadow on the Sea' (*S* 47)

In discussing a woman poet creating female figures, and any meaning the poem might suggest, the issues of both intention and poetic strategies arise. We need to understand that a subjective poetic voice is not one-dimensional, with gender the only focus, as Ní Chuilleanáin herself maintains. Any poetic voice is a construct and as such needs to be distanced from the voice or life of the author, although in Ní Chuilleanáin's case, as the following chapters will illustrate, the people and places in her own life sometimes provide the specific subjects and settings of her poems. Likewise, a poem should not always be seen to represent a collective voice representative of a specific group. How, for example, could a woman poet be seen to necessarily represent 'women's experience' or reflect the identities, beliefs and experiences of all women? With the evolution of feminist theories and the development of new and varied approaches to reading poetry, questions of sex and gender, as these may be reflected in poetry, have also become much more complex. The hard lines dividing sex and gender definitions and the question of whether an emphasis on women creates a reductive, essentialist category became the centre of much valuable discussion. While this led to some serious academic debates illustrating different theoretical positions, it was the natural evolution of new approaches to critical reading. Analysing the implications of the social constructs that influence gender definitions, responding to demeaning images of the female body while finding positive ways to represent that body, examining traditional distinctions between man and woman, male and female, sex and gender, understanding the implications of culture, race, ethnicity, all affect analyses of images and representations of sexual and gender identity. They also come into play when critiquing poetry by women.

Contemporaneous with this, the rise of philosophical challenges to traditional epistemological theories of human subjectivity, as well as the function of language to reveal identity, undercut earlier assumptions about representation, subjectivity and voice in poetry. The questions of whether one can assume that a speaking voice represents a unified subject or whether one identity, like gender, supersedes the multiple identities a person has have led to more questions about representation, choice, intentionality and meaning in a poem. An emphasis on a fluid identity, or multiple identities, rather than a stable one, challenges assumptions about authorial voice. Postmodern and psychoanalytic theorists complicated the issues further by presenting convincing evidence that it was not easy to clarify what one means by female identity.

Equally important, especially for poetry, were arguments raised about language. One of the issues for some early feminist critics was the emphasis in Irish poetry on male voices and male personae and what was often seen as a traditional male poetic language. Attempts were made to understand and differentiate how women's experience could be illustrated in writing. Seeking to counteract what were seen as masculinist hierarchies of power and language, some critics sought to define a specifically female language, labelled early on as *écriture féminine*, which is seen as more fluid and open, and different from the more closed, 'rational' language of the male. A critic like Borbála Faragó, on the other hand, in describing some responses to 'the maleness of language' which 'contributes to the invisibility and subordination of women', also sees a problem with defining a specifically female language. Faragó argues that poetic techniques which 'demonstrate a preference for upsetting the discursive constructivism of linear thought and language' can ultimately create a 'gendered segregation' of public and private spheres which 'devalues the female by rendering her public morality inadequate'.[1] Assigning women to a 'private sphere' has in the past devalued both their voices and experiences. As a poet for whom public space and public morality are important issues for both women and women poets, and who in one sense uses language structures in more traditional ways, Ní Chuilleanáin's should not be categorised as a specific female language. The issues of the fluidity and openness of language, however, and her capacity for deconstructing language in her poetry, will be demonstrated in later chapters.

Another group of theorists maintains that poetic voice is determined by language norms and systems of social discourse and that, in effect, it is discourse, not the intention of the poet, which creates the voice we hear, thus undercutting the more traditional concepts of subjectivity and poetic personae. Judith Butler, arguing against the 'myth' of a unified subjective voice, describes what we hear as 'linguistic acts of performative resistance'.[2] Speculating about any gender, autobiographical, historical or contextual implications embedded in the poem, therefore, is often seen as counterproductive. Those postmodern formalists, for whom language is a closed system of discourse, and the unified speaking subject in a poem an illusion, are challenged by theorists loosely grouped under Cultural Studies. New Historicists, Postcolonialists and others object to an ahistorical approach in which emphasis on language systems questions the concept of a unified subjective voice or any cultural or historical context in a poem. Likewise, some feminist critics argue that language critics, in eliminating any sense of a specific female persona, are undercutting the women's movements' attempts to challenge the dominance of male voices in poetry. Seyla Benhabib, for example, criticised Butler for what she called deterministic theories, claiming that the lack of stable subject worked against women's voices as it denied authority, self-reflexion and agency to women.[3]

In the light of different contemporary theories and debates, reading a poem and discussing poetic strategies becomes much more complex, and reading poetry by women raises issues of gender, voice, genre, image, figure, form and language. In poetry, can we speak of a specifically female persona? Can we connect a female persona with a woman poet? Is there ever a unified subjective female voice? Can one see a specific political or cultural context or meaning in a poem? Does a female voice ever represent a collective concern or experience of women? Is there a specific way in which women write? Can we consider the intention of a poet? In the case of Ní Chuilleanáin, there are many answers to these questions, most of them positive, as she clearly writes as a woman about the experiences and concerns of women, and also writes about herself and those around her. At the same time, she attempts to rise above the limitations created by traditional gender categories and essentialist approaches. It can be helpful to look at Ní Chuilleanáin's poetry in terms of how her poetic strategies address many of the theoretical questions and issues raised over the years, but to understand her poetry we must acknowledge the possibility of subjective voices, female personae and the significance of autobiographical and cultural contexts in her work.

Ní Chuilleanáin's work, however, can be analysed using some of the above theories. Irene Gilsenan Nordin, in her book *Reading Eiléan Ní Chuilleanáin, A Contemporary Irish Poet: The Element of the Spiritual*, for example, addresses her poetry from a postmodernist position. On self, voice and subject, Nordin sees in the poet's work a 'de-centred, deconstructed self' and a 'fragmented post-humanist subject'. Significantly, however, she also explores a spiritual element in Ní Chuilleanáin's poetry, and describes Ní Chuilleanáin's subjects as inhabiting a 'secret space beyond articulation, in silent spaces filled with promise waiting to be released'. For Nordin, this is also a liminal space 'outside the constructs of society and the limits of designated conceptual structures'.[4] Nordin sees Ní Chuilleanáin creating a 'dialectic between inside and outside space', and her analyses emphasise the many images in Ní Chuilleanáin's work, like windows, which mark the divisions between different realms. On the issues of intention and meaning, this study also illustrates Nordin's belief that Ní Chuillenain has an ethical position.[5] And Nordin's work offers a valuable perspective to clarify the many themes and images in Ní Chuilleanáin's work derived from traditional religious and spiritual beliefs.

Ní Chuilleanáin works from the position that any vision or voice is always limited; that the journey towards understanding never ends, partially because there are things we cannot know, a world beyond the physical of which we get hints, but not full revelation. That world beyond is what critics like Nordin correctly see as the spiritual dimension in Ní Chuilleanáin's work; it is spiritual in the broadest terms, and should not be seen as dogmatically religious, even though it is sometimes expressed with traditional religious imagery. The past, for example, becomes a version of this world, and history is full of secrets that may never be revealed to us. Folklore and myth also deal with the immaterial world and give us narratives and characters, stories, rituals and images by which to confront what we cannot logically understand.

We might imagine Ní Chuilleanáin the poet as exisiting in a liminal space mediating between the material and immaterial worlds. The value of art, and especially of poetry, is its ability to offer imaginative creations when our access to knowledge is limited. What we cannot know, we can imagine, and a poet like Ní Chuilleanáin, working from the particulars of the physical world, shows us how that world gives us glances and flashes of something beyond. However, because these are fluid and fleeting, controlled by time and change, Ní Chuilleanáin imagines what we see as always open to new and enhanced perspectives and additional meanings. Such a vision underpins the female figures in her poems, where their lives and experiences are not necessarily fixed, nor necessarily limited in the way that conventional images, both past and present, represent them. Thus they are open to both renewal and revision.

Ní Chuilleanáin's vision of the female figure in poetry, often with emphasis on the material body, starts from a basic principle which she explains: 'as a woman writer it has always been hard for me to accept the idea that women's lives are inherently duller and less readily articulated than men's.'[6] Her response over the years has been to create an assortment of female figures and female voices whose hallmark is their diversity. In addition to a single lyric voice which we can identify with her, her poems present many other voices, speaking from many different times, places and spaces. Explaining this, Ní Chuilleanáin says that she is attracted to the 'oddest women, geniuses or martyrs or lunatics or women with power'[7] from the past. For her poems, she has delved into history and myth, opening up conventional images to new interpretations and illustrating that an image is always ripe for both challenge and revision. In choosing to focus on some historical women, like Rosa O'Doherty, who moved from Ireland with her husband in the Flight of the Earls, or her own aunts, who worked in Europe during the Second World War, Ní Chuilleanáin also stresses the heroic contributions and achievments of women, sometimes little known, who worked under difficult circumstances. Added to this, her choice of subjects from contemporary and her own personal life and work create not only multi-dimensional images of women's lives but broad implications of how these apply to all human lives.

One way in which Ní Chuilleanáin opens up new potential for interpretation is by presenting alternatives to female and male gender stereotypes. Starting with particular and sometimes unrecognised details of her figures' lives, Ní Chuilleanáin often shifts the focus from negative to positive image, or from positive to negative, working from popular perception to new insight. From the Gaelic tradition, for example, Ní Chuilleanáin often draws on the female figure of the *cailleach* (Irish for 'veiled one'), the original source for many of the female figures which became popular in Ireland in the eighteenth and nineteenth century.[8] In Gaelic the *cailleach* takes many forms, but is essentially a wise old woman with healing and prophetic powers, usually of divine origin, and described as both powerful and passing through several incarnations, outliving the males with whom she mates. In one version of these stories, the *cailleach* turns from old woman into beautiful maiden. Seeking to emphasise the image where the older wiser woman is not subsumed into a younger one, and her wisdom is respected, Ní Chuilleanáin portrays her as both speaker and subject in her poems. Referring to such images, Ní Chuilleanáin maintains that to speak as a prophetic woman may 'be to take the place of the female figure in the *aisling*' thus creating a female speaker or subject to set beside the idealised female of the male poet's dream vision.[9] Referring to the older figure, Ní Chuilleanáin has said that 'the *cailleach* is really there',[10] describing the ways in which this figure can embody value and meaning in a contemporary context. In such poems as 'The Informant' (*SP* 62), 'Daniel Grose' (*SP* 78) or 'Borders' (*SP* 118), the *cailleach*, as will be discussed in later chapters, plays major roles, not the least of which is to provide good advice.

Other reimagined figures also come from folklore, as illustrated by the poem 'In the Desert', from *The Sun-fish* (*S* 50), whose subject is the archetypal princess/woman imprisoned in a tower, her life and body controlled by others. Isolated in a sandstorm, the woman looks down to see a man walking in the desert and soon becomes, unlike the mythic female, the observer rather than the observed. As speaker in the poem, the woman gives the man a role in a narrative which suggests not only his, but her own, feelings:

> Coming to the well he lifts
> Its wooden covering. Night
> And coolness are still down there.
> The snakes lie in the well, males
> And females coiled together, wet.
> Before he lowers his cup to drink

He salutes them saying, happy
Snakes, like the poor people
Who have only the comfort men
And women find in each other.

In the beginning of this poem, the female speaker says that the man 'must be half blinded' by the sand. She wraps her eyes and body with her red scarf as the storm blows up, but when she uncovers her eyes, she sees the man, with something 'bright' on his head 'masking the face', emerging in the dawn light. The recurring images of covered and uncovered eyes, scarfs and masks, light, dark and shadow, dawn and night not only repeat typical Ní Chuilleanáin images of an emerging illumination but also reinforce the emphasis on the woman's point of view and her own sexual consciousness, symbolised by those 'happy' snakes, 'males / And females coiled together, wet'. The speaker's assertive voice, 'I hear him praying, I see him drink', in the emphatic final couplet shifts a conventional emphasis from the seen to the seeing woman. The images of divided halves, and the woman imprisoned in the tower, suggest the impossibility of 'the comfort men / And women find in each other', if they are separated like this, with the female imprisoned in the tower. The woman imagines the man speaking, 'Let me fill my cup, let me rest', an ironic description of what she herself is also doing in watching the man. The allusions to sandstorms, mirages, something unclear which here is brought into the light, and to the snake's traditional connection with sexual sin, add to the weight of the woman's voice. Most significantly, this poem addresses the limitations of the image of mythic female whose life, body and sex is controlled by others, as it also challenges the validity of images of silent, asexual women. Eliminating the boundaries created by gender constructs, she creates a female figure to match the more conventional male.

'In the Desert' is from the 2009 volume *The Sun-fish*, and in Ní Chuilleanáin's earliest poetry one is not necessarily conscious of the predominance of such unique female figures; looking back over the body of her work, however, we see poems gradually featuring more female subjects and speakers in a vast array of contexts and spaces. In the early volumes, 'Lucina Schynning in Silence of the Nicht' (*SP* 13), 'Wash' (*SP* 15), and 'The Apparition' (*SP* 20) from *Acts and Monuments* (1972); and 'The Lady's Tower' (*SP* 29), 'The Absent Girl' (*SP* 30), and 'Odysseus

Meets the Ghosts of the Women' (*SP* 35) from *Site of Ambush* (1975) all focus on women subjects. In *The Magdalene Sermon* (1989), the poems are devoted almost entirely to female figures, as well as to the female voice, and numerous images of women appear in the subsequent volumes, *The Brazen Serpent* (1994), *The Girl who Married the Reindeer* (2001) and *The Sun-fish* (2009). Increasingly over time, the female figures become less generalised and more specifically identifiable from myth, history, folklore, sacred narratives and Ní Chuilleanáin's own life. As interest in the rights of women, and such revelations as the abuse of women in the Magdalene Laundries in Ireland highlighted the need for Irish culture to cxamine its images and treatment of women, more female figures appeared in Ní Chuilleanáin's poetry, many portrayed as alternatives to traditional images of women.

In moving beyond conventional boundaries, Ní Chuilleanáin's characters, like the speaker in 'In the Desert', step outside conventional gender constructs and roles. Two poems illustrate how she demonstrates this with different voices. The 'I' speaker in 'Swineherd' (*SP* 16), for example, is a male who tells us that, when he retires, he desires another life:

> I intend to learn how to make coffee, at least as well
> As the Portuguese lay-sister in the kitchen
> And polish the brass fenders every day.
> I want to lie awake at night
> Listening to cream crawling to the top of the jug
> And the water lying soft in the cistern.

Another early poem, 'Wash' (*SP* 15), which precedes 'Swineherd' in both *Acts and Monuments* and Ní Chuilleanáin's *Selected Poems*, presents another perspective on this. In this poem Ní Chuilleanáin creates the image of a woman washing a fish at a sink where the voice, subject and tone are very different from those in 'Swineherd'. An unidentified speaker observes the woman in the scene:

> Wash the man out of the woman:
> The strange sweat from her skin, the ashes from her hair.
> Stretch her to dry in the sun
> The blue marks on her breast will fade.

Unlike the swineherd, who imagines the lay sister's life as filled with apple blossoms and a conversation 'mainly about the weather', the speaker in 'Wash' expresses an undertone of violence in the scene, describing a woman whose 'flat curious eyes reflect the squalid room', connecting her with the dead fish. Observed by this speaker, the woman is seen in a simple domestic act of washing a fish, but something more frightening, the specifics not disclosed, is embodied in the observer's vision. While not necessarily noticeable at first, the juxtaposition of these two early poems creates different images and perceptions on the lives of men and women, as the swineherd focuses on what he sees as a comforting domestic life while the woman in 'Wash' is dealing with the dark underside of life in a home.

As the above poems illustrate, one of the important things we should notice about Ní Chuilleanáin's female figures has been her attempt to get beyond traditional gender stereotyping. Included in this is her challenge to the image of the domesticated woman homemaker so pervasive in cultural images of Irish womanhood.[11] Over time, Ní Chuilleanáin's poems have consistently portrayed women working outside the home or living in female communities, like convents, not associated with conventional marriage and family. She describes her poem 'Woman Shoeing a Horse' (*SP* 77) as 'a celebration of a woman who could do that, and also a call for other women to do that' as she describes the female blacksmith in terms of her physical strength:

> I could see by her shoulders how her breath shifted
> In the burst of heat, and the wide gesture of her free arm
> As she lifted the weight and clung
>
> Around the hoof. The hammer notes were flying.[12]

Another poem, 'The Liners' from *The Sun-fish* (*S* 55), pictures a woman who spent her whole life working at sea but is now back on shore remembering her job: 'Close print of cabins, listed laundry, echoes of command. / It hung like a cloud of midges, like sparks, the bubbles / In her glass. A living face'.

At the same time, Ní Chuilleanáin acknowledges and respects the often unrecognised value of the domestic work that many women do. In her poems there are women in kitchens, working to keep homes comfortable: the sister who played the violin in the London Philharmonic with the 'skill of the left and the right hand' (an image of Ní Chuilleanáin's sister Máire) is also the one whose hands, in the elegy 'A Hand, A Wood' (*SP* 88) produced the 'script curls on the labels of jars' in a kitchen press. Seeking to create diverse and multi-dimensional images of women, she emphasises their materiality with images like the hands portrayed in this poem or 'the living face' in 'The Liners' quoted above. Ní Chuilleanáin imagines female figures both as inside and outside traditionally defined roles, just as she sometimes depicts males involved in activities which have often been defined as 'women's work'.

The male figures in her poems, moreover, step outside patriarchal systems to challenge a conventional warrior hero or proud male of many Irish narratives and poems. In the poem 'A Revelation, for Eddie Linden' (*S* 20), the scene is a gathering where those seated 'listen to the lines / Praising their lives, the voice that trembles / Eloquently holding them in place'. The speaker looks away and notes another figure in the room, outlining him against a background of books:

And I spot you, Eddie,
Stepping back from the spillage,
Imprisoned against glass bookcases
Where the spines in a row slide from *Assyrian* to *Hittite*
(No script more strange, no dragon a more
Outrageous presence than yours) and you draw breath,
Because your retreat is partial, and when you speak
A draft from a city of broken windows
Will come razoring under the door.

Eddie Linden, whose poem 'The City of Razors'[13] depicts the sectarian struggle on the streets of his native Glasgow, is portayed as 'imprisoned' against books focused on Assyrian and Hitttite cultures, an 'outrageous presence', a 'dragon', who, unlike the audience, is more concerened as poet with peace in a 'city of broken windows' than with the wars described in the books. Many of the males in Ní Chuillenáin's poems, like Eddie Linden, the hermits in 'Studying the Language' or the sculptor who is memorialised in 'Séamus Murphy, Died October 2nd 1975' (*SP* 40), are singled out for a different type of heroic role.

In addition to reimagining stereotypical gendered images with alternative figures, Ní Chuilleanáin uses other poetic strategies to express her views, including poetic genres ranging from dramatic to narrative and lyric. Her dramatic and narrative poetry creates what Christian Michener, alluding to ancient drama, calls a 'sacred chorus' of saints and sisters.[14] As many critics have pointed out, a story or a short scene from a narrative often underpin a Ní Chuilleanáin poem; these scenes carry embedded dramatic meaning. An enormous collection of imagined actors and voices – from history, myth, religion, contemporary life – focuses our attention on scenes which range from the performance of rituals and ceremonies, to pilgrims visiting shrines and cathedrals, to a woman in 'Passing Over in Silence', who 'kept the secret of the woman lying / In darkness breathing hard, / A hooked foot holding her down' (*SP* 71). Ní Chuilleanáin also uses narrative plots from folklore, as in 'The Girl who Married the Reindeer', changing parts of the plot, as well as the sex and nature of some of the characters, to present a different idea, and sometimes a new ending.

One of the difficulties of Ní Chuilleanáin's work is that we often get just part of these dramatic narratives; we begin in *medias res*, as it were. However, one objective of this strategy is to suggest the limitations of what we can know, to raise a question or imagine a scene, given that the entire story is unavailable to us. The poem 'London' (*SP* 54) from *The Magdalene Sermon* is a good example; its opening lines set the tone: 'At fifty, she misses the breast / That grew in her thirteenth year / And was removed last month'. As two people sit in a 'random' bar talking, the woman who has had the mastectomy scans the bar 'looking along the jacketed line of men's lunchtime backs' to note reflections in the 'polished curve' of a large urn at the end of the bar. As the two speak, one asks and the other answers:

> What are you staring at? That polished curve,
> The glint wavering on steel, the features
> Of our stranger neighbour distorted.
> You can't see it from where you are.
> When that streak of crooked light
> Goes out, my life is over.

There are no quotation marks to indicate the speakers' words, just the dialogue represented by 'you' and 'my', and the meaning of the poem is expressed in the images. The curve of the urn distorting the stranger's features suggests the lost breast, which the woman uses as a metaphor for her own body, its 'features' 'distorted', and more now like the jacketed line of men's backs than her former body. Her words to her friend, 'You can't see it from where you are', refer not only to the urn but also to the situation the woman is in. Her clothes cover where the breast has been removed, and her friend can neither see the changed body nor quite understand how the woman feels. While the poem ultimately expresses the fear of death hanging over anyone who has to live with the potential consequences of cancer, it also highlights the specific issues for a woman whose body is changed so dramatically by such an operation. The understatement in the short poem, tightly controlled by three 6/5/6 line stanzas, is reinforced by this quiet scene of a woman trying to come to grips with a situation over which she has no control.

With Ní Chuilleanáin, it is difficult to ignore the preponderance of 'she' and 'her', the predominance of identifiable female voices and the importance of seeing the dramatic 'I' in her poems as illustrating the many voices in her work focused on different women's experiences. The speaking voices and snatches of conversation in her poems are complicated and often shift within a single poem. At times, as in the traditional lyric, the first person 'I' or 'we' is expressed by an unidentified, non-gendered speaker. In other poems, an unidentifiable speaker is recording another voice, or other voices, both female and male, in an overheard dramatised conversation. However, in many poems, a clearly defined female persona is dramatised as an 'I', sometimes unidentified, sometimes associated with an historic, religious or mythic female, sometimes related to Ní Chuilleanáin herself, sometimes to a woman poet. It is difficult therefore not to see a unified subjective voice in her poems. Ní Chuilleanáin once explained that when she first started to write she had to 'invent strategies for saying "I" in a poem, but eventually did not need to do that'.[15] Her first-person speakers, however, are varied and diverse; her voices, many.

When asked about recent literary theories on the poetic voice and the concept that any subjective voice is an illusion and that meaning in a poem, therefore, is difficult to assess, Ní Chuilleanáin answered that she was not entirely convinced by poststructuralist arguments,[16] and she felt that her poetry had a coherent subjective voice which she recognised as her own. 'I can hear a coherent voice in my own and other poets' work,' she says, suggesting further that a poem is 'not ready' if you can not hear a distinctive speaker.[17] The question of voice, or of subjective material, therefore, is significant when examining Ní Chuilleanáin's work. In discussing the poems in her collection *The Brazen Serpent*, and responding to a question about an autobiographical voice in her work, Ní Chuilleanáin says: 'In a few cases, I am speaking', citing 'Fireman's Lift', a poem about the death of her mother. In other poems she explains that she uses the third-person pronoun: 'That's one way to make the distinction about whether or not I am using a persona. I try to make that clear from the context of the individual poem.'[18] The context of some poems, clearly illustrating experiences from her own life, connect the speaking 'I' to the poet. At other times the 'I' is more indeterminate or clearly a persona in a dramatic monologue.

The use of a dramatic monologue creates the voice in 'The Lady's Tower' (*SP* 29), where a female speaker describes her delight in the natural world. In a poem like 'The Informant' (*SP* 62), we hear snippets of a conversation between two people as an old woman answers the questions of a young man about what happens after death. At times the poems present voices within the context of a dramatic scene, marked by italics, as in 'J'ai Mal à nos Dents' (*SP* 60), a poem written in memory of Ní Chuilleanáin's aunt, Sister Mary Antony, where a nun, having gone to France to serve in the war, writes letters back in the French she is learning. There is no doubt that one of Ní Chuilleanáin's intentions is to let these women speak in their 'own' voice, which though created for them by the poet, allows them and her to articulate the diverse and numerous experiences of not only women's, but all people's, lives.

In moving beyond image and voice to other formal elements of Ní Chuilleanáin's poetry, the influence of both English and Gaelic poetry is apparent, an indication of her sense of herself as inheritor of two cultures and two languages, and of her willingness to borrow from both traditions. Her emphasis on narrative often determines the form of a poem, for example in 'The Second Voyage' (*SP* 18) or 'Michael and the Angel' (*S* 22), where the traditional long line and loose form of narrative poetry carry the poem. More often, as Peter Sirr notes, in general Ní Chuilleanáin 'blocks the poems in self-contained sections rather than a single, seamless narrative flow';[19] many times these units develop one specific image in detail. Ní Chuilleanáin sometimes uses conventional English stanzaic forms; however, the regularity is interrupted in the course of the poems. For example, while some poems are written in quatrains ('A Bridge Between Two Counties', *S* 12) or tercets ('Agnes Bernelle, 1923–1999', *SP* 117), and 'Troubler', *SP* 104), she also combines different stanzas in a single poem, alternating tercets and couplets, for example in a poem like 'The Crossroads' (*SP* 92), or quatrains and tercets in 'Fireman's Lift' (*SP* 64). In some of her poems, the last stanza will have an extra line or two ('In Her Other House', *SP* 97); in others, a couplet will finish off a series of tercets ('Permafrost Woman', *SP* 51; 'Ballinascarthy', *S* 16; 'Tower of Storms, Island of Tides', *SP* 111).

Most of these strategies involve techniques which undercut an expected regularity in the poem to reinforce its theme, which like her reimagining of myths and narratives, illustrates another example of Ní Chuilleanáin's new version of older forms. The alternating long and short lines in the quatrains that make up 'The Cure' (*S* 37), for example, with their carefully crafted end-stopped and run-on lines, highlight the interruption and continuation of the two isolated and very different conversations which the poem highlights. Variations of the fourteen-line English sonnet stanza, in 'The Water' (4/2/2/6) (*S* 38), 'Studying the Language' (8/4/2) (*SP* 89), 'Celibates' (5/5/4) (*SP* 17) or 'The Angel in the Stone' (4/4/3/3) (*SP* 94), illustrate her reworking of conventional forms with little attention to traditional meter or rhyme. Reinforcing the images and themes involving borders and edges prevalent in her poetry, such forms illustrate a technique the speaker in 'Borders' (*SP* 118) describes: 'I leap over lines that are set here to hold'.

Other formal elements of Ní Chuilleanáin's work owe more to Gaelic poetry, which does not use end rhyme or meter but depends on internal rhyme and assonance, illustrated in lines such as those from 'The Sun-fish' (*S* 44) which depict the yearly appearance of the basking sharks off the west coast of Ireland: '… A fin a fluke / And they are there, the huge Sun-fish, / Holding still, stencilled in the shallows'. Ní Chuilleanáin's phrasing often consists of small units controlled by commas and mid-line breaks and she explains that she sometimes counts syllables in parts of a poem, a characteristic of Gaelic poetry, because 'that's a conspicuous but inconspicuous and secretive thing to do', while rhyme, unless it is subtle, can dominate. At the same time, she also believes that every poem should have its own shape and 'ideas would have precedence over words', though the words should have 'a weight and shift' of their own. Ní Chuilleanáin also says that she sometimes borrows rhythms from other languages like the alexandrine or the eleven-syllable line from Italian.[20]

With words as well, and this may be the most unique characteristic of her poetry, Ní Chuilleanáin is always exploring potential meanings and how words can both retain and lose meaning, as well as represent several possible, even contradictory, meanings. Drawing numerous associations from English words, she demonstates how the many meanings embedded in langauge become an asset for the poet. She also illustrates the ways in which different languages express similar objects and ideas, fluidity and potential being essential assets of language, especially for the poet. In the poem 'The Sun-fish' (*S* 44), for example, the subtitle gives the name of the fish in other variations and languages: basking shark, another English name for the Sun-fish; *An Liamhán Gréine*, its Irish name; and *Cetorhinus maximus*, its scientific Latin name. The central theme in the four-poem sequence focuses on the migratory fish's seasonal appearances off the Irish coast, with its arrival eagerly watched for and its disappearance regretted, as it once provided the livelihood for a seaside community on Achill Island. The same fish carries different names in different cultures and contexts, its meaning not limited to one word, or even in these poems to one meaning, as the basking sharks in the collection *The Sun-fish* become a poet's symbol for both presence and absence, loss and memory.

The speaker in 'Their Shadow on the Sea' (*S* 47), a poem of couplets within the sequence, also connects language to the basking sharks, describing the many things the sharks can represent:

> I watch for the outline, widening the maritime stare.
> The angles are a scattered puzzle. I will not
>
> Let it take shape yet, trying
> To freeze the dappled light and foam.
>
> But they are there already, as the watcher saw them
> Once, craning as they nosed in under the cliff,
>
> Suddenly present, a visitation,
> Like the faces of my two parents looking at me
>
> From the other side, from the outside
> Of the misty screen of winter.

In this poem, the memory of the speaker's dead parents, like the sharks, is 'Suddenly present, a visitation … / From the other side'. However, the poem also associates the sharks with numerous other words and different languages: '*Krill, Bloom, Copepods, Thermocline. / Elasmobranch. Liamhán Gréine*', suggesting that 'In troops of words they form, a gulp dissolves them'. Like the sharks that suddenly show up on the coast, or dead parents who reappear in memory, words can suddenly disappear and reappear, 'Suddenly present'. The speaker 'watches for the outline', wills not to 'Let it take shape yet, trying / To freeze the dappled light and foam', a good description of the process of writing a poem. In a complex set of images Ní Chuilleanáin connects animals, people, words, poems in the 'scattered puzzle' of presence and absence, while also highlighting the diverse meanings and feelings words and images can express. Although the speaker in these poems is not clearly identified, the image of the dead parents is repeated in other poems in the volume ('The Polio Epidemic', 'Ballinascarthy', 'On Lacking the Killer Instinct') where they are identified with Ní Chuilleanáin's parents. Knowing this, we can connect the speaker in 'Their Shadow on the Sea' with the poet herself, seeing the finished poem as moving from a 'scattered puzzle' to 'suddenly present'.

As the above poems show, Ní Chuilleanáin often starts with a convention and then gives it a new turn, opening up the several possible variations contained in a word, an image, a line. A myth is refocused to reverse the roles of predominant male and subordinate female, a saint is reimagined in a new context, a basking shark symbolises presence and absence, visitations 'from the other side'. Words are plumbed for numerous meanings, varieties of the English sonnet are created, a poem becomes a scene from a drama, a poem in English adopts a Gaelic technique of syllable counting. As the following chapters will illustrate, there is often an element of surprise as Ní Chuilleanáin draws material from history, sacred narratives, folklore and literary and artisitic traditions, exploring the potentiality of word and image. Likewise, in her large collection of female figures, Ní Chuilleanáin ranges across a vast landscape to take advantage of the potential for reviving and renewing images for an imaginative presentation of women's lives. She would maintain, however, that these images, and the themes and meanings they embody, apply to all humans as they confront such mysteries as time, absence, change, loss, memory and language.

CHAPTER 3

Imagining History

Our history is a mountain of salt
A leaking stain under the evening cliff
It will be gone in time
Grass will grow there –

Not in our time.

'History' (*MS* 11)

Ní Chuilleanáin's interest in history is apparent in all of her work, but hers is a historiography defined in its broadest sense from the political history of Ireland and beyond, to her own personal and family history, and to the history of women, until recently an often unexamined and under-documented field. With Ní Chuilleanáin, however, these all intermingle and cannot be easily separated, and often her explorations into history lead to the conclusion that not only is it difficult to understand the past, because a particular history will not reveal its secrets and its voices, but also that the arbitrary lines we draw between past and present can be illusory. Although this was one of Ní Chuilleanáin's areas of undergraduate study, history as fact-finding, as evidence for pinning down the 'true' nature of the past, of recording events, people and cultures so we understand what and who they were, is not ultimately Ní Chuilleanáin's primary concern.

Working from the belief that our vision is always limited, that we can view history from multiple angles and that facts are both selective and open to different interpretations, Ní Chuilleanáin takes a different approach to looking back. As a poet, she chooses often to imagine events, scenes and figures from the past, to speculate on what is hidden, what lies beyond the surface, what might be, metaphorically, on 'the other side'. Moreover, as Helen Emmitt explains, Ní Chuilleanáin's moments of revelation are ironically balanced by another theme in her work, 'the omission of the history that could explain the situation'.[1] As we have noted earlier, often with Ní Chuilleanáin there is the start of a narrative, or a glimpse of a scene, and we are encouraged to draw some meaning from a partial story, realising that we can never fully understand the whole.

In this process, Ní Chuilleanáin's imaginative recreations often interrogate traditional roles assigned to men and women as these are reflected in some historical accounts, and she revises well-known figures and narratives, sometimes using the present, or her own personal experience, as an entrance into the past. Acts and monuments – as the title of an early volume suggests[2] – are often a starting point. As Ní Chuilleanáin says, 'the past is there. It is there in the present. In one sense, it is the only thing that we actually do know.'[3] Events and specific places and spaces are extremely important, whether an Italian kitchen, her native city of Cork, the cathedral at Parma or the ruins of Bessboro, a Mother and Baby Home in Cork. A recurring motif in all of these poems is the approach to the edge, to the borders of recovery and understanding, to the threshold of a mystery or secret. There is some information to be gained, glimpses into the past, yet the emphasis often falls on limited access to facts. Ironically then, Ní Chuilleanáin begins a journey of discovery, uncovering bits and pieces, only to let us know that there is something there that we can never fully understand, a mystery at the heart of any history. On the other hand, this opens up opportunities for the poet to imagine and recreate worlds we cannot see.

Ní Chuilleanáin has described history as 'that sort of hologram where now you see it, now you don't, now you see further into the background and then you don't',[4] depicted metaphorically in the mists, veils and shadows we see often in her poems. As a poet, Ní Chuilleanáin uses this to advantage, with imaginative scenes of what might have been. An artist and not an historian, she profits from the ambiguity poetry affords, from the complexity and multiplicity of meanings that art and language allow. One can certainly argue that this is not a conventionally reliable way of viewing the past, but, as we will see, her strategies give us not only some understanding of the past but also a sense of what has been selected, left out, or misrepresented in traditional historical visions. All of this is important in terms of representations of women's lives. As she says, 'I'm interested in female roles, especially historically.'[5]

In his essay contrasting Ní Chuilleanáin's formulation of history to that of Irish poets like Derek Mahon and Seamus Heaney, Nicholas Allen suggests that there is a 'gendered difference between alternate ways of processing and representing history' and suggests that Ní Chuilleanáin 'sidesteps … what we more typically think of as history, that harmony of discordant dates that allows for representable translation between the private and public spheres'. Allen correctly argues that Ní Chuilleanáin 'seems acutely aware of history's limits. Her poetry acts as an incantation to voices from the margin; her words are much like a scribe's asides, her commentary oblique, personal, mysterious.'[6] By ignoring the conventional separation of public and private spheres, by connecting figures from past and present, by reflecting on her own experience as an Irish woman, and by focusing on female figures, Ní Chuilleanáin creates poetry in which, in Allen's words, 'history is a constant present, a text of versions'.[7]

The telling of Irish history in the past was often very much focused on political and military events. Describing this with the term 'patriarchal history', Joan Hoff explains that the criteria for this kind of history were 'power, prestige and periodization' which resulted in the general exclusion of women. The result, says Hoff, was emphasis on confrontation between powerful male figures or on the search for heroes who illustrate certain narrowly defined standards of power and prestige. Women, Hoff argues, generally do not fit these patriarchal criteria, thus the lack of female heroes. At the same time, she explains, important issues and events in women's lives were also ignored or devalued.[8] When we look at Ní Chuilleanáin's poems, we see an attempt to move beyond the limits of patriarchal history, to question the celebration of confrontations over power, especially as this applied to nation-building, and to highlight the lives of many women left out of Irish histories. Ní Chuilleanáin also insists that many lost women's lives and works are recoverable in some yet to be published texts.[9] Responding in an interview to Irene Gilsenan Nordin's questions about this, Ní Chuilleanáin replied: 'The texts are often there much more frequently than popular perception realises … certainly in the seventeenth century there are large numbers of unpublished women's autobiographies, diaries, letters and so on'.[10] One advantage of Ní Chuilleanáin's academic work in literature is that she has read many of these, and she argues, for example, that the autobiographical texts of females in the Renaissance contrast those who surface in biographical writing by men which often describe women in the most general terms – 'modest', 'a shrew', 'a whore'.[11]

Ní Chuilleanáin's allusive and stylistically imagist poems are never easy to understand, and the ways in which her views on Ireland's history are expressed can be missed in casual readings. Also, despite her republican family ties,[12] Ní Chuilleanáin's images of Irish political history portray the complexity of problems and often relate more to other social issues, or to individual human experiences, than to specific political ideologies or allegiances. A good example of this can be found in her poem 'Borders' (*SP* 118), an elegy in *The Girl who Married the Reindeer*, where the generality of the title image allows for multiple levels of meaning. The subject of the poem, John McCarter, was a teacher in St Patrick's School in Armagh and later in Letterkenny, Donegal, whom Ní Chuilleanáin describes as a man of 'great fun'.[13] Two interesting aspects of this poem are the highlighting of female figures in the elegy, including a clearly defined female speaker, and the memorialising of a man who does not fit the criteria for a conventional patriarchal hero.

When the speaker in the poem is driving from south to north to McCarter's wake, she remembers how often the dead man crossed this Irish landscape, from north to south and back again. The map of a divided Ireland provides the setting when the speaker describes passing the north-south border at a town 'under the soldier's lenses at Aughnacloy'. Counterpointing this political allusion is the description of McCarter crossing the map 'in a toil of love / … from Dublin to Portadown or Armagh to Donegal', all important sites in Irish political battles. The individual's journeys of love, contrasted to the conflict underpinning the Irish Troubles, are not only a tribute to the dead man, but also a comment on what may be lacking in an Irish political landscape, and in certain versions of Irish history.

In the poem 'Borders', two other images also highlight boundaries analogous to the political borders, and involve images related to gender. In both cases, the speaker-poet describes breaking through literary traditions and restrictions: 'I no longer own a ribbed corset of rhymes', and 'So I leap over lines that are set here to hold and plan / The great global waistline in sober monoglot bands'. The woman poet here will not be restricted by traditional poetic conventions of rhyme ('ribbed corset') or by the characteristics of a single language ('sober monoglot bands'), allusions on some level to the English language and poetic conventions which replaced the earlier Irish as the English drove further through the Irish landscape. These literary allusions are introduced early in the poem with the narrator's comment: 'I must start at the start, at the white page in my mind', an image which reappears in other Ní Chuilleanáin poems.

In 'Borders', she blends two literary traditions: she uses a traditional English quatrain but breaks the 'ribbed corset of rhymes' with repeated irregular and off-rhymes ('hand'/'mind', 'land'/'Strabane') and a recurring, but not uniform, thirteen-syllable line, syllabic verse being more typical of Gaelic poetry. Likewise, the final lines of the second and third quatrain literally leap over the lines on the printed page as extra syllables carry them into a fifth line. Leaping over lines, then, can be seen as both political and linguistic and a clear case of the form of the poem embodying its theme. Borders are being crossed, as a female speaker/ poet, without a restrictive 'ribbed corset', memorialises the man able to move between Northern Ireland and the Irish Republic.

Explaining 'I follow the road that follows the lie of the land', the persona crosses a stream called Fairy Water, again representing a border and evoking Irish legends of fairies, 'to come to the bridge at Strabane'. A town in County Tyrone between the Irish Republic and Northern Ireland, Strabane was the centre of much paramilitary activity at the end of the twentieth century, and the bridge represents another political boundary. But a number of borders, between fact and legend, between myth and history, between Irish and English cultural and literary traditions, between male and female, are also highlighted. Transgressing boundaries, this poem poses the question Ní Chuilleanáin has also raised in her essay 'Borderlands of Irish Poetry', which focuses on the significance of borders for a writer:

> What other borders, of class, gender, religion, language, does the political fence cut across? How far does political and institutional division mask unity of interests and attitudes? Since nobody is going to suggest that British influence stops short at Clones, or that the Gaelic language abruptly begins to interest writers and readers at Aughnacloy or Keady, what do the terms 'state' or 'province' or 'region' mean when applied to the writers or readers of poetry and the climate they inhabit?[14]

In the poem 'Borders', Ní Chuilleanáin crosses constructed gender boundaries as well, apparent in her choice of female images to memorialise a man's death, and also to add a female voice to a commentary on Irish politics. McCarter's crossing the map is compared to 'Lir's daughter driven to the Sea of Moyle / By spells'. In Irish myth, Lir's daughter

Fionnuala was turned into a swan by Aoife, her stepmother, whose curse meant that Fionnuala would spend three hundred years on the straits of Moyle, freed only after a man of the North mated with a woman of the South. In this poem, the myth becomes a political allegory for the centuries of wars that created the borders, while inherently suggesting the possibility of a potential reconciliation between Northern Ireland and the Irish Republic, one that involves women as well as men.[15]

In an important allusion in the poem, the speaker sees herself as 'the witch who stands one-legged, masking one eye', a version of the female *cailleach* figure in Irish mythology. With her image of the witch/*cailleach* speaker, Ní Chuilleanáin creates an active female voice, an 'I' in a positive female figure, ironically referring to herself in the more negative image of the witch. The *cailleach* is linked to the landscape in Irish mythology, a landscape redefined by the borders which divided Ireland. A female of great wisdom, the *cailleach* pre-dates a separated Ireland and was also known to leap great distances across the landscape, giving additional meaning to the line in 'Borders': 'so I leap over lines that are set here to hold'. Avoiding the image of Mother Ireland, the passive female exploited by Irish revolutionaries as a political victim, Ní Chuilleanáin restores the *cailleach*'s authority; she is the wise woman who will not be contained, and who, even with one eye masked, sees more than the soldiers' lenses which the female speaker has to pass under as she drives to the wake.

Patricia Coughlan, in an excellent reading of 'Borders', suggests that with 'her uncanny powers, the poet can also 'leap over' the virtual corset of longitude (making a comic *cailleach*-as-the-land-of-Ireland equivalence between the ample 'global waistline' of territory and of an older woman) and thus 'follow the road that follows the lie of the land'. Coughlan continues:

> The matter of the nation becomes much more than before a question of resistance to internal oppression, and Ní Chuilleanáin's feminist feeling – always evident, if, as has often been noted, never readily detachable from other aspects of her complex and subtle poetic thought – flows together with passionate social critique.[16]

This critique is expressed in many other Ní Chuilleanáin poems; at the centre of her use of female figures is the desire to include women in 'the matter of the nation'. And this wise old woman/*cailleach* figure appears in other poems, sometimes connected, as in 'Borders', with the female poetic voice asserting its value.

On first reading, it is not always clear that Ní Chuilleanáin's poems are exploring events or figures from Ireland's history, and often such poems require careful deconstructing before such meanings are clear, but a concern with Irish history has been apparent from her earliest works. As she has said, 'History has been particularly alive for me as for many Irish people. We are lectured occasionally by benevolent advisers and told this is bad for us. But like others who share my linguistic background, I am always aware of the presence of the past and of the strangeness, the untypical edge on the way I read history.'[17] That 'untypical edge' is illustrated as she imagines an Ireland in poems that present surprising twists and untraditional views of past events. Most of these, however, need not be read only in terms of conventional Irish political history, as their themes and imagery have broader application, to social and family history and to gender issues as well. Two poems, *Site of Ambush* (*SV* 5), a poem in eight sections, and 'On Lacking the Killer Instinct' (*S* 14), set in Cork, Ní Chuilleanáin's native city, comment on different political ideologies as Ní Chuilleanáin explores the way events have sometimes been presented. Because both also involve the soldier/warrior/hero celebrated in patriarchal Irish history, her strategies include placing female figures in the poems. She also spotlights males in domestic settings, within the more stereotypically female private sphere, thus challenging the validity of certain gender constructs.

An early poem, *Site of Ambush* is a good example of these strategies, what Thomas McCarthy calls 'a history lesson through evocation; the elliptical autobiography of a war-torn county'.[18] Divided into eight sections, which range from a narrative of a specific military manoeuvre to reflections on and descriptions of pastoral places, the poem becomes both a meditation on what one section calls 'Time and Place' and an exploration into the consequences of war and military strategies, deconstructing the conventional hero by juxtaposing soldiers with the female figures in the poem. The poem raises questions about gender roles, and how the celebration of the masculine soldier figure leaves women out of the story. A major narrative in the poem is set in Cork in the 1920s when the Black and Tans, British troops brought in to reinforce the Royal Irish Constabulary, battled with the Irish Republican Army and *Sinn Féin*, forces who supported the Irish Republic declared by the *Dáil* in 1919. The Black and Tans became synonymous with military brutality, which was particularly evident in Ní Chuilleanáin's childhood home, Cork City, the centre of which was burned in December 1920.

Part 2 of *Site of Ambush*, 'Narration', describes a planned military ambush by the Black and Tans which is calculated with minute-to-minute precision between daybreak and noon as 'enemy commanders synchronised their heartbeats'. The ambush turns into a disaster in which both the soldiers and a young innocent boy are killed. The poem focuses on the aftermath of the event; the lorry the soldiers rode in is now 'rusting in the stream' and the soldiers and the boy 'all looked the same face down there: / … coiled / By scythefuls limply in ranks'. Contrasted to the human dead, a watch still 'vibrates alone in the filtering light'. Ní Chuilleanáin emphasises the reaction of the natural world to the disaster: 'The pine trees looked up stiff', 'the birds shoaled off the branches in fright'. In Section 6, 'Voyagers', these soldiers are compared to other voyagers: the Irish hero Maelduin and the Greek heroes Odysseus and Anticlus, all of whom devised ambushes and strategies to return from sea wanderings to their island homes, but who are represented here as hemmed in, 'penitential', 'crouching' and 'suffocating'.

In Part 3, with its ironic title 'Standing Man', a beautiful passage, alternating short and long lines which control the movement and rhythm of the poem, contrasts the images of garden and cemetery in describing an excavated history:

> The last bed excavated, the long minute hand
> Upright on the hour,
> The years in pain scored up are scattered and their tower
> Down: time at a stand.
>
> And upright on horizons of storm the monumental crosses,
> Lone shafts like the spade
> Hunting the furrow's end, flourish when man's unmade
> Wedged in stones, sunk in mosses –
>
> Aching an upright femur can feel the tough roots close
> Gently over bone, stick
> Fast holding a smooth shaft. Only the flesh such strict
> Embraces knows.

The crosses that 'flourish' when 'man's unmade' have universal significance in their evocation of military cemeteries, and the image of an upright femur suggests something right below the surface, a hint of what has happened in the past. This is an image Ní Chuilleanáin will use again, to suggest a history still to be uncovered: in a later poem, 'The Real Thing' (*SP* 68), a nun's hidden history is described as 'the one free foot kicking / Under the white sheet of history'.[19]

The phrase 'man's unmade' while referring specifically to the dead men, has significant other meanings as well, not only in deconstructing the model of the warrior/hero but also when considered in the light of the female figures who become major subjects in the poem. In the last section, 'Site of Ambush', the boy who was killed by the soldiers in the narration returns, resurrected as a young girl. Imagining this girl as both 'soaked from her drowning' and as a phoenix that 'turns to flame', the speaker urges: 'Lay fast hold of her / And do not let her go', as she

> Comes back from her sleep
> – troubling for a minute the patient republic
> Of the spider and the fly
> On the edge of the aspic stream
> Above the frail shadows of wreckage.

The lines 'troubling for a minute the patient republic / of the spider and the fly' evoke both the narrative of the soldiers who disrupted the natural world, and the new life that the young girl represents. The soldiers killed here, along with their fellow Black and Tans, were ultimately unable to suppress the formation of a 'patient' Irish Republic, which came into being in 1949, the year mentioned in another section of the poem, 'March in a garden', where the branches of a cherry tree 'host a songbird'.

Subtle shifts occur in *Site of Ambush* in the movements from a military narration to descriptions of the timelessness of the natural world, and from the focus on the soldiers to the female figures whose lives and habits are different from those of the soldiers but who are equally affected by political turmoil. The resurrected girl in the final section, who has replaced the dead boy, is connected to the young girl in Section 5, to the female speaker walking beside the strand in Section 7, and, in Section 4, to a 'weakened creature in a dirty cream coat', walking across the decimated landscape:

She fingers three coppers in her pocket;
The wind scratches her face –
Dryskinned, these skeleton days
No more aware than wind of the passage of sand,
Tolling of dead bells.
. . . .
Her parcel of bread grows mouldy
The milk in her jug sours fast under the sun.

One hears echoes here of Pádraic Colum's poem 'Old Woman of the Roads', whose wandering female, a stock character in Irish narratives, seeks 'a little house, a house of my own / Out of the wind and the rain's way'. Ní Chuilleanáin's figure is a step more desperate than Colum's sentimentalised old woman who could 'be busy all the day / Clearing and sweeping hearth and floor'. With her mouldy bread and sour milk, Ní Chuilleanáin's 'weakened creature' is disconnected from the real world, not aware of 'the passage of sand, / Tolling of dead bells'. With the use of this figure, Ní Chuilleanáin challenges the romanticising of an image like Colum's, contrasting her to the real women of the time. Like the young girl who appears at the end of *Site of Ambush*, the old woman is also an attempt to illustrate that the battling males were not the only tragic figures in the war-torn landscape.

In *Site of Ambush*, many metaphors call attention to females: 'Pale widowed houses', 'breasts of hills criss-crossed', as do images of 'dark knitting', 'shady presses', and 'dated jamjars'. The ultimate effect of all of these images is to suggest a narrative which includes female figures to counterpoint both the male soldiers and warriors and the stereotypical female figures who have dominated narrowly focused modern Irish narratives. It is as if the poet tells us, as the poem says of the resurrected girl: 'Lay fast hold of her / And do not let her go'. Turning the young boy who was killed into a resurrected girl, and highlighting the old woman, Ní Chuilleanáin presents a different story – one in which the consequences of war on men, women and children are highlighted.

Looking at the sections of *Site of Ambush* as interrelated, we can also see the first-person speaker in the poem as a unifying female voyager or wanderer, visualising and collecting a series of scenarios, moving from the site of the Black and Tan ambush, past the old woman with her bread and milk, then to Sandymount Strand, in so doing creating a bit of an ambush herself on male-dominated Irish narratives. The image of the male voyagers reinforces this, when the narrator addresses them in Section 6:

> You look sad entering your dream
> Whose long currents yield return to none.

While, on one level, the poem is about the passage of time ('the lorry now is soft as a last night's dream'), it also integrates women into the narratives of Irish history, culture and literature, which Ní Chuilleanáin has continued to do throughout her career. While readers might not notice this at first, one effect of the narrator in *Site of Ambush* is to strengthen the structural connection between the parts of the poem, unifying them through images and themes as Ní Chuilleanáin asks us to consider the lives and behaviours we celebrate and record, and the effects of war on all the Irish people. The female narrator is an important device to bring this about as we get the sense that she too has arrived at a new understanding of what she has seen. Moreover, as in 'Borders', the voice of the female poet is injected into representations of Irish military history.

Allied to the female figures in this poem are males the narrator spotlights whose lives and vocations contrast those of the soldiers. Juxtaposed with images of the men plotting and battling are those in Section 5, 'March in a garden' where Michael Barry tends the spring flowers, or in Section 7, 'Now', where the speaker is walking beside Sandymount Strand and sees Maurice Craig reading a book in his window. 'March in a garden' recreates a scene in 1949 when Ní Chuilleanáin lived as a young girl at University College Cork, and Michael Barry was the college grounds superintendent, described in the poem as 'a dark male figure' and known as the man 'who threw the bowl / And hit the Chetwynd Viaduct'. This feat, celebrated as a great achievement in Irish sport, occurred on St Patrick's Day, 17 March 1955, when Barry threw a bowl over the ninety-foot viaduct on the Cork–Bandon Road, a place known in Ireland as the 'Everest of Road Bowling'. Barry became an instant celebrity because of the difficulty of what he had accomplished. Contrasting the skill required for such an achievement to the failed manoeuvring of the dead soldiers, Ní Chuilleanáin gives us another kind of hero, one whose actions hurt no one. We should also note that 'March in a garden' is set in 1949, when the 'patient' Irish republic came into being. The spades in Barry's garden, as the quotation noted earlier highlights, are contrasted to the crosses standing upright which mark the soldiers' graves.[20]

Maurice Craig, the other man noted in the poem, was a well-known architectural historian. Born in Belfast, Craig spent much time in London before settling in Dublin to write several books, including a history of Dublin buildings from 1660 to 1860 and *The Architecture of Ireland from the Earliest Times to 1800*.[21] An article in the *The Irish Times* on 15 October 2009 refers to Craig as 'a conservation warrior', and a 25 June 2006 *Times* of London feature on his photographs of Irish buildings calls Craig 'the ideal explorer to navigate and chart the hidden features of Ireland',[22] certainly a contrast to some of the other explorers the poem highlights, and one reason Ní Chuilleanáin would have alluded to him in this 1986 poem. Craig has also crossed those borders Ní Chuilleanáin highlights, having moved between Belfast, London and Dublin. And we should not fail to note both that the Belfast-born Craig's books on Ireland's buildings go back to the seventeenth century and the beginnings of the modern conflicts between England and Ireland, and that he, like the gardener Barry, is more interested in preserving than in destroying landscapes.

While *Site of Ambush* was a relatively early poem of Ní Chuilleanáin's and one which examines the English Black and Tans' behaviour, a later poem interrogates the modern Irish troubles by examining certain republican actions and viewpoints, also from a woman speaker's point of view. 'On Lacking the Killer Instinct', in the 2009 collection *The Sun-fish* (*S* 14), opens with an image of a hare the persona sees as she walks to the place where her father is dying. She then describes a later newspaper image of a hare escaping two greyhounds, and, at the end of the poem, compares this to her running off from her dying father:

> And I should not
> Have run away, but I went back to the city
> Next morning, washed in brown bog water, and
> I thought about the hare, in her hour of ease.

On a narrative level, this is a poem about deserting the dying and seeking personal comfort, but the centre of the poem creates another scenario where the hare fleeing the greyhounds is compared to the speaker's father running from a lorry of soldiers in 1921, 'cornering in the narrow road / Between high hedges, in summer dusk' as the lorry approaches:

The lorry was growling
And he was clever, he saw a house
And risked an open kitchen door. The soldiers
Found six people in a country kitchen, one
Drying his face, dazed-looking, the towel
Half covering his face. The lorry left,
The people let him sleep there, he came out
Into a blissful dawn.

Ní Chuilleanáin explains the background and inspiration for this poem, an action of her own father, who at age nineteen had joined the Irish Republican Army during the War of Independence, describing an incident when he was running from the Black and Tans:

> He had to shave off his beard on the train back to Cork because he couldn't face his mother. He had described to me what it felt like running away from his lorry, and he ran into a house and the lorry came up and pulled up alongside the house. He had bolted into the kitchen and he saw a towel and some water. He picked up the towel and put it up to his face and looked as bleary-eyed as he could. And they looked around the kitchen and those there said they hadn't seen anybody and the lorry went on. He said he never felt so well in his life as when he was running, so I've been trying to put that into a poem.[23]

From one political point of view, this action was 'clever' strategy in war time, one about which the speaker's father felt 'never such gladness'. But the poem brings up another question about seeking personal safety or shelter at the expense of others:

… Should he have chanced that door?
If the sheltering house had been burned down, what good
Could all his bright running have done
For those that harboured him?

Subordinating the larger safety of a family to personal need, or the welfare of kind people to individual safety, complicates both the memory of her father's cleverness and the actions of the deserting daughter who 'should not / Have run away' as her father was dying. The speaker acknowledges that her father, clever as the hare that like him 'should never have been coursed' needed to save himself; like the hare, he had to choose the time 'to spring away out of the frame, all while / The pack is labouring up'. The persona nevertheless raises the larger issue of war strategies: how does one measure individual need with the risk to, or safety of, others? Interrogating certain attitudes, including republican, Ní Chuilleanáin typically leaves us with an unanswered question, but one which has universal significance not only for war experience but also, beyond family and nation, for all human experience. As in many of Ní Chuilleanáin's poems, there are no easy answers to questions she raises.

The 'frame' described in the poem is literally the newspaper image, but it can also represent the frames of history or of the speaker's father's portrait, where one has to examine the motives and tactics of those who go to war, as well as the overall consequences to all those that war affects. And, like the poem 'Borders', this poem illustrates a need to get beyond the restricting frame, as a daughter interrogates both a national and family history, relating this to her own motivations in seeking personal comfort in a difficult situation. The title here, 'On Lacking the Killer Instinct', alludes to the female speaker but suggests that one's victories must be weighed in the context of consequences to all people involved. The recorded history of Ireland since the 1920s, troubled as it has been, demonstrates that the larger goals of the various factions have not yet been totally met, but more importantly that the 'killer instinct', having caused much harm, should not be celebrated.

With her emphasis on the fate of the family in the farmhouse, and the potential for them or their home to be destroyed, Ní Chuilleanáin puts the spotlight on the broader issues of the consequences of continual fighting. The female subject-speaker here sees her own actions of running away from her father's deathbed as morally debatable, as she also questions the morality of the soldier's strategy. This poem makes clear, as does *Site of Ambush*, that the tragic consequence of such tactics, clever or not, were not restricted to male soldiers – they affected women, young children and families as well. And when history becomes primarily a recording of dates and figures connected with such conflicts, celebrating military victories, it ignores other types of suffering, heroism and history. Both of these poems are set in Cork and the autobiographical overtones suggest that Ní Chuilleanáin is presenting her own perspective on events in Ireland's and Cork's past.

Ní Chuilleanáin's journeys into Irish history, however, and into the place of women in that history, are by no means restricted to twentieth-century Ireland, as the poem 'In Rome' (*SP* 59) illustrates. The speaker here is Rosa O'Doherty, the wife of Cathbar O'Donnell, who joined her husband in the famous Flight of the Earls, when the Gaelic Ulster leaders Hugh O'Neill and Rory O'Connell and their families left Donegal in 1607, fleeing encroaching English armies. They headed for Spain and their Spanish allies but ended up in France and moved eventually on a difficult journey through Switzerland to Rome, where the pope had offered them asylum. Though the women were integral to this long journey, they have often been given less attention in recorded Irish history and narrative and are seen primarily as wives and helpmates.[24] Ní Chuilleanáin, however, chooses to imagine their hidden lives and says of women like O'Doherty: 'One is constantly having to uncover women who were quite celebrated in their day but were then covered up by the process of historical change or the writing of history by men.'[25]

In the poem 'In Rome' Ní Chuilleanáin imagines O'Doherty domiciled in a small space and dependent on men, the pope's musketeers living on the floor above ('The captain lowered some charcoal / Last night') and others:

> Indeed, only an hour after the markets close
> The deaf runner from the palace climbs
> With two silver pieces and odd coppers.

O'Doherty contrasts her present situation to her former life in rural Ireland:

> When we were at home it would have been three sheep –
> Work for the troop, skinning, washing the guts,
> Digging the pit for the fire. When the meat was eaten,
> The wool to card and spin.

Characteristically Ní Chuilleanáin focuses on the value of the often-unacknowledged work of women; at the same time she imagines, in the voice of O'Doherty, the restrictions on their lives which O'Doherty and the women with her now face:

... my poor girls are cooking eggs now
Behind the screen. Soon they must wrap
And veil up for the street, for the hours lounging
Nibbling bread in the Cardinal's front hall,
Twisting to keep their heels out of sight.

Basically forced to remain invisible, the women here, including O'Doherty, are reduced to dependence on men; in this case having fled Ireland and living in a foreign country. In recovering women from Ireland's past, Ní Chuilleanáin is trying to broaden our view of history, shifting the focus from the rebellious (and controversial) earls to the difficulties for the women who helped to make their journeys possible.

It is interesting to compare and contrast the poem 'In Rome' with another poem that appears earlier in *The Magdalene Sermon*, 'The Italian Kitchen' (*SP* 56), to illustrate Ní Chuilleanáin's contention that the past lives in the present and 'is the only thing we know'. The speaker in this poem creates a totally different atmosphere but one which describes a kitchen furnished by someone who has also moved frequently: 'One more of your suddenly furnished houses' refers to Eilís Dillon, Ní Chuilleanáin's mother, who, like O'Doherty, had moved from Ireland to Rome when her husband Cormac Ó Cuilleanáin was ill with rheumatoid arthritis. Ní Chuilleanáin also alludes to another of her mother's homes, in 'California where you are now', as Eilís, after she married Vivien Mercier, had spent parts of each year in California, when he was teaching there. 'The Italian Kitchen' evokes Rosa O'Doherty's residence in Rome, but the circumstances are very different. In 'The Italian Kitchen' there is a man asleep upstairs, as opposed to the pope's musketeers above O'Doherty, whose reeking cooking smells and 'retching' caged doves O'Doherty must endure. And in contrast to O'Doherty, here are two women, the speaker and her mother, who have not been dependent on others for their food and kitchen supplies:

Eighteen years since we discovered, cash in hand,
Anonymous, the supermarket pleasures
Stacked and shinily wrapped, right
For this country, where all wipes clean,
Dries fast.

Displacement here is by choice and the comfort of this kitchen contrasts with the hardship ('cooking eggs now / Behind the screen') described by O'Doherty in 'In Rome'. Images of the poet/speaker in 'The Italian Kitchen' suggest a sense of plenty, of women who have their own money ('cash in hand'), and of peace and fulfilment. These women are also able to combine different kinds of work, including that beyond the domestic, which the opening lines suggest:

> Time goes by the book laid open
> On the long marble table: my work
> In the kitchen your landlord painted yellow and white.

The connections between these women, one in the eighteenth century, the others in the twentieth, are made through the images in the poems. 'I've brought blankets and firewood; we live here now,' says the speaker in 'The Italian Kitchen' as opposed to O'Doherty, who must depend on the pope's musketeers for charcoal for her fire. O'Doherty is recognised for the difficulty she endured and for her competence surviving the horrible circumstances that the Flight of the Earls created, but in Rome she was also economically dependent on others who controlled the resources she needed. By focusing on O'Doherty, and, more importantly, by giving her voice as the first person narrator of 'In Rome', Ní Chuilleanáin highlights the heroism and competence of women who have been overshadowed in Irish political and cultural history as the exploits of militant men and Irish political leaders are recorded. Suggesting that none of these activities would have been possible without the work, courage and perseverance of women, Ní Chuilleanáin unveils a forgotten history of Irish women's deeds and lives, by connecting past and present. The meditative conversational tone of the speaking voice in 'In Rome' is created by many long lines, between eight and thirteen syllables, echoing the Gaelic syllabic verse of O'Doherty's time.

While the plight of Rosa O'Doherty is described in *The Magdalene Sermon*, 'Kilcash' (*SP* 90), a poem in the 'Coda' to *The Girl who Married the Reindeer*, is a translation from the Irish of a traditional lament for Margaret Butler, Lady Iveagh, of the Butler family which resided in Kilcash Castle, County Tipperary. Like her mother, who translated from the Irish Eibhlín Dubh Ní Chonaill's 'The Lament for Art O'Leary', a *caoineadh* and love poem memorialising her husband who had been killed,

Ní Chuilleanáin chooses a poem which focuses on a lament for a woman in Irish history. Lady Iveagh was known both for her generosity and her support of Gaelic Catholic causes.

'Kilcash', written in the early eighteenth century, begins with a description of the loss of Kilcash, the Butler family home, and its surrounding forests, which, according to John and Phil Flood in *Kilcash: A History 1190–1801*,[26] date back to the late twelfth century. Kilcash, the poem tells us, a house 'where the lady lived with such honour', now is missing not only its family but also the streams, animals and trees which once marked the property, as the abandoned residence lies in ruins. The speaker in the poem suggests that, while this loss is great, it is not the worst of 'our troubles':

> She has followed the prince of the Gaels –
> He has borne off the gentle maiden,
> Summoned to France and to Spain.
> Her company laments her
> That she fed with silver and gold:
> One who never preyed on the people
> But was the poor souls' friend.

The poem ends with a prayer for Lady Iveagh's return to Ireland, 'to dancing' and 'to fiddling' when the house is rebuilt. Ní Chuilleanáin's translation tells us, in its reference to France and Spain, that Lady Iveagh had joined in the Flight of the Earls, but her leaving is described as 'a summoning', like in a fairy tale, where her prince has 'borne off the gentle maiden'. Ní Chuilleanáin makes a connection between 'Kilcash' and 'In Rome', highlighting the two women, but by translating the poem from the Irish she also forefronts the different cultural heritages embodied in Irish history and language, including the Anglo-Normans from which the Gaelic Butler family descended.

Similar images appear in both poems, and the changed situation of the women is stressed: in 'Kilcash', the speaker tells of how Lady Iveagh fed the poor with silver and gold which is now gone, an image reflected in 'In Rome', where an impoverished Rosa O'Doherty speaks of the plenty she once enjoyed. In 'Kilcash', Lady Iveagh's 'company laments her' because of her generosity; in 'In Rome', we see Rosa O'Doherty reduced to the poverty she had worked to alleviate in Ireland, but still trying to keep a household going. By looking at these two poems together, we note that emphasis is more on the historical plight of the women than that of the earls, as well as on the women's basic goodness helping others. In her own poem, 'In Rome', however, unlike her translation of the original 'Kilcash', Ní Chuilleanáin is able to give a first-person voice to O'Doherty, telling her own tale, a choice 'Kilcash' does not provide, as Lady Iveagh's voice remains lost to the speaker though her generosity is remembered. Most significantly, both poems see these women as important figures in their own right and as concerned with the people around them. By highlighting their actions and values in her poems, Ní Chuilleanáin gives them a higher status in Irish history and links them, through their work, to contemporary women, suggesting a more multidimensional view of women's roles, unrecorded in most versions of Irish history.

To counteract the dearth of historical accounts of the ordinary lives of women and to offer a view of Irish womanhood which would include social and family histories, Ní Chuilleanáin often focuses on women in her own family – her mother, grandmother, aunts and sister. In these poems, Ní Chuilleanáin is often clearly identified as speaker, and the poems can be seen as a record of her own life and her family's lives. She succeeds in turning these experiences into poems with a restrained lyric voice, quiet yet powerful, the stanzaic framing and most especially the images carrying the weight of feeling. One of the most beautiful of these poems is 'A Hand, A Wood' (*SP* 88) in *The Brazen Serpent*, a short two-part lyric on the death of her sister Máire, who also figures in the poems 'Autun' (*SP* 106) and 'Crossing the Loire' (*SP* 108) in *The Girl who Married the Reindeer*. 'A Hand, A Wood' is a poem about grief and the ways in which one tries to deal with the inevitability of loss. Máire, a violinist with the London Philharmonic who lived in London, died from a brain tumour in 1990. In the first section of the poem, the speaker describes how, in returning to her sister's home and washing up, she is trying to prise her sister from under her nails, as she notes the words on labelled jars and the dates in a diary, written records, a part of a woman's history, in the woman's own hand.

In the second stanza, the scene shifts to a wood where the dead one's ashes have been scattered: 'the wet leaves are blowing, the sparse / Ashes are lodged under the trees in the wood'. Ní Chuilleanáin has said of the biographical aspects of this poem:

> 'A Hand, A Wood' is factual, about the physical absence of Máire from the house in Palmer's Green, the sense that every time one washed, one was washing away something of her, and every time one used up something from a jar she had labeled. The second half was written in Italy after her death and the scattering of her ashes in a little wood on our land beside our Italian house.[27]

Images of time appear frequently in this poem, three days, diary dates which 'come and pass', the changing weather, reminding us of the limits of mortality. Ironic images portray continuous life and activity in the natural world: a rattling stream, hunters scattering shot, birds spreading out. Despite the fact that the speaker tries to prise the lost one from under her fingernails, she says at the end:

> I am wearing your shape
> Like a light shirt of flame;
> My hair is full of shadows.

'A Hand, A Wood' is a moving elegy for Máire Ní Chuilleanáin which also gives us a clue that we should read this poem at different levels. The hands highlighted in the poem are those of the professional violinist, but we can see them also as the hands of the speaker who was washing away small details of her sister's life, and the hands of the poet recording her own response to her sister's death. Likewise, the wood is both the 'little wood' on the land in Italy where Máire shared a house with her sister, and where her ashes are scattered, and an image of the wood of the violin she played. This tribute to Ní Chuilleanáin's sister becomes, then, with its compact images, not only an elegy for one life but also a validation of the different roles that women have played in history, both inside and outside the home. In short lines running between six and eleven syllables, with their alliterative and assonantal sound patterns, 'something of her', a biography in images, is recorded by the hand of the poet.

Using her own family history, Ní Chuilleanáin works against the stereotype of woman's limited role as caregiver, whose sole domain lay within the domestic realm; at the same time she acknowledges the collective experiences of caregiving many women are involved in. The speaker in 'Early Recollections', a poem in *Acts and Monuments* (*SP* 24) says: 'do not / Investigate my adult life but try / Where I started', stressing the importance of family and of memory for constructing a history. By drawing connections between historical figures like Rosa O'Doherty and her own mother, or the 'dated jamjars' mentioned in *Site of Ambush* with those in the press in her dead sister's home, Ní Chuilleanáin connects women to one another and imagines a tradition of women's lives by creating linked poetic images. Deborah Sarbin suggests that an emphasis on legendary figures, or on male-dominated history, 'has created a distance, a tendency to remove history from the realm of the everyday' and 'to value large-scale action while dismissing the ordinary and domestic'. Sarbin sees Ní Chuilleanáin's use of metaphor and imagery as working against this tendency.[28]

Nicholas Allen's judgment that Ní Chuilleanáin's words are much like a 'scribe's asides'[29] might best be illustrated in Ní Chuilleanáin's poem 'Ascribed' from *The Sun-fish* (*S* 21), in which a woman tries to write, 'as if a voice had spoken', telling her to: '*Write / For those who never made it to the promised shore*'. Describing an historical situation where people struggled through a flooded landscape, with children and their toys, to come to a stone pillar built after the Williamite Wars, the writing woman stops:

> And the voices of the drowned did not reach her at all
> But instead it came to her in silence,
> An instant: her grandmother remembered in old age
> Her long hair down, her wide shoulders bare
> Before her basin in the early light
> While the cat lapped a basin of fresh milk,
> And how as a child she watched without moving.

Allusions to the Williamite Wars in Ireland, where the armies of William of Orange defeated those of James II, are connected here to a disastrous flood where parents carrying their children are drowned, linking the tragic consequences of both military conflicts and natural disasters. When the writer/recorder cannot hear the voices of the dead to write their story, however, she describes instead a vision of her grandmother which came to her in silence: an 'instant' recovered from memory and personal history.

This beautiful, painterly image of a remembered older woman can be set against the many images of the drowned in Ní Chuilleanáin's poetry, those described in this poem, and those taking us all the way back to the drowned soldiers and boy and girl in the earlier poem *Site of Ambush.* Like a medieval scribe who could be an historian, a poet, a painter, the female writer in 'Ascribed' imagines her grandmother as her link to the past and as another version of the resurrected young girl, 'soaked by her drowning', who appears at the end of *Site of Ambush.* The admonition in that poem, 'Lay fast hold of her / And do not let her go', applies here as well. If 'Our history is a mountain of salt' which 'will be gone in time', the poet's words and images can record bits of it for posterity, just as the medieval scribes did. But for Ní Chuilleanáin, those images include women across time, *cailleachs*, young girls, historical figures, grandmothers, mothers and sisters. In the poem 'Sunday' (*GMR* 13), the speaker says of the past, 'I can't go there, but I know just how it will be'. Using her own family history, military events in Cork, women like Rosa O'Doherty and Lady Iveagh, wives, widows, the stories, legends and secrets that she has absorbed, Ní Chuilleanáin creates female figures who work against stereotypes and cut across all kinds of borders.

CHAPTER 4

Fictive Women: Myth and Folklore

> The woman turned and under the towel as if
> Shrouded by the mantled oxter
> Of a heroic bird was a girl's mother-of-pearl sheen,
>
> A girl's hesitant body, sheltered by the bird's broad wing.
>
> 'The Married Women', *The Sun-fish* (*S* 54)

An interesting debate has developed over the differences between myth and history and each as a source of knowledge. In an essay on 'Myth, History and Theory', Peter Heehs sums up the debate: 'positivist historiography declares that myth has nothing to do with history; academic mythology replies that history has nothing to do with myth. Certain contemporary historians study myth as an object or category of historiography. Others go so far as to view history as a sort of myth.'[1] Heehs argues that the two are connected, and although historical narratives should correspond in some ways to actual events in the past, historians must consider the 'culturally conditioned – and therefore mythical – nature of the reality-grid through which they view the past' and be aware that it is sometimes difficult to draw an absolute line between fact and fiction. Citing the value of metaphor, allegory and symbolism, Heehs maintains that myth often allows people to create a vision of the past more meaningful than an accumulation of facts.[2] When we also consider that myth and folklore fit into the general category of the storytelling art involving both oral and written traditions, the intersection of history, myth and art can lead to revealing aspects of specific cultures.

If we apply this idea to Irish culture, where women have by and large been left out of many historical narratives, it is not surprising that women writers have so often turned to myth for both subject matter and female figures. As she has done with her use of historical material, Ní Chuilleanáin employs the values of myth and folklore to develop many of the images and themes in her poems. In addition, as in these other areas, she also highlights female figures found in mythic and folklore narratives. Angela Bourke, whose work on Irish folklore is well known, explains the value of folktales and the preponderance of women found in them in her essay 'Language, Stories, Healing'. Her description can be applied to Ní Chuilleanáin's work:

> Stories like these deal with ambivalence and paradox, with transitions in human life and situations that are beyond human control. Their protagonists stumble into a world where everything is other, and emerge either mutilated or enriched. Fairy legends ... are meditations on change, reassuringly rooted in the past ... Many, if not most, are about women and children.[3]

In general, we might distinguish myths from folktales by suggesting that in myth the emphasis is more on human responses to divine worlds and folklore is more centred on describing mysteries and obstacles humans face. For a poet like Ní Chuilleanáin, however, this distinction can be less important than their narrative or dramatic function, which depend on the artistic strategies of symbolic representation to carry embedded meanings and lessons. Significantly in Ireland, where connections can be drawn between some religious rituals and traditional folklore, as in the case of devotion at holy wells, the cultural importance of folklore should not be underestimated. Like myth, the recurrence of folklore and legends in Ní Chuilleanáin's work suggests a link with the past which is extremely important to any understanding and representation of Irish culture, but these narratives, as is usual in her work, can also be used to express ideas about contemporary life.

Diarmuid Ó Giolláin argues in his book *Locating Irish Folklore: Tradition, Modernity, Identity*[4] that folklore also provides a body of material which challenges conventional attitudes and thus provides a way not only to connect past and present but also to interrogate authoritative views and traditional perspectives, an appealing aspect given Ní Chuilleanáin's interest in revising images of the female. In this regard, Ní Chuilleanáin often uses such tales to spotlight women subjects and figures; as her poetry developed, the women in myth and folklore moved front and centre. As she says: 'folk tales are so full of themes of quest, and Irish folk tales quite often have women who go on quests, or undertake tasks, which are important.

So, again, that would be a way of putting a feminine presence into a poem.'[5] However, for Ní Chuilleanáin, Irish folktales are also part of a collective mythic heritage in a transnational cultural spectrum which includes classical myths as well. In her poetry, allusions to figures in both mythology and folklore appear quite often. Like words and images, these tales are always open to renewal and new interpretations.

The classical myth of Ceres and Persephone, for example, demonstrates the symbolic value of such figures. One of the best-known myths centring on female figures, the narrative describes how a young girl playing with her friends is snatched from her mother and taken by Hades to the underworld. When Ceres protests, Persephone is allowed to return each spring in a myth which marks the seasonal cycle from dark winter to spring rebirth. Taking advantage of its associations with the landscape, Ní Chuilleanáin uses this myth in the beautiful poem 'Sicily: Ceres and Persephone' from her 2009 volume *The Sun-fish* (*S* 24). Sicily has been associated with Ceres, and evidence in literature, including from Ovid, as well as historical remains of a temple devoted to her in Catania, suggests that worship of Ceres was quite strong there. The modern celebrations of St Agatha, popular in Catania, are traced by some to the pre-Christian Ceres figure, reinforcing the anthropological connections between classical and modern beliefs and the way in which legends and tales appear in different forms and cultures.

In Ní Chuilleanáin's poem, the speaker is first seen on a ferry sailing away from Catania where she has witnessed a contemporary scene similar to the mythic Persephone's frolicking with her friends:

> Catania, where the girls in their circle
> In the gymnasium held hands,
> Embracing, kissing, smiling at me
> Like a heavenly ceiling …

The remembered scene begins to fade, however, as the traveller leaves the island behind:

> What seemed at hand (earth
> Blooming with orange-trees and hotels)
> When the train rounded the headland was revealed
> In shadow, far away
> On the other side of the straits.

The parentheses mark the diminishing view of the tropical landscape, and the imagery evokes not only the disappearance of Persephone but also the persona's disappearing vision:

> I can see through a round hole: water
> Racing, laughing, and on the dappled ceiling
> Shadows in backward flight.

In this movement from pleasure to loss, the 'heavenly ceiling' associated with the smiling young girls in the early lines of the poem becomes the 'dappled ceiling' at the end as the shadows begin to close in and the land becomes for the speaker 'far away / On the other side of the straits'. The recurring images in Ní Chuilleanáin's poems of shadows, waters and 'the other side', especially evident throughout the *Sun-fish* collection, reinforce her continuous emphasis on the inevitability of change and loss, a theme the Ceres and Persephone myth illustrates as well.

However, the poem also fits into a pattern of poems about mothers and children throughout Ní Chuilleanáin's work: 'Balloon' (*MS* 21), a poem related to Ní Chuilleanáin's own experiences with the adoption of her son; 'St Margaret of Cortona' (*SP* 72), who after her husband's death sought refuge for herself and her son with her father, who would not take her in; 'Translation' (*SP* 102) and 'Bessboro' (*SP* 103), about women whose babies were taken from them; and 'The Girl who Married the Reindeer' (*SP* 99), who loses her son after she leaves her mountain home, to be reunited with him in the end. Connecting the mythic Ceres' loss of her daughter with the actual experience of a trip to Sicily, the speaker in this poem demonstrates how Ní Chuilleanáin links mothers to their children and uses the female figures of Ceres and Persephone to symbolise the frightening possibilities of loss Ceres experienced.

Ní Chuilleanáin also uses myth both to question the figure of a conventional heroic male and to highlight females who have been subordinated to males in classical tales. In two poems, 'The Second Voyage' (*SP* 18) and 'Odysseus Meets the Ghosts of the Women' (*SP* 35), we find a perturbed Odysseus, a version of the Tennysonian hero caught between land and sea. Ní Chuilleanáin's figure, however, frustrated by his inability to tame the sea, rails at the waves in 'The Second Voyage':

If there was a single
Streak of decency in these waves now, they'd be ridged
Pocked and dented with the battering they've had,
And we could name them as Adam named the beasts.

Reminding us of the soldiers in *Site of Ambush*, discussed in Chapter 3, who had little respect for the natural world, Odysseus seeks control over nature, like Adam's naming gave him control over animals. Gerardine Meaney also notes that in 'The Second Voyage' 'Penelope is entirely absent' and believes that the 'struggle is between an ordering, naming heroic and masculine subject and an intractable feminine ocean which will not stay to be named, ordered, objectified'.[6] In the poem, Odysseus decides to leave his ship, plant his oar in the sand and 'organise my house then'. But the hero is unable to resist the challenge of the sea: the 'unfenced valleys of the ocean still held him', and the sea 'was still frying under the ship's side'.

At the end of the poem, Ní Chuilleanáin contrasts this image of water as battleground to a settled Irish landscape where water flows peacefully through the land: in water-lilies, in fountains, lakes, canals and horse troughs. Imagining a more domestic world of tea kettles and 'housekeeping' spiders and frogs, and of settling on land with herons, silent valleys and farmers who feel none of the stress of Odysseus's voyages, the poem emphasises what Odysseus is missing, in not favouring the home base over the rigours of the sea. There are similarities to *Site of Ambush*, especially in the images of water and the way soldier-warriors value control over nature. Both Ní Chuilleanáin poems present an alternative to their heroes' quest for glory and adventure in the form of a quiet, almost paradisial Irish landscape of birds, spiders, frogs and 'the black canal, pale swans at dark'. Again challenging the conventional image of the mythic male hero, Ní Chuilleanáin offers an alternative.

In a companion poem to 'The Second Voyage', 'Odysseus Meets the Ghosts of the Women', Ní Chuilleanáin introduces female figures as it focuses on Odysseus' search for his mother. The poem opens with an allusion to the underworld scene in *The Odyssey* where the hero comes upon a group of women, like Homer's figures, whom Ní Chuilleanáin describes in her poem as 'daughters, wives, / Mothers of heroes or upstanding kings' and 'women who had died / Of pestilence, famine, in slavery'.[7] Among the group, Odysseus sees his mother, Anticleia, but she passes him by. With his 'long sword fending them off', Odysseus again becomes the hunter, chasing futilely after the women; not recognising the hero, however, they turn on him, their voices a 'hiss like thunder'. Afflicted with 'the habit of distress' (a phrase that Ní Chuilleanáin borrows from Pope's translation of *The Odyssey*), Odysseus is another frustrated warrior in Ní Chuilleanáin's work, and in this poem he is subordinated to women long overshadowed by the males with whom they are associated. By putting emphasis on these women, and on his mother, Ní Chuilleanáin not only questions the great importance assigned to the Odyssean-type adventurer but also calls attention to the millions of women, imagined as ghostly, who suffered unrecognised through pestilence, slavery and famine. With its reference to famine, Ní Chuilleanáin also acknowledges the suffering of Irish women in the famines that devastated the country from the 1840s on.

In other poems, Ní Chuilleanáin also humanises female figures from mythic narratives, often beginning a poem with an image of a contemporary woman. Ní Chuilleanáin's continual connection of present to past, and physical to spiritual, especially as this applies to the female body, is seen clearly in 'The Married Women', a poem from *The Sun-fish* (*S* 54) in which a speaker remembers her aversion as a child to the married women she saw with bangles, 'stiff new hats at Easter' and 'weddings and honeymoons in the Channel Islands'. Avoiding such women all her life, she saw them as 'made out of timber and steel'. The female speaker later sees a woman in a swimming pool dressing room and discovers something beneath the hardness she had perceived:

> She saw a woman, that timber face
> Her towel as crisp as ever, her jeans
> So stiff and brisk on their hook she thought of the new hats.
>
> The woman turned and under the towel as if
> Shrouded by the mantled oxter
> Of a heroic bird, was a girl's mother-of-pearl sheen,
>
> A girl's hesitant body, sheltered by the bird's broad wing.

This image of the 'girl's hesitant body', in a last emphatic line preceded by seven tercets, highlights the importance of the image. Words like 'sheltered', 'shrouded', 'running from' and 'feared' refer to the ways women have perceived or covered their bodies, as well as to how women's bodies can be objectified and imagined. The young child had seen them in negative terms, as hardened and bruised: 'Stiffened by a dose that had penetrated their flesh, / Poisoned and tinged them lightly purple', but the older speaker sees and appreciates the natural beauty of the unclothed female body.

The mythic allusion to the heroic bird in this poem brings to mind the story of Leda, a 'girl's hesitant body', which was 'shrouded by the mantled oxter' of Zeus's wing as the god swept down upon her. The insight the speaker gains here is like the one Ní Chuilleanáin describes when she first saw Correggio's 'Leda and the Swan' in a Berlin art gallery and recognised the physical beauty of Leda's body as the artist imagined it.[8] The poem connects real and mythic women on a physical level, as sharers of the same body. Ní Chuilleanáin's poem might be contrasted to Yeats's 'Leda and the Swan'[9] in terms of its portrayal of the female figure. Yeats's Leda, struck by a 'sudden blow' and 'the great wings beating', is described as victim of an assault by Zeus: 'staggering', 'helpless', 'terrified', 'caught up', 'mastered', by the overwhelming power of the 'feathered glory'. Yeats's sexual imagery, the 'loosening thighs', a 'shudder in the loins', the 'burning roof and tower', emphasises the violent intercourse between the godly Zeus and the human Leda, and its final question leaves the female's plight unanswered: 'Did she put on his knowledge with his power / Before the indifferent beak could let her drop?' In Yeats's poem, Leda's body becomes the vehicle for exhibiting the great power of the gods, and the sexual act is seen as a cause for Agamemnon's death. Presenting a different perspective, Ní Chuilleanáin shifts the emphasis to the beauty of the female body, with its 'mother-of-pearl sheen'.[10] We have the sense in 'The Married Women' that the persona's new insight, a change from a childhood fear generated by her image of married women ('what she was running from'), is to see the female body, underneath its many coverings, from a new angle, as something beautiful. One might also see in the background here the image of the asexual Virgin Mary at the Annunciation, where a young girl, also 'shrouded by the mantled oxter' of a descending angel (a 'heroic bird' might also refer to the Holy Spirit, imagined in Christian imagery as a bird), is miraculously proclaimed to be the mother of God with no reference whatever to her 'girl's hesitant body' or her participation in a sexual act of intercourse.

While the above poems draw material from classical mythology, the sources for many of Ní Chuilleanáin's poems are figures in Irish culture and folklore. Ní Chuilleanáin often finds similarities between different systems of belief, for example those of pre-Christian and Christian Ireland, suggesting that 'religious narrative is very folkloric'.[11] In 'A Midwinter Prayer', a narrative poem focused on exiles from her early collection *Acts and Monuments* (*AM* 24), allusions to Celtic, medieval and modern narratives illustrate the ways in which different cultures respond to human needs and the way stories can be borrowed and renewed. The poem opens with Fionn, Irish leader of the Fianna warriors, pictured at the royal hall at Tara at *Samhain*, the festival where ceremonies mark the end of the harvest and commemorate the dead. In the poem Fionn, a symbol for other exiles tested by challenges and obstacles, including the questing medieval knight who 'catches light from chapel doors', is described as a man whose life 'seemed like a funeral journey / And all his company a troop / Of anxious gravediggers'. The midwinter Fionn/exile walks the streets where 'trampling feet remind his ears of hammers / Of a hundred smiths constructing the new model of the world'. That new model of a hero has traditionally been embodied in tales of the heroic Fionn, the saviour Christ, the medieval knight who finds the chapel.

In the middle of her poem, however, Ní Chuilleanáin introduces female figures: the exile's mother, who carried him 'through the wet and dry months', is connected to Mary, the girl who 'gave birth in a ruin … As the year swung round to a new birth'. Both women are integrated into a narrative which acknowledges their role in creating and nurturing new life, an integral part of a 'new model of the world'. When juxtaposed with 'The Second Voyage', 'A Midwinter Prayer' can also be seen as suggesting alternatives not only to the importance of the mothers but also to the warrior's construct of the world. Fionn is a version of Odysseus: 'Fionn stood all night, his eyes open / For well-armed demons, for fire, music and death'.[12] The mother's important question in the poem: 'is that the young son / I carried through the wet and dry months?' suggesting a soldier she does not recognise, again raises the question of the value of different kinds of heroism and presents the female figure as a wise questioner who should be listened to.

Many of Ní Chuilleanáin's poems that deal with myth and folklore respond to images identifying Ireland with the female figure. The poem 'Permafrost Woman' (*SP* 51) from *The Magdalene Sermon* presents a version of the female landscape, but this one has clearly-imagined sexual organs. Evoking the conventional trope of Ireland as woman, landscape and body are integrated here as a man travels from desert to mountain where a face:

> Unfolds among peaks
> Of frozen sea, …
>
> Dumb cliffs tell their story, split and reveal
> Fathomed straits …

The male traveller feels:

> His hair bend at the fresh weight
> Of snow, the wind is an intimate fist
>
> Brushing back strands: he stares at the wide mouth, packed
> With grinding ash: the landslide of his first dream.

Mother Nature here has a sexual life, and when her body 'opens its locks', the male faces her exposed vagina.

In this poem Ní Chuilleanáin alludes to the *sheela-na-gigs*, stone figures, often of older women, found on churches in Ireland; these figures have a frontal orientation and their hands hold open their vulvas. Used on sacred buildings, they inspired, or were intended to inspire, horror and fear. The *sheela-na-gig* is a fascinating figure, found also in Britain and dating from the Middle Ages, though there is some evidence that it might have been a pre-Christian image assimilated into Irish Christianity.[13] Carved on walls and over doors in churches, convents and castles, *sheela-na-gigs* have been interpreted variously as warnings against lust, fertility figures, a version of the crone associated with the three-part Celtic goddess (maiden, wife and crone) and misogynist representations of female sexuality. What is most remarkable about them is their overt sexuality, with enlarged genitalia their most prominent feature.

Whatever the original intention of their placement in churches and convents, it seems clear that they were, within a Christian context, intended as negative images of the female and certainly a threatening representation of female sexuality. Ní Chuilleanáin has said that:

> The *sheela-na-gig* … is a very interesting, but a very masculine, image. It is an image that men made to express their fear of women; if you notice in Irish folklore, the image is found over the doors of churches and in places where it would seem to have a protective function … But I think it is very much an image made by men, even the very fact that it is the stone masons who made it.[14]

With the title 'Permafrost Woman' and her allusion to the *sheela-na-gig*, Ní Chuilleanáin highlights both the landscape and an image of female sexuality as the confused and terrified male in the poem stares at the female body. As the permafrost thaws in this poem, the 'body opens its locks'. The male moves beyond all 'the lapping voices', and the 'dumb' cliffs 'split' to 'tell their story' as the woman reveals herself. The opening body is imagined as both the exposed vagina and an opening mouth, counterpointing a male gaze with a female voice and body.

'Permafrost Woman' can be linked to other poems in *The Magdalene Sermon*, including 'Pygmalion's Image' (*SP* 49) where Pygmalion's statue of Galatea merges with the female landscape and with the figure of Medusa to become a woman speaking. Described as an awakening woman where 'the wind knifes under her skin and ruffles it like a book', Ní Chuilleanáin creates a ('real') body and voice:

> The crisp hair is real, wriggling like snakes;
> A rustle of veins, tick of blood in the throat;
> The lines of the face tangle and catch, and
> A green leaf of language comes twisting out of her mouth.

In a similar poem, 'A Voice' (*SP* 58), a man follows a woman's voice and 'downfaces the shimmer' as he 'shakes to hear the voice humming again'. The poem begins with his hearing a 'distant wailing' and discovering another version of the female landscape, imagined as a trapped woman: a 'human skeleton … clasped / In the grip of a flowery briar'. As the man approaches, the voice invites him in: '*You may come in – / You are already in*'. The woman is pictured buried in a stream: 'She lies in her bones – / Wide bearing hips and square / Elbows. Around them lodged, / Gravegoods of horsehair and an ebony peg'. As the man wonders what he is looking at, questions reveal his confusion:

'What sort of ornament is this?
What sort of mutilation? Where's
The muscle that called up the sound,
The tug of hair and the turned cheek?'
The sign persists, in the ridged fingerbone.

The ridged fingerbone, as well as the wide hips and the square elbows, create a picture of a real woman, with an emphasis on her materiality, not the idealised, constructed female, the 'ornament', the frightened man in 'A Voice' is seeking. At the end of the poem, the man hears the woman's voice as 'a wail of strings', because of the way she is perceived. The ebony peg, the ridged fingerbone and the wailing strings develop the images of voice and music in the poem, the peg a tuning peg for a violin and the ridged fingerbone the mark on the fingers after years of continuous playing. As Carmen Zamorano Llena suggests, 'a female voice leads the male listener to perceive the female image in a different light – as a mutilated body that, forced to be merely an 'ornament' needs to be (re) membered'.[15] The 'distant voice' and 'wail of strings' stress that this voice has not been heard. 'A Voice', as a poem in the *The Magdalene Sermon*, emphasises women speaking ('the muscle that called up the sound'), and connects voice with body. Like 'Permafrost Woman', it challenges the stereotypes of a passive mythic Mother Ireland and portrays the fear of female sexuality which the *sheela-na-gig* came to represent.

In examining such images of the female, both Catriona Clutterbuck and Patricia Coughlan point to poems by Irish males, with Clutterbuck suggesting that 'the menacing aspect of women sited in hidden, therefore private, locations is one of the most consistent threads running through contemporary Irish poetry by men'. She notes Seamus Heaney's 'Sheelagh-na-Gig' and Richard Murphy's figures in *The Mirror Wall* as examples.[16] Patricia Coughlan describes similar figures in John Montague's work, citing 'Sheela-na-Gig' from *Mount Eagle* and Heaney's bog queens and goddesses in *North*, as well as 'Sheelagh-na-Gig' in *Station Island*. Coughlan argues that, 'in the narrative of personal identity or that of nationality … it remains very difficult for men, when they imagine self-formation as a struggle, to escape conceiving that struggle, however metaphorically or virtually as *against* the feminine'.[17]

Coughlan likewise suggests that some of the poetry produced in Ireland in the twentieth century 'requires an implicit assumption of the inescapability of a gendered allocation of subject-positions, by means of which rationality, speech and naming are the prerogatives of the autobiographically validated male poet'. As a consequence, Coughlan maintains, 'various female figures dwell in oracular silence, always objects, whether of terror, veneration, desire, admiration or vituperation, never the coherent subjects of their own actions'.[18] In 'Permafrost Woman' and 'A Voice', Ní Chuilleanáin works against this by using folkloric images of the female to question a conventional cultural image of Ireland as an objectified woman upon whose body negative and frightening images are inscribed. The numerous awakening female bodies and speaking women in her poems, often from myth and folklore, are presented as alternatives.

Ní Chuilleanáin's interest in such figures as the *sheela-na-gig* is complemented by her allusions in other poems to folktales, legends and fairy tales in which women play a part. Ní Chuilleanáin has noted that her father collected folklore and had contact with folk narrators, and that her mother, as a children's writer, was a great influence on her early reading: 'When I was a child, she was looking at what I was reading, fairy stories and things like that, with the eye of a practitioner ... I am fairly sure that even though I am trying to depict adult images, my childhood is very prominent.' But Ní Chuilleanáin also notes that many women writers have chosen to make use of folklore in their work:

> I was particularly cheered by coming across other women writers using folklore; I think women in general are inclined to use folklore ... the folk imagination is never able to leave women out. The structures and institutions find it easy to omit women, but I think that because of the way the folk imagination works, it always seems to come up with striking female images. They very often may be negative ones but they are there.[19]

In fairy tales found in the work of many women, revision of the female is an important component. Joyce Carol Oates, in a study of classic and contemporary fairy tales, notes the number of women writers who have drawn from these in their work: 'The fairy tale, as a literary/cultural genre, has traditionally been associated with women; and women have, in different times and in distinctly different ways, impressed upon these tales the nature of their deepest fantasies.'[20] Oates explains that, while fairy tales have been collected by men like Charles Perrault, the Grimm Brothers and Hans Christian Andersen, most of their material was provided by women. She describes the tales as a 'rich storehouse of mysterious, luminous, riddlesome, and ever-potent images, a vast Sargasso sea of the imagination' providing miniature narratives which 'spring from a diverse and anonymous communal source, mysterious in their origins as language itself'. Distinguishing it from the traditional, Oates explains that the contemporary tale has evolved into a subversive art form suggesting that for women, 'the romance of fairy tales is an illusion to be countered by wit, audacity, skepticism, cynicism, and eloquently rendered rage'.[21] Suggesting that women writers are sometimes reacting to the stereotyping found in fairy tales (missing mothers, wicked stepmothers, old witches, and such), Oates sees the revising as a strategy for reimagining the role of women in society.[22] Much of what Oates describes can be seen in Ní Chuilleanáin's work.

The title of Ní Chuilleanáin's collection *The Girl who Married the Reindeer* alerts us to her use of folklore themes, and the title poem of the collection (*SP* 99) employs the plot of a folk narrative in which a young girl walks into the mountains and, as she is picking sloe berries from a blackthorn bush, is approached by a reindeer. She joins him and rides on his back to his mountain home, but later returns to her former home for her sister's wedding, having given birth in the mountains to a son she leaves behind with his reindeer father. Prodded by the old queen, the bridegroom's mother, those at the wedding:

> … slipped a powder in her drink,
> So she forgot her child, her friend,
> The snow and the sloe gin.

As a consequence the girl stays, failing to return to her mountain home. The reindeer eventually metamorphoses into a young man with an old man's face 'scored with grief' and dies when their child is ten, having cursed the old queen for her tricks. After his father's death, their child, 'led by the migrating swallows', searches for his mother and finds her hammering beans and tossing them into a pot. A miraculous change occurs when she sees him, and mother and child are reunited:

She knew her child in that moment:
His body poured into her vision
Like a snake pouring over the ground,
Like a double-mouthed fountain of two nymphs,
The light groove scored on his chest
Like the meeting of two tidal roads, two oceans.

Variations of this folk tale appear in different cultures and suggest many border crossings and meetings between different worlds: valleys and mountains, human, animal and spirit worlds, fantastic and ordinary, all reflected in this poem by the integrative, doubling imagery in the above lines. Irene Gilsenan Nordin sees as a source the Scandinavian folktale of Meandash whose mother lived among reindeer and gave birth to a son.[23] Ní Chuilleanáin herself mentions a Native American folk tale called 'The Girl Who Married the Bear', and says that she may have heard that at one time, but she does not make a direct correlation between her poem and a specific version of the tale.[24] Helen Emmitt has suggested that Ní Chuilleanáin's story brings to mind the well-known Irish legend of Fionn Mac Cumhaill and Sadhbh, the deer mother of Oisín.[25] In this tale, Fionn, hunting, comes across a deer; rather than kill it, he takes it home and that evening the deer turns into a beautiful woman, Sadhbh, who tells Fionn that she had been transformed into a fawn by a Druid whose love she refused. Fionn marries her and, as long as she stays within his dun, she will remain a woman. While Fionn is away fighting, however, a pregnant Sadhbh is tricked into leaving the dun and she disappears, never to be seen again. Several years later, Fionn comes across a young boy who resembles Sadhbh and who tells him the story of a deer who had raised him until she was carried off by an angry man. Recognising his son, Fionn names him Oisín and he becomes poet/bard of the tribe.

While this version of the tale is not a direct source for Ní Chuilleanáin, it has similar narrative elements, and contrasting her poem to the Irish Fenian tale illustrates her very different emphasis. In Ní Chuilleanáin's poem, the female protagonist meets a male reindeer as opposed to the Fenian tale where the hunter carries home the female deer. The changes in the traditional tale, from deer to woman and back to deer, are echoed in Ní Chuilleanáin, but in her poem it is the male reindeer that changes: 'naked in death his body was a man's'. In Ní

Chuilleanáin's poem, the girl makes the choice to ride off with the reindeer, but then loses her son when she travels back into the more conventional world she had left. After she stays in that world, she takes care of children, prepares meals and nurses the sick queen who had cursed her. Finally in the Fenian tale, Sadhbh is kidnapped by an angry man and disappears forever, but in Ní Chuilleanáin's poem the woman is miraculously reunited with her child ('like the meeting of two tidal roads, two oceans'), unlike in the Fenian narrative where Fionn finds and names his son Oisín. In choosing to focus on the tale of a girl who married a reindeer, Ní Chuilleanáin shifts the emphasis which we see in a tale like the male-dominated Irish Fenian tale to a narrative with a female subject, and from the prevailing father figures in such tales to the often-invisible mothers.

While Ní Chuilleanáin chooses a folktale which makes the female the central subject of her narrative, in the poem the girl's choices are still controlled by others who would like her to lead a more conventional life. In this sense, Ní Chuilleanáin also brings the tale into the present where similar issues for women can still exist. In 'The Girl who Married the Reindeer', when the girl returns from the mountains, those in her hometown 'put her in a scented bath, / Found a silk dress, combed her hair out' and then put powder in the sloe gin drunk at her sister's wedding, suggesting the trappings of a modern conventional marriage ceremony and celebration. Eventually, however, the reunion of mother and son, when the reindeer's curse brings about the old queen's death, culminates in a miraculous scene, where she gets her child back, as 'his body poured into her vision'. Unlike the Fenian tale, the reunion of mother and son, not father and son, is at the centre of Ní Chuilleanáin's poem.

Most importantly, Ní Chuilleanáin's use of folklore here must also be seen in the context of other poems in the volume *The Girl who Married the Reindeer*, especially the two poems that follow it, 'Translation' (*SP* 102), which memorialises the tragedy of the Irish Magdalenes, and 'Bessboro' (*SP* 103), focused on abuses in the Mother and Baby Homes in Ireland. As discussed later in Chapter 5, both poems highlight the tragedy of unmarried women whose children were taken from them and the Irish bureaucracies which enforced repressive social policies with regard to women, children and marriage. Pregnant outside of marriage, the women in these institutions can be related to the girl who chooses to ride off with the reindeer and bears a child, only to be punished when she returns to a conventional family wedding. Unlike many of the women who ended up in the Magdalene Laundries and Mother and Baby Homes, however, the woman in the 'The Girl who Married the Reindeer' eventually gets her child back.

Much of Ní Chuilleanáin's interest in myth and folklore involves rituals and tasks, and in her poems these are often carried out by women; as Lucy McDiarmid explains, many of these women 'perform their rituals out of the sight of male authorities'.[26] A good example of a task poem is 'The Water Journey' from *The Brazen Serpent* (*SP* 70) where the speaker tells of sending a girl on an uphill journey to a well; the girl comes back with 'her eyes fixed on the level of the water / Cushioned in her palms'. Young boys on bicycles cheer her on as she tries to keep from losing the water, and present a contrast to, as Irene Gilsenan Nordin notes, the young girl's deliberate movement.[27] The girl succeeds in bringing the water to a threshold where the speaker drinks, stressing the significance of this ritual:

> I said to the other sisters, each of you
> Will have to do the same when your day comes.
> This one has finished her turn,
> She can go home with her wages;

Citing as a source for this poem the tale where a young girl is sent to a well by a woman for whom she works, Ní Chuilleanáin explains: 'All she has to do is go to the well and bring back water in her hand, but the poem tries to suggest how fairly simple things have their stress built in.'[28] The final lines of the poem, 'She would hardly make it as far / As the well at the world's end', also suggest William Morris's 1896 novel *The Well at the World's End*, where the son of a king journeys to find the magic well which would guarantee immortality. Along the way he is assisted by a woman who has drunk from the well, a prototype for the subjects in Ní Chuilleanáin's poem. Typical of Ní Chuilleanáin, however, it is the girl and her sisters who are the central subjects in this poem, illustrating Ní Chuilleanáin's desire to use folklore, as a 'way of putting a feminine presence into a poem'.[29] In this she says she was also influenced by the Renaissance tales of women questers 'who take on the impossible burdens of their tales as male heroes do, having in fact no choice'. 'And it was that inescapable burden that I wanted to stress in my poem,' Ní

Chuilleanáin adds, 'where the speaker is an older woman who sets the girl her challenge: she has only to carry water a short distance in her hands.'[30] The opening line, 'I sent the girl to the well', creates the voice of the old woman as she matter of factly tells her version of the journey.

In most of Ní Chuilleanáin's task poems women performing rituals are highlighted, counterpointing many narratives of rituals where males are featured, like Pádraic Colum's *The King of Ireland's Son* or the king's son featured in Morris's *The Well at the World's End*. In 'The Liturgy', from *The Magdalene Sermon* (*MS* 10), this is most obvious, even though the poem opens with a scene of a male who has been invited to officiate at an ancient ceremony, the 'Farewell to Fire'. When he leaves his house to carry out the ceremony, however, the two women on the ground floor perform their own ritual: 'They know the length of the ceremony, they know / They have just forty minutes'. As in many other Ní Chuilleanáin poems, we are not told what their secret 'ceremony' is, just as we are not given many of the details of the water journey. It is the task or ritual itself, rather than the specific details, that Ní Chuilleanáin wants us to consider, and it is the women who secretly conduct their own ritual, working around the more visible male, that is of interest. Ní Chuilleanáin has said of these poems: 'I have written quite a few poems that try to imagine alternative systems … where I use ideas about ceremony which have no direct connection with Christianity other than that they use the ecclesiastical calendar or hierarchy or similar references.'[31] Many of these poems are connected to the task poems in that there is a pilgrim or an exile carrying out a specific act or ritual.

The female figures in the task poems often include the folkloric figure of the wise old woman, variations of the Hag of Beara or the *cailleach* who appear frequently in Ní Chuilleanáin's work as sources of knowledge, often in a modern context. An interesting poem in this regard is 'The Informant', from *The Magdalene Sermon* (*SP* 62), another voice in a collection dedicated to speaking women. In this poem, a young man is listening to a taped interview he has made of an old woman, where she is explaining what happens when a man dies:

'The locks
Forced upward, a shift of air
Pulled over the head. The face bent
And the eyes winced, like craning

To look in the core of a furnace.
The man unravelled
Back to a snag, a dark thread'.

Throughout the poem, Ní Chuilleanáin uses italics for the young man's questions about what the old woman is describing: '*Did you ever see it yourself? … And then what happens? … Then he is gone?*' and the older woman confidently explains that the dead man does not disappear right away but speaks in the voice of a child; and that one must leave him food, and watch, after washing her feet, where to throw the water.

The poem opens with a description of a photograph of the woman, which Ní Chuilleanáin has commented on, noting that under the photograph the woman is identified in terms of her name, age and her dead husband's occupation, not her own.[32] As the young man listens, the tape recorder breaks, and there is 'a tearing, a stitch of silence' where 'Something has been lost'. Signalling a movement from the scientific world of technology to the world of folklore, the poem tells us that her voice 'resumes as she begins to explain what she has seen'. At the end of the poem, the man asks the old woman, '*You find this more strange than the yearly miracle / Of the loaf turning into a child?*' and she answers, 'Well that's natural, … / I often baked the bread for that myself'.

Ní Chuilleanáin explains that the background for this allusion is a medieval image from the Mass of St Gregory, noting that there are many legends from the thirteenth century of people who doubted the real presence of the body of Christ in the Eucharist. In one, a woman says she cannot believe in the actual presence of Christ in the Eucharist because she baked the bread for the Eucharist herself, but when she goes to Mass and sees at the Elevation that the priest has a child in his hands, she believes in the miracle.[33] Ní Chuilleanáin transfers this legend to a modern Irish setting: 'in another parish, near the main road'. Picturing the informant with the fairy cake she had baked that morning, Ní Chuilleanáin juxtaposes the young man, dependent on the tape recorder, with a wise woman who is the source of tales which describe what happens when someone dies. Ní Chuilleanáin has pointed out how such tales embody elements of both pre-Christian and Christian culture, found often in Ireland, and that she is more interested in the rituals and patterns themselves than the spiritual.[34] Combining imagery from religion, like the Catholic dogma of transubstantiation, with the pre-Christian folklore the woman expresses, and titling the poem 'The Informant', Ní Chuilleanáin portrays the value of images and rituals to confront the mysteries science can not quite explain.

In the dedicatory poem in *The Sun-fish* (*S* 9) we can see the ways in which Ní Chuilleanáin relates folklore to her own experiences as she creates an epithalamium celebrating the 2009 marriage of her son, Niall Woods, to Xenya Ostrovskaia. The speaker is another version of the *cailleach* or the informant who gives advice, her accumulated wisdom as it were, to the young couple. The poem imagines their new life as a journey in which they set out with 'half a loaf and your mother's blessing', but suggests that what they leave behind, they will find again 'in the stories'. The talking cat of Sleeping Beauty in her tower will tell them tales about 'the firebird that stole the golden apples', and about The King of Ireland's Son, folktales in which couples live happily ever after. The speaker imagines her son and his new partner as the characters in Pádraic Colum's *The King of Ireland's Son*[35] in which a young man wins the hand of his beloved Fedelma after a series of tests which her father, the Enchanter, sets for him. Connecting Colum's tales, published in 1916, with the story of the firebird and the gray wolf, a Russian fable which alludes to the newly married woman's background, Ní Chuilleanáin links the two cultures which the married couple represent, by way of cultural narratives or 'stories':

When the cat wakes up he will speak in Irish and Russian
And every night he will tell you a different tale
About the firebird that stole the golden apples,
Gone every morning out of the emperor's garden,
And about the King of Ireland's Son and the Enchanter's Daughter.

The final lines of the poem suggest that there is another story, however, which Sleeping Beauty's cat does not know, from the Book of Ruth in the Old Testament. Of this tale, the speaker says:

And I have no time to tell you how she fared
When she went out at night and she was afraid,
In the beginning of the barley harvest,
Or how she trusted to strangers and stood by her word.

The story of Ruth provides the basis for this mother's advice. After her husband died, Ruth showed her loyalty and devotion by returning to Bethlehem with Naomi, and she persisted through a series of trials in a new land by trusting to strangers and standing by her word. The story of Ruth and Naomi, two female figures in the stories of the Old Testament, symbolic of love, loyalty and commitment, are offered as models of the possibility of happiness for the young couple, even through difficult times they might encounter in the future. Comparing the tasks embodied in folktales with the Biblical story of Ruth's difficult experiences, the poem offers a mother's blessing and advice to the young couple about the future in the emphatic final line: 'You will have to trust me,' the speaker says referring to the story of Ruth, 'she lived happily ever after.'

In this poem Ní Chuilleanáin illustrates her faith in 'the stories', in folktales, myths, legends and fictions from different cultures which provide relevant lessons across time. The two young people here are setting out on a journey, the quintessential folklore theme, and there inevitably will be obstacles they must confront. Adding the narrative of Ruth, Ní Chuilleanáin validates the Biblical story as a source dealing with fear, trust, love, loyalty and commitment. The poem blends past, present and future, the mythic and the real, the personal and impersonal, as this young couple, beginning their new life, now 'look out across the fields / And … both see the same star / Pitching its tent on the point of the steeple'. Ruth, who also 'went out at night' 'afraid' at the start of her new life, is offered as a counterpoint to the more conventional Sleeping Beauty, and a symbol of how to live happily ever after, despite the difficulties she encountered.

The speaker here, as in many other Ní Chuilleanáin poems, is a female figure, a mother giving advice to her young son and his new partner in a voice reminiscent of the wise woman, the *cailleach*, but clearly identified also with this female poet. The autobiographical details are subsumed under the folkloric as the speaker presents the young couple with models for their long journey, a combination of Biblical story, fairy tales and folklore narratives. The value of stories in illustrating love, trust, commitment, the possibility of happiness even through difficult times ahead, is seen clearly in this marriage poem, offered as 'a mother's blessing'. This poem is also a response to traditional customs seen in tales like *The King of Ireland's Son*, in which young men and women must seek a father's blessing. Ní Chuilleanáin here offers an alternative to what

Moynagh Sullivan describes as 'the preoccupation of father-son relationships in Irish cultural and critical production'.[36]

Ní Chuilleanáin's updating of myth, folklore and legend, the connections she makes between the events of the present and stories from the past, are a unique characteristic of her poetry, a kind of double vision which moves us between different worlds to suggest multiple ways of viewing human experience and confronting mysteries we cannot understand. Angela Bourke in 'The Virtual Reality of the Irish Fairy Legend' explains that folktales deal with 'much of the betwixt-and-between – the liminal, the marginal, and the ambiguous, whether in time, in the landscape, or in social relations – making them important cognitive tools'.[37] Ní Chuilleanáin's use of folklore can be seen in this way; in assuming the voice of the *cailleach* or retelling a task legend or fairy tale, she works against the idea that truth about people is always contained in the 'believable'. Rather, she says, there is much to be learned from fictional figures: 'Witches, viragos, martyrs, hermits – I do admit their humanity and their femininity; I do not think they have dissolved their women's bodies because they may be eight feet tall or dressed in knightly armour. I cling to romance almost as tightly as to history.'[38]

The poet Seamus Heaney says of this poet that there is 'something second sighted, as it were, about Ní Chuilleanáin's work, by which I don't mean that she has any prophetic afflatus, more that her poems see things anew, in a rinsed and dreamstruck light. They are at once plain as an anecdote told on the doorstep and as haunting as a soothsayer's greetings.'[39] In seeing things anew in this way, Ní Chuilleanáin also gives us numerous female fictive figures creating what she describes in 'A Midwinter Prayer' as a 'new model for the world'.

CHAPTER 5

Women and the Sacred

> She still prayed for them all by name. I remember
> When she would give me an hour of her visions,
> When she would levitate – she was always deaf –
> When thin pipe music resounded beyond the grilles
>
> 'Anchoress' (*SP* 93)

One of the more intriguing aspects of Ní Chuilleanáin's work is her interest in the sacred and the spiritual, demonstrated often through traditional religious imagery. The connections with history are highlighted when she says: 'I am interested in the sacred in history'; she has also defined herself by way of religious heritage as 'a Gaelic-speaking female papist'.[1] However, as in much else, it is difficult to pin Ní Chuilleanáin down in terms of a specific religious vision. Her poetry and critical writing on such topics as Donne's sermons,[2] or in such essays as 'The Debate Between Thomas More and William Tyndale, 1528–33, Ideas on Religion and Literature',[3] reflect not only her academic work in Medieval and Renaissance literature, but also a continuing exploration of the interconnections between the spiritual and the literary. Using her word 'sacred', we can examine her vision and use of Christian imagery, understanding that this is related to her sense of the sacred in the stories and rituals of myth and folklore as well.

Given the institutional church's resistance to both feminist thought and gender equity, and its promulgation of very narrowly defined roles for women, it is interesting to examine Ní Chuilleanáin's challenges to models that the Christian, and more specifically the Catholic, church has presented as ideal females. Especially important is her response to the negative images of female sexuality the church has helped to promote. As is typical of Ní Chuilleanáin, she often separates sacred imagery from paternalistic contexts to give us new visions of religious rituals and female saints. At the same time she challenges the institutionalised church's treatment of women. In an interview with Deborah Hunter McWilliams,[4] Ní Chuilleanáin describes the sacred as a way to highlight 'the history of injustice, deprivation, victimisation', and, in her images of religious figures and issues, the injustice to and victimisation of women are often highlighted. As we shall see, the spiritual for Ní Chuilleanáin has broad and multiple meanings, and reimagining sacred figures is significant in developing these.

In examining Ní Chuilleanáin's later poetry, Catriona Clutterbuck places this work within a Roman Catholic religious context and, invoking Sartre, makes a distinction between bad and good faith, seeing Ní Chuilleanáin as focusing on the 'liberating potential of religion' in an age when the Catholic Church is increasingly under criticism. Ní Chuilleanáin, she says, uses religious tradition as 'a forum that connects aesthetics and politics through its facilitation of communal awareness'.[5] Noting that as 'issues of gender and sexuality have come to the forefront in the disintegration of the traditional authority of the Irish Catholic Church',[6] Clutterbuck believes that some of Ní Chuilleanáin's wariness about the institutional church comes from its treatment of women. Linking this with issues of political identity, Clutterbuck argues that the 'impossible language of good faith is one where the divisiveness of gendered and national identity is eradicated in order to restore the possibility of desire and its unconfirmed but real promise of fulfillment'.[7] Applying this definition, Clutterbuck reads Ní Chuilleanáin's *The Magdalene Sermon*, *The Brazen Serpent* and *The Girl who Married the Reindeer* as involving 'a positive reassessment of religion'.[8]

Patricia Coughlan argues from a slightly different point of view. Discussing Ní Chuilleanáin's images of nuns, relics, miracles, saints and devotional practices, Coughlan says that Ní Chuilleanáin employs all of these 'not in order to propose a re-mystification of the world (in the teeth of postmodern secularism), still less to reinstate Catholic hegemony, but to set up a thematic viewpoint which is both specifically feminist and allows a kind of symbolic intelligence which is alternative to current Anglophone norms to operate'.[9] Agreeing with Clutterbuck that gender identity is a problem within the institutionalised church, Coughlan also sees Ní Chuilleanáin as conducting 'a thematic exploration … of the role and psychological functions of the sacred, including religious manifestations from the subaltern realm of popular devotional practice'.[10]

While mysteries involving the sacred are at the centre of much of her poetry, it is also the concrete responses to those mysteries that interest Ní Chuilleanáin, which is clear from her own comments on how ritual is connected to her poetry:

> … what really attracted me always was the surface of the religious life. The bits and pieces: the prayer books, manuals, holy pictures, the holy water fonts, all those things that get thrown out whenever anyone dies in Ireland … The way in which religious rituals and religious groupings, like the Confraternity or the convent or whatever, sometimes provide metaphors for life; to me anyway they always seem to provide powerful metaphors, and that could be partly because of my background, the nuns and family and all.[11]

In much of her poetry, the images taken from religion and the spiritual life do become what she calls 'metaphors for life'.

In her explorations into 'the sacred in history', Ní Chuilleanáin has written poems about female saints, and two, 'St Mary Magdalene Preaching at Marseilles' (*SP* 61), from *The Magdalene Sermon*, and 'St Margaret of Cortona' (*SP* 72), from *The Brazen Serpent*, involve reconstructions of the historical images of these saints while also connecting them to the female figures in other poems, including 'Translation' (*SP* 102) and 'Bessboro' (*SP* 103). All of these poems focus on women who have been tagged within the church as either prostitutes or promiscuous, labels Ní Chuilleanáin challenges to present these figures in a different light. On one level, she humanises female saints as alternatives to the idealised ways in which they have been presented; on another level, she connects the saints to contemporary women who have been punished for what has been considered immoral sexual behaviour. Rather than accepting views of the saints as repentant sinners converted to asexualised women, Ní Chuilleanáin emphasises many of their other characteristics, including the materiality of their bodies.

In 'St Mary Magdalene Preaching at Marseilles', the saint is imagined at the end of her life in the French city, where according to legend she went with Martha and Lazarus to preach after the death of Christ. Ní Chuilleanáin has said that she was drawn to John Donne's image of Magdalene in the opening lines of the 'Sonnet Cycle for Lady Magdalen',[12] where Donne describes the saint in an untypical representation of her significance:

An active faith so highly did advance,
That she once knew more than the Church did know,
The Resurrection; so much good there is
Delivered of her, that some Fathers be
Loth to believe one woman could do this;
But think these Magdalens were two or three.

Noting that Mary Magdalene witnessed and announced the resurrection of Christ, Donne credits her with knowing 'more than the Church did know'. The Fathers of the Church, unable to accept that as a woman she would have this role, confused believers by maintaining that there was not a single Magdalene but several by that name, thus subverting her individual identity and authority. The complicated history of Mary Magdalene, which Donne alludes to, resulted from the fusing of different Marys named in the Bible. Moreover, although there were different versions of Magdalene's life and various legends connected with her, the image of the saint that moved to the forefront in the church involved her role as repentant prostitute.[13]

Working against a patriarchal image of Magdalene passed down through church history, Ní Chuilleanáin follows the poet Donne to emphasise Magdalene's role as the miracle bearer who announced Christ's resurrection. Emphasising Magdalene in this poem as preacher/ saint, Ní Chuilleanáin counterpoints the sexualising and almost exclusive emphasis on the image of converted prostitute and sees Magdalene as someone who 'stands for the border between the sacred and the profane because she is a person who transgressed'.[14] Although there is little historical evidence that Magdalene preached in Marseilles, and little that she was a prostitute, Ní Chuilleanáin uses the legend of Magdalene in Marseilles to remake the saint imaginatively into what she calls 'a strong feminine presence in the Christian tradition, a woman who is presented as there, as active, as being where she wants to be. The legends have her migrating to France and first converting Marseilles and then withdrawing to the desert – because that's where she wants to be'.[15] Ní Chuilleanáin also describes being attracted to the 'sensuous vibrant spirituality' of Magdalene[16] and sees her as 'somebody who was not doing what was expected of her and was not remaining in her category'.[17]

In the poem, Ní Chuilleanáin draws on the medieval legend that, as preacher in Marseilles, Magdalene converted many to Christianity, eventually retiring to the desert. She imagines Magdalene at the end of her life as a speaking 'voice / Breaking loose from the secret shroud of her skin'. The saint is also presented as a female version of John the Baptist, but, as contrasted to his 'crying in the wilderness', her voice is 'glittering'. Most importantly, Magdalene is portrayed in all her physicality, and not as some immaterial, iconic saint. Her 'loose red hair' is highlighted, 'a cataract flowing and freezing', and she is pictured as a real and independent woman wandering by herself late in the evening:

> The hairs on the back of her wrists begin to lie down
> And she breathes evenly, her elbows leaning
> On a smooth wall ...

Noting that her image of Magdalene has been influenced also by different paintings of the saint, for example Correggio's, Ní Chuilleanáin explains:

> ... she is wonderful in art. I have a Mary Magdalene postcard – I think the cleaners don't like it – they keep on turning it to the wall! But she is an important symbol as the woman speaking, as the woman surviving, and I have to say, because of the long hair, there is quite a strong identification.[18]

As the subject of the title poem in the collection *The Magdalene Sermon*, the saint becomes one of the many female voices speaking in that volume, important especially in that she is given not only a voice, but also equal stature in Christ's life to a figure like John the Baptist.

The second poem, 'St Margaret of Cortona' (*SP* 72), continues this theme of a woman surviving, focusing on a saint named patroness of the Lock Hospital in Dublin. The hospital, centred in Monto, the one-time brothel district of the north inner city, often served prostitutes, many of whom suffered from sexually transmitted diseases and died at the hospital. Given Margaret's image within the church, turning from sexual transgressor to a life of prayer, she became in the church's eyes the ideal saint for the women who entered the hospital. The thirteenth-century daughter of an Italian farmer, whose mother died when she was seven, Margaret is remembered in church narratives for her elopement with a man with whom she lived unmarried for nine years, until he was murdered in 1274. Left with a child, Margaret was rejected by her father who, because of her actions, refused to let her come home. With her son she took shelter in a Franciscan institution, eventually ministering to poor and sick women. Always the object of gossip for her immoral elopement and pregnancy, Margaret is redeemed when she devotes the rest of her years to penance, eventually joining the tertiary Franciscans for a life of prayer.

The setting for Ní Chuilleanáin's poem is an 'annual panegyric' of Margaret's life at her shrine in Cortona, where her preserved body is still displayed under the main church altar. A preacher discusses the 'riddle' of the woman who was 'neither maiden, widow nor wife', three images of women basic to some Irish views of female roles. The poem describes a preacher who reminds his listeners that hers was 'a name not to be spoken'; it also tells us that the 'word *whore* [is] prowling silent / Up and down the long aisle'. Honouring the saint while simultaneously identifying her as whore, the preacher praises and condemns her at the same time. Like Magdalene, however, St Margaret in Ní Chuilleanáin's poem is an active presence at the shrine, and a very different figure from the one the preacher celebrates:

> In the mine of the altar her teeth listen and smile.
>
> She is still here, she refuses
> To be consumed. The weight of her bones
> Burns down through the mountain.

Seeking to portray the saint as a more realistic and material female figure with teeth, bones and 'hollowed' eyes, the speaker in Ní Chuilleanáin's poem rejects the preacher's judgment and presents her as a woman who had to suffer the murder of her partner, doors locked against her, ongoing gossip, and subsequently the church's primary emphasis on her sexual sins:

> The names flew and multiplied; she turned
> Her back but the names clustered and hung
> Out of her shoulderbones
> Like children swinging from a father's arm,
> Their tucked-up feet skimming over the ground (*SP* 72).

Interestingly, Ní Chuilleanáin ends this poem with a metaphor comparing the names St Margaret has been called to children swinging from a father's arms, undercutting the image of sexual transgressor with the more positive image of parenthood, emphasising the role of loving family which Margaret, her murdered partner and her child once represented.

These final lines also connect Margaret of Cortona to Magdalene whom Ní Chuilleanáin imagines in Marseilles looking down on a piazza, where 'boys are skimming on toy carts, warped / On their stomachs, like breathless fish'. Shifting the emphasis from sexual sinners converted to saints by their penitential and redemptive acts of self-repression, Ní Chuilleanáin revises the images of both saints to make them humanised active presences and a challenge to the virgin/whore stereotype embedded in church tradition. As Patricia Coughlan writes: 'This poem is a particularly good example of Ní Chuilleanáin's moves towards the re-negotiation of feminine modes of agency and towards the salvaging, from the current wreck of institutional Catholicism in Ireland, of a range of images of female holiness and transcendence which resist the virgin-or-whore patriarchal binaries.' Coughlan adds that the effect is to 'propose a feminine integrity – embodied, quite literally, in the saint – distinct from and other than its instrumental use as a mere *exemplum* of moral teaching'.[19] Counteracting the preacher's word '*whore*' or the names 'that flew and multiplied' around both Margaret of Cortona and Magdalene, Ní Chuilleanáin uses her words to suggest of both saints, 'She is still here' and ready to be re-imagined.

It is not hard to see connections between these saints and the mothers in two poems in *The Girl who Married the Reindeer*, whose subjects are the Bessboro Mother and Baby Home in Cork and the Magdalene Laundries which operated all over Ireland, places where women also became exempla of the church's moral teaching. In these institutions, women and girls who were pregnant and unmarried, or considered to be promiscuous, were hidden from public scandal. Many of the women in these institutions, run by nuns and supported by both church and state, lost their children in what were often manipulative adoption systems. Puritanical moralistic views about women's sexuality allowed the women and girls to be shuffled off to institutions and hidden behind closed doors as church and state collaborated to keep their plight secret. We can connect these women with the figures of Mary Magdalene and Margaret of Cortona in that they have all been defined through their penance for sexual transgressions. As role models for young women, both the saints and their Irish counterparts in the homes and laundries became useful to propagate a repressive sexuality and the threat of punishment for those who transgressed, creating what the speaker in 'Bessboro' calls 'a hammer-note of fear'.

The story of the Irish Magdalenes is the subject of Ní Chuilleanáin's poem 'Translation' (*SP* 102), which memorialises the reburial of more than 150 women who had lived and died behind the walls of a convent laundry at High Park, Drumcondra, run by the Sisters of Our Lady of Charity. Uncovered in 1993, when the site was excavated in preparation for selling the land, the remains of these women were reburied eventually in a ceremony in Glasnevin Cemetery, for which Ní Chuilleanáin wrote this poem. The Magdalenes had been taken, often by family members or parish priests, to do penance for their sins in laundries named after the repentant saint. They worked without pay, often staying years beyond the birth of their children. These laundries existed all over Ireland, the women working in them mostly invisible to surrounding communities.[20]

In 2009, a report issued by the Ryan Commission to Inquire into Child Abuse,[21] eleven years in the making, detailed years of physical, sexual and emotional abuse in the industrial schools and residential institutions in Ireland, run primarily by religious communities. A massive report, it outlines the conditions in these homes and schools, and volume III, section 18, which describes the Magdalene Laundries, quotes witnesses describing for the commission their lives in the laundries, including harsh working conditions in imposed silence, shaved heads, public ridicule and beatings. The testimony reveals the demeaning treatment to which the Magdalenes were subjected; in the words of one witness, 'When I got there they [religious staff] … took all your clothes off … crying … Cut all your hair off and bandaged you … [breasts] … up so that you wouldn't look like a girl, because your body was sin and belonged to the devil' (18.57). One witness tells of being put into the laundry when she was ten; another, at twelve. The report notes that three residents described those who had given birth as 'constantly denigrated', and another witness told the commission that her baby was placed in foster care without either her consent or knowledge (18.63). Many of the children born in the laundries were placed for adoption, with mothers sometimes coerced into giving them up; and, while the average time spent in the laundries has been estimated between two and four years, some of the women spent their entire lives there, thus the bones uncovered on the site of the Drumcondra convent.

Ní Chuilleanáin's 'Translation' describes the women gathered from all over Ireland for the reburial ceremony, emphasising a female community which links past and present:

> The soil frayed and sifted evens the score –
> There are women here from every county,
> Just as there were in the laundry.

Ní Chuilleanáin's laundry metaphors imagine the daily activities of the young women within them:

> White light blinded and bleached out
> The high relief of a glance, where steam danced
> Around stone drains and giggled and slipped across water.

Images of bleach, soap and drains, of temporary names and infants' cries, recall the lives of women whose identities and children were stolen from them. The 'high relief of a glance', or 'every grasp', symbolic of the Magdalenes' efforts to communicate, are described as 'bleached' or 'melted', not only in the atmosphere in the laundries but also in the disconnection between them and the outside world, and between these women's lives and recent attempts to identify them and record their story. In a prayerful tone ('Assist them now', 'Allow us now to hear it'), the speaker asks for help for the children still searching for lost mothers and for the nuns who must come forward to reveal the secrets and hidden histories of the laundries.

Most important in this poem is Ní Chuilleanáin's image of words rising, of attempts to hear what the Magdalenes might have said, had they not been denied a voice. The final stanza, a sestet which follows five carefully controlled tercets, opens up the form as the poem's 'I' shifts from an observer at the reburial to a resurrected Magdalene speaking. Those present are connected to the dead as the risen woman speaks, reminding us of St Margaret of Cortona who also 'refuses to be consumed':

> Washed clean of idiom · the baked crust
> Of words that made my temporary name ·

A parasite that grew in me · that spell
Lifted · I lie in earth sifted to dust ·
Let the bunched keys I bore slacken and fall ·
I rise and forget · a cloud over my time.

With the metaphors of 'baked crust' and 'sifting' relating not only to words but also to both the excavated earth and domestic chores usually performed by women, Ní Chuilleanáin imagines the temporary name as a parasite that destroyed the Magdalenes' identities. The speaker here describes death as release from the spell of the laundries, from the imprisonment which confined her. Her voice simultaneously represents a resurrected individual and a cloud over the present time, an allusion to the ongoing scandal of the laundries. The rhythmic alliteration and assonance of beautiful ten-syllable lines like 'Lifted I lie in earth sifted to dust · / Let the bunched keys I bore slacken and fall · ' emphasise the double sense of loss and resurrection, of attempts to name the nameless. The line stops, punctuated with raised dots in the middle of the line, echo the rhythm of ecclesiastical prayers and litanies.

In this poem, the tragic fate of the Magdalenes repulses even the natural world, illustrated in the excavation metaphor of the opening lines where 'the soil frayed and sifting evens the score', and in the final lines, where the 'earth sifted to dust' suggests the Magdalenes' graves, as well as the destruction of the convents where the Magdalenes and nuns lived. With the reburial ceremony as focus, and with women from all over Ireland present, Ní Chuilleanáin places the Magdalenes in a larger context where time and nature defeat all human attempts to keep their tragedy secret, an ongoing theme in many of her poems. With the shift to the first person Magdalene persona, Ní Chuilleanáin employs a poetic strategy to focus on individual identity; by imagining what one of them might say, she creates a voice to cut through the silence which has surrounded the women's lives and deaths. In alluding to the 'edges of words grinding against nature', to 'idiom' and the 'crust / Of words', Ní Chuilleanáin insists on the importance not only of names but also of words, of voices, including the poet's, in breaking the silence. The poem describes 'one voice … rising above the shuffle' and we can imagine this with multiple meanings: the voice of a Magdalene, of a speaker at the reburial, and last, but not least, of the female poet who incorporates the voices of all of these women in her poem. Written for a public ceremony acknowledging the lives of the Magdalenes, Ní Chuilleanáin's poem becomes a public testament for the losses these women suffered.

In examining the sacred in history, Ní Chuilleanáin also alludes to another sad chapter in the treatment of Irish women within the Catholic Church in her poem 'Bessboro' (*SP* 103). Bessboro was the site of a Mother and Baby home opened in Cork in 1922 and operated by the Sisters of the Sacred Hearts of Jesus and Mary; it was, according to a local government report, 'for the reception and reformation of girls who for the first time have had illegitimate offspring, or as they are usually designated – first offenders'.[22] According to this report, these 'first offenders' were usually kept in the homes for a year after their babies were born, spending time in religious instruction and training in domestic and agricultural work. Brian Titley, however, writes that many of these women spent at least three years at the homes, unless they were able to provide £100 to buy their way out. Like the Magdalenes, they received no money for their labours, and were, Titley maintains, 'indentured slaves'.[23] A 1984 *Dáil* report indicated that there were still twenty-four children under age two living at Bessboro,[24] and a 2003 report from the Commission to Inquire into Child Abuse found that infants at Bessboro had been used in a controversial experiment with polio vaccine in the 1960s.

Ní Chuilleanáin's poem begins with a speaker standing at the gate of the former home, noting what has been lost:

> The white barred gate is closed,
> The white fence tracks out of sight
> Where the avenue goes, rain
> Veils distance, dimming all sound,
> And a halfdrawn lace of mist
> Hides elements of the known:
> Gables and high blind windows.
> The story has moved away.

The barred gate, the rain that veils the distance, the lace of mist, the blind windows are images in other Ní Chuilleanáin poems which suggest a secret story or a history that we cannot see ('elements of the known'), in this case stressing the difficulty of understanding how the church could have supported these homes because 'Earth is secret as ever'. The reference to veils, like that used in 'Translation', also evokes images of the nuns who managed these homes.

The story which has 'moved away', however, also has a personal dimension for this speaker and other women in Ireland, as Bessboro is described as a name and a place which represented a warning to them:

> Of what might happen a girl
> Daring and caught by ill-luck:
> A fragment of desolate
> Fact, a hammer-note of fear –

The name Bessboro becomes, therefore, a symbol for the fear instilled in Irish girls from a church which threatened them about pre-marital sex and the consequence of illegitimate offspring. Like the Magdalenes and their babies described in 'Translation', the women and children are now gone from Bessboro, and a history is lost: 'The blood that was sown here flowered / And all the seeds blew away'. The opening line of 'Bessboro', 'This is what I inherit', suggests, however, that something has been left – a lace of mist, we are told, is only 'halfdrawn' and while it hides the 'elements of the known', it also gives us a look, if only a very limited fragment of fact, into the past. In an interesting connection, the poem is tightly structured into four eight-line stanzas, with most lines of seven syllables combining two and three syllable feet – an illustration of both the Gaelic syllabic and English accentual traditions. We might see this as giving added meaning to the opening line of the poem, 'This is what I inherit'.

All four poems discussed here, 'St Mary Magdalene Preaching at Marseilles', 'St Margaret of Cortona', 'Translation' and 'Bessboro', focus on negative images and repression of female sexuality and the institutional church's representation of women as sexualised bodies. Emphasis only on purity and chastity, and the consequences for women of failure to adhere to the church's views on them, are spotlighted in these poems as Ní Chuilleanáin seeks to challenge some traditional images of the female and to restore a sense of identity and humanity to the individual women described. If, as Clutterbuck maintains, Ní Chuilleanáin's poetry illustrates that 'good faith involves an enquiry into how religion – alongside the despotism of many of its institutional forms – can host a vision of fruitfulness and liberation that both serves and is expressed in art',[25] the above poems illustrate how this is done. Ní

Chuilleanáin's definition of the sacred as dealing with victimisation, deprivation and injustice is demonstrated clearly in the situations of the female subjects and speakers in these poems.

Reading the poems about the saints, as well as 'Bessboro' and 'Translation', one might conclude that Ní Chuilleanáin has only a negative view of religion, and of nuns, given their part in administering the Magdalene Laundries and Mother and Baby Homes. This, however, is not the case. Some of the more interesting, and one might argue ironic, female figures who appear in Ní Chuilleanáin's poems are nuns, often considered powerless within the patriarchal structure of the Catholic Church. Ní Chuilleanáin, however, also sees nuns in a more positive context, leaving family to live in communities of women who on some level control their own lives. In her essay 'Nuns: A Subject for a Woman Writer', Ní Chuilleanáin maintains that a history of women can be seen in the history of nuns. After detailing some memories of her own three aunts who entered the convent, Ní Chuilleanáin explains that the life of nuns is even more in the shadows than that of other women. Writing about her poems about nuns, Ní Chuilleanáin explains:

> I record all these things because they suggest so much to me still about women and their history. In my aunts' lifetimes there is another, better known, story of Irish women's lives, the story of their confinement to home and maternity, of their defeat or marginalisation as workers, of Magdalens and typists, of mental patients, tuberculosis sufferers, of teachers and farmers. But there were also the women who lived in the enclosed world they had chosen, the communities of sisterhood. Their history is no odder, surely, than the history of armies.[26]

Speaking of some typical Irish attitudes toward nuns, Ní Chuilleanáin adds: 'An uncle said to me, commenting on the subject of a few of my poems, "When I see a nun, I always think 'none'." The feminine as lack and privation, most intensely seen in women, most intensely seen in women who have neither man nor need for man.' Reacting to such perspectives, Ní Chuilleanáin has said that her choice of nuns as subjects for poems also arises out of a desire to show women working outside the realm of the Irish home.[27] More than anything, her goal is to present a more comprehensive and complex view of religious women who have chosen to dedicate their lives not only to prayer but also to the service of others.

Her images of nuns are complex, however, including the one in 'J'ai Mal à nos Dents', from *The Magdalene Sermon* (*SP* 60). The subject of this poem works all day in France with the sick and injured during the Second World War, alongside fellow nuns who fortify their patients and themselves with 'jugs of wine to hold their strength' while planes fly overhead. Accepting the sacrifice of the self involved in the convent life she has chosen, this nun, not yet fluent in French, once complained to a dentist, '*I have a pain in our teeth*'.[28] The incorrect use of the plural pronoun symbolises not only her acceptance of community life but also the consequence of her detachment: what the poem calls 'her body dissolving out of her first mother, / Her five sisters aching at home' (*SP* 60). The male figure in the poem, her brother, 'could not see her / Working all day with the sisters' as he listened to the radio for news of the war because, we are told, 'her name lay under the surface'. Before her death, as the Irish nun lost her French accent and returned home to care for her sister, 'they handed her back her body, / Its voices and its death'. The opening lines, 'The Holy Father gave her leave / To return to her father's house', emphasise the paternalistic boundaries inscribed for nuns, and Ní Chuilleanáin's use of pronouns, 'I', 'our', 'her', 'their', 'he', 'they', as well as the English and French words in the poem, highlights the issues of gender self-identity and language the poem addresses.

'J'ai Mal à nos Dents' was written in memory of Anna Cullinane, Sister Mary Antony, who lived at the Franciscan convent in Calais and was the first of Ní Chuilleanáin's aunts to enter convent life. As Ní Chuilleanáin insists, however, the image of the nun here can be read in the context of a larger women's history where the caretaking nuns are almost invisible. Although their work and courage are invaluable in many areas in wartime, these are overshadowed by the more clearly acknowledged realm of male soldiers, brother and Holy Father. At the end of the poem, 'They handed her back her body / Its voices and its death' as she is 'Going home in her habit to care for her sister Nora', 'habit' suggesting both the nun's dress and her continual caretaking. On the one hand, the invisibility of the convent involves individual choice, but the poem makes clear that the failure of society to note the very positive contributions of nuns, seeing 'nun' as 'none' for example, accounts for the nun's name falling 'under the surface' of recorded history, whether of nation or church. As Ní Chuilleanáin says in the introduction to her collection of essays, *Irish Women: Image and Achievement*:

'The image created by woman herself may supersede the one presented to her by history and society, but she remains a member of society, an interpreter of history, and thus can never ultimately separate herself from a historical image of the feminine.'[29] By dedicating this poem to a specific nun, and focusing on the difficult and selfless work nuns engage in, Ní Chuilleanáin seeks to challenge that image by focusing here on the value of women within the church.

The courage and perseverance of nuns are highlighted in a later poem, 'The Sister' (*S* 56), where Ní Chuilleanáin describes a young woman setting out by train to the unknown but difficult life of the convent. The question, 'How on earth did she manage / That journey on her own?' opens the poem, contrasting this woman to the men who went off on trains:

> Built for strapping fellows
> Flinging their big bundles
> Easily on to high shelves –
> Real men.

Different from them, the sister 'turned up at the station, / Small, her clothes, once elegant, / All black'. As the nun leaves the train at the end of her journey, 'a lump of a lad' hands her bag down and she walks to the convent to find a 'leathery kiss', a bed and silent meals, 'veiling herself for good'. The veil, a traditional way to cover the female head, is used here to suggest not only the nun's habit and sacrifice of body and voice to the convent's community values, but also the covering over of the achievements of religious women, their lives and their works. The veil, as noted before, is an image Ní Chuilleanáin uses often to suggest something that is concealed or obscured, and shows up in many poems, including 'Translation'.

'The Sister', like 'Bessboro', illustrates Ní Chuilleanin's use of traditional poetic forms, blending three seven-line stanzas with a sonnet. In section 1, the stanzas each create a single scene and end with an emphatic short line ('And held on', 'Real men', 'A cormorant') as the lyric repetitions of assonance and alliteration work with dramatic scene: 'She turned up at the station, / 'Small, her clothes, once elegant, / All black. Past the train window / Slid the suburbs, a fast river'. The sonnet in the second half of the poem, combining two quatrains and a sestet (4/6/4), continues the lyric rhythm as the nun is again placed in the context of the landscape she is leaving behind:

> But the cold woke her, and a subtle mist, as fine
> As gauze, hung on the glass. In the freezing dawn
> She dragged a web just as light across her skin,
> Veiling herself for good, and she slept on.

Images of mists, gauze, webs and veils are familiar in Ní Chuilleanáin's work; in 'Bessboro' we read: 'rain / Veils distance … and a halfdrawn lace of mist / Hides elements of the known'. Lace also appears in 'The Sister', which describes nuns, 'sitting up, working in pairs, / To finish the stitching, tacking the last of the lace'. Using lace as both literal and metaphoric ('lace of mist'), Ní Chuilleanáin mediates between the known and unknown worlds, suggesting how we cannot always access 'elements of the known' when, as 'Bessboro' says, the 'story has moved away'. Ní Chuilleanáin takes it upon herself, however, to give us imaginative insight into the hidden lives of such women.

Ní Chuilleanáin is fascinated not only by religious women, saints and nuns, but also by what she has called the 'surface of the religious life', such as sacred relics and the devotion they inspire. Following 'Saint Margaret of Cortona' in *The Brazen Serpent*, the poem 'Our Lady of Youghal' (*SP* 73) focuses on a small ivory statue of Mary and Jesus from the fifteenth century. Although Dominican records indicate there is no certainty about its origin, a sixteenth-century text suggests it was washed up on the shore of the Dominican Priory in Youghal in County Cork embedded in a large piece of wood, where it became a very popular artifact and the subject of different legends. When Walter Raleigh ordered the Dominican Priory destroyed, supposedly the statue was saved by Honoria Fitzgerald, the daughter of Sir James Desmond, who also had a silver case made for it. In 1832, a Dominican priest found it in a safe in Cork and it resides today in St Mary's Priory, still in its case.[30]

Working with the facts and legends about this icon, Ní Chuilleanáin's poem imagines its discovery by a lay brother:

> Flowing and veiling and peeled back, the tide
> Washed the bulk of timber
> Beached on the mud, so heavy
> Twelve horses could not pull it.

A lay brother rose at dawn, and saw it moved,
The weight melted away,
To the shore below the water-gate.
He rolled it easily as far as the cloister.

The poem compares the 'virgin's almond shrine … bursting out of the wood' to the mystery of a blind man's fingers finding water in a tree's elbow, which allows him to see a leaf 'cutting its way to the air / Inside a tower of leaves'. In 'Our Lady of Youghal', Ní Chuilleanáin gives us multiple images of secrets or mysteries hidden within enclosures. Relics develop sacred meanings for the faithful, and it is this, as well as the rituals which surround them, that attracts Ní Chuilleanáin's attention. Anchoring her images in the real world, she nonetheless emphasises the miraculous which such icons represent; a virgin bursting out of the wood is as marvellous, one could say, as a leaf bursting out of a branch, connecting the spiritual with the natural world and the human with the spiritual. Jefferson Holdridge maintains correctly that in all of her work, Ní Chuilleanáin is 'profoundly interested in the subtle intersections of nature and the sacred'.[31]

It is interesting to note, however, that in other poems, like 'Permafrost Woman' (*SP* 51), 'Pygmalion's Image' (*SP* 49) and 'A Voice' (*SP* 58) from *The Magdalene Sermon*, similar images of 'unveiled' or 'opening' female figures appear: in 'A Voice' a body discovered in the bed of a stream; in 'Pygmalion's Image' a statue coming alive with a 'rustle of veins, tick of blood in the throat'; in 'Permafrost Woman' a figure unfolding 'among peaks / Of frozen sea' when 'The body opens its locks'. As discussed in Chapter 4, in each of these poems, images of opening female bodies suggest both voice and female genitalia, thus moving them beyond the realm of the abstract. Connections between these images and those dealing with the sacred, like those in 'Our Lady of Youghal', should be made. Ní Chuilleanáin has said that relics and reliquaries often are seen as something you enclose, adding, 'I can, of course, also see that this is a kind of feminine image … As in my earlier poem, 'The Lady's Tower', anything hollow or enclosed can suggest the feminine, a body that contains and then reveals.'[32]

The significance of artistic representations like Pygmalion's statue or the relic of Our Lady of Youghal should not be missed, as they suggest ways in which Ní Chuilleanáin sees art and artifacts as connecting physical and spiritual worlds. While 'Permafrost Woman' and 'A Voice' can be seen in terms of the trope of woman as landscape, they also allude to the *sheela-na-gigs*, noted earlier, artistic representations of women's sexuality, which, with their open vaginas, were hung as warnings over the entrances to churches. The statue of Our Lady of Youghal emphasises Mary's fertility, and in Ní Chuilleanáin's 'Pygmalion's Image', the silent figure created by the male sculptor is replaced by another whose locks are also opening as 'a green leaf of language comes twisting out of her mouth'. In each of these poems, the materiality of the female figures is emphasised, much like the poems in which the bodies of Saints Mary Magdalene and Margaret of Cortona are highlighted, all in a positive way. Challenging social and cultural conventions which insist on veiling or controlling the female body, or on images of silent women, Ní Chuilleanáin expresses the value of that body, even – and one can say especially – within the realm of the sacred and religious. Alluding to sacred artifacts which celebrate rather than denigrate women's bodies, Ní Chuilleanáin works against negative religious views of women.

Another poem which focuses on religious icons and, by extension, on women's control over their own lives is 'The Real Thing' (*SP* 68), in which a nun, Sister Custos, lives in a convent where the bishop has 'ordered the windows bricked up on one side' (much like the blind windows of Bessboro). On Palm Sunday, Sister Custos unwraps a relic of the brazen serpent, maintaining that it is the 'real thing'. This is one of many treasures in the convent, including '*Bones / Of different saints. Unknown*', or 'The Book of Exits, miraculously copied / Here in this convent by an angel's hand'. The image of the brazen serpent, as the epigraph to the volume notes, is from the Old Testament, Numbers, XXI, 6–9, where God, having sent fiery serpents to destroy the Israelites, then tells Moses to create a brass serpent to cure those who have been bitten. Sister Custos claims that hers is a fragment of the original brazen serpent; her name, Custos, which in Latin means 'guardian' or 'keeper', reinforces her role as protector of the relic.

Ní Chuilleanáin explains that in the course of research on sixteenth-century religious life in Italy, she discovered regulations for the labelling of relics and for the discipline of nuns: 'These seemed very like each other, so I thought I'd put the two together in the same poem. I see Sister Custos as a hidden voice.'[33] The regulations for the labelling of relics such as a fingerbone or a lock of hair became necessary when questions about their authenticity arose. Catholic authorities like Carlos Borromeo, the Bishop of Milan, established rules on their dating, documentation and provenance. Of particular importance was the need for sealing relics in a reliquary so that they would be safe from misidentification and plundering of the type that occurred during the Reformation. Many of these relics ended up sheltered in monasteries and convents. The bricked-up convent in 'The Real Thing', symbolic of the male hierarchy's control over the nuns' lives and the rules of discipline created for them, also suggests the sealed reliquaries that were required to protect the relics.

The history of the use and misuse of relics – or artifacts purported to be relics – would make one challenge whether Sister Custos's relic is actually the 'real thing'. But that is not the point of this poem; as symbol of her belief, as a concrete artifact, the relic represents a way to approach life's mysteries, the embodiment of faith at the centre of someone's life. As Helen Emmitt says, relics are important to Ní Chuilleanáin 'because they are the meeting place of the historical, the mystical, and the physical'.[34] The poem's lines, 'True stories wind and hang like this / Shuddering loop wreathed on a lapis lazuli / Frame', pay homage to the attraction of such artifacts and to the reality of the brazen serpent's effect on people's lives. And Sister Custos's role as guardian, her ability to cover and uncover it, gives her a sense of self-importance within a patriarchal church.

The final stanza, repeating imagery in other Ní Chuilleanáin poems, focuses on the nun's life:

> Her history is a blank sheet,
> Her vows a folded paper locked like a well.
> The torn end of the serpent
> Tilts the lace edge of the veil.
> The real thing, the one free foot kicking
> Under the white sheet of history.

Because the serpent in the Old Testament is both a destroyer (a 'real' serpent) and a healer (the brass serpent), the complexity of Ní Chuilleanáin's images points to the significance of stories, rituals, symbols and artistic representations to represent the sacred and mysterious. Though the bishop has control over Sister Custos, and though the episcopal seal is stamped on all the reliquaries, Sister Custos asserts her authority as she guards 'her major relic'. As Dillon Johnston writes, the image of blankness suggests 'that the acting out and writing of history depend on such emblems of faith or such "unreasonable fictions" freely chosen, which therefore are "the real thing", as Sister Custos says'.[35]

Her history, however, is 'a blank sheet' – her convent vows, her life, are 'a folded paper locked like a well' though the 'torn end of the serpent / Tilts the edge of the veil'. As in 'Translation', the veil image serves many purposes, not the least of which is to cover both a woman's body and an unwritten life: 'the one free foot kicking / Under the white sheet of history'. Blank sheets of paper suggest something yet to be written, as the poet continues to explore the nature of reality, the mystery of the sacred, the 'true stories' that flow from religious rituals and relics. Implied also is the unwritten history of the nun, and by extension, as Ní Chuilleanáin herself has suggested, the unrecorded history of women of which the nun is a part. Ní Chuilleanáin has identified Sister Custos as typical of girls who would have been sent to the convent at eight or nine years of age, and, when legislation eventually ruled out such practices, nuns like Sister Custos would remain as one of 'a generation that doesn't get liberated, the people who remain in whatever situation they had been in previously'.[36] Like the 'lace of mist' in 'Bessboro' which 'hides elements of the known', or the high walls of the Magdalene Laundries, the veils in 'The Real Thing' are to remind us of the lives of invisible girls and women.

While what we might call the 'imagery of the sacred' runs throughout Ní Chuilleanáin's poetry, it is most pronounced in *The Magdalene Sermon*, *The Brazen Serpent* and *The Girl who Married the Reindeer*. *The Girl who Married the Reindeer* was published in 2001 and the poems reflect the difficult period following the deaths of Ní Chuilleanáin's stepfather, Vivien Mercier, in 1989, her sister Máire in 1990, and her mother, Eilís Dillon, in 1994. The first six poems in *The Girl who Married the Reindeer* resonate with the loss and isolation of one searching for a haven in a threatening world, and sacred imagery, especially Christian imagery involving liturgical seasons and church rituals, is integral to them. The female subjects help to create the tone of grief and loss, and the search for acceptance, which permeate the poems.

The opening poem, 'The Crossroads' (*SP* 92), sets the tone and introduces images which recur in subsequent poems in an eighteen-line poem alternating tercets and couplets. The poem is set in the interval between Shrove Tuesday and the feast of the Assumption, a period in the Catholic calendar that marks both the death and resurrection of Christ at Easter and the feast of the Assumption of Mary into heaven (August 15). The speaker opens the poem with the statement: 'I have been at the crossroads now / All the time without leaving'. While this should not be read strictly as an autobiographical poem, it was inspired by Ní Chuilleanáin's mother's death, which occurred in July of 1994, a month before the feast of the Assumption; her death was preceded by a lingering illness. This is reinforced by a poem that forms the epigraph to *The Brazen Serpent*, 'Fireman's Lift', which, written in 1993–4, also uses the image of Mary's Assumption as a metaphor for her mother's illness and death, an interpretation Ní Chuilleanáin has discussed.[37]

The speaker in 'The Crossroads' is somewhat removed from the rituals of the season, isolated from other people:

> They brought me the blessed ashes
> Wrapped in tissue paper.
>
> When I awoke on Palm Sunday
> The palm branches had been left
> On the damp stones of the stile.

She mentions hearing people at Easter 'across the ploughed fields', stressing in these images her distance from the rituals of Ash Wednesday, the day that marks human mortality, as well as from the celebration of the risen Christ at Easter. In the final lines, the speaker retreats to memory and, significantly, it is her mother who will come:

> To collect me in her pony and trap
> And we will go calling on all our cousins
> And take tea and sherry in their parlours.

This will happen on the feast of Mary's Assumption which, we are told, is a long time away. We can read this poem as dealing with the loss of a mother, with the speaker unable to move beyond a 'crossroads', but it likewise suggests the possibility of the healing rituals symbolised by the Christian season of death and resurrection which, significantly, includes the Assumption of Mary. The retreat to memory, however, turns this poem into something more than a validation of Christian optimism. Crossroads symbolise those liminal spaces between presence and absence, life and death, as a person tries to deal with loss and grief. In the space between death and the difficult acceptance of that death, the speaker remains unable to move forward. Even the young girls described in the poem, who 'stood / A short way off' showing their 'embroidered dancing costumes', cannot inspire joy.

In the poems that follow 'The Crossroads' in *The Girl who Married the Reindeer*, the images reinforce a sense of loss as the subjects and narrators look for comfort in rituals, in the protective enclosures of cloisters and convents ('Anchoress', *SP* 93); in mountain chapels ('The Chestnut Choir', *GMR* 14); in small towns ('In Her Other Ireland', *SP* 98); or in memories of family gatherings ('Sunday', *GMR* 13). These poems are again filled with female figures, both subjects and personae, and the settings are often religious spaces. In 'The Anchoress', the 'pilgrim'/ speaker journeys to a cloister where, set away from the world, the anchoress would 'give me an hour of her visions' and levitate when 'music resounded beyond the grilles'. In 'The Chestnut Choir', the subject listens in a convent chapel to the female choir singing of the Biblical story of Daniel in the lion's den:

Behold how wide are the doors
That open beneath the furnace
Where the flame dives under the stone.

The images of the Biblical den, of cloisters and blank walls, and of chapels, are picked up again in 'The Cloister of Bones' (*SP* 95)where the speaker, describing terraces 'scuttling down / As if they hunted something buried', tells us:

I am searching for a shape, a den, watching
For the cloistering blank of a street wall,
A dark reticence of windows
Banked over an inner court,
Especially rooves, arched and bouncing
Naves; a corseted apse,
And always, even if the chapel sinks
Deep inside, lit from a common well,
I search for hints of doors inside doors.

The search for enclosure, the chapel, the inner court, naves and apses, for 'doors within doors' to find an 'avid presence', resonates on many levels. On the one hand, it can be read as a comforting haven for the faithful seeking the presence of God; on another, a search for the presence of an absent or dead person, a reading reinforced by the 'bones' of the title. The comforts of such sacred places and liturgical rituals are clear, but they are also limited, as we see in 'The Chestnut Choir' where a woman lets herself into a box pew at the back of a convent chapel to close off the outside world as she listens to the nuns singing. At the end of the poem, this visitor (a 'wanderer') is ironically 'free to be away' but she must confront what lies beyond the convent walls:

> The bar would be shut, and some beast
> Was snuffling outside,
> But she got up and left them to their vigil.

The beast is a variant of the lion alluded to in the song the nuns in the choir sing, and their songs and vigils are ways for them, like Daniel, to deal with what the lion or the beast represent. The nuns in another poem, 'In Her Other Ireland' (*SP* 98), sent by the mistress of novices 'to practise / The service for deliverance from storms and thunder', present another variation of the ways in which religious rituals address the threats of the natural world. In visiting these convents and cloisters, the pilgrim in these poems connects at least temporarily to what she calls her 'other Ireland'. The rituals, vigils and silent chapels become a source of solace for the 'wanderer' in these poems. The solace, however, is only temporary as the wanderer must return to the other world where 'The names are lonely, the shutters blank –/ No one's around when the wind blows'.

Another in these initial poems in *The Girl who Married the Reindeer*, 'The Angel in the Stone' (*SP* 94), repeats the imagery we see in 'The Cloister of Bones', with an emphasis on death in both. As in 'The Chestnut Choir', 'Where the flame dives under the stone', the stone in 'The Angel in the Stone' calls out from 'darkness / Where moss and spiders never venture', evoking again the 'something buried' in 'The Cloister of Bones'. Characteristic of Ní Chuilleanáin, the stone lies below a 'hard threshold'; the bones suggest a buried body, but the image is also another variation of Daniel looking into the flames of the lion's den ('You look down where the high peaks are ranging, / You see them flickering like flames'), which sets the tone of the poem. The literal image is of an angel carved on a gravestone; and this one, 'trampled in the causeway' has been 'passed over' by builders. The stone speaks as if human, describing disintegrating bones: 'You see our affliction, / You know / How we were made and how we decay', tying this poem to others which focus on the cycle of life to death. The final plea, 'Give me rest for one long day of mourning', can be easily transferred to a human voice, dealing with death and grief. It also connects to the tone of the speakers in the other early poems in the volume, at a crossroads and needing time for mourning.

With the image of the angel in the stone, however, we are also reminded of Michelangelo's statement about sculpture, mentioned in Vasari,[38] that he had seen an angel in the marble he was working with and carved the block to set the angel free. The angel in Ní Chuilleanáin's poem, who symbolises in religious terms a world beyond the human, has also been 'carved' literally on a tombstone, a marker to represent the dead. In addition, that angel has been carved as an image in this poem and given voice as a speaker. With this allusion to the angel in the stone, Ní Chuilleanáin validates the importance of art, in this case to make abstract ideas concrete, to allow the visible to represent the invisible. The poet here is also seeking to carve a shape, the poem as work of art, which in the case of 'The Angel in the Stone' happens to be a sonnet, of two quatrains and two tercets. In this context, we can also read the opening lines of 'The Cloister of Bones', 'I am searching for a shape', as referring not only to the dead persons the speaker is mourning but also to the shape of the poems which their deaths inspired. It is hard not to connect these initial poems in *The Girl who Married the Reindeer* to Ní Chuilleanáin's own reaction to the deaths of her mother, sister and stepfather, but they also move beyond the personal to universal themes about loss and grief, to the mysteries of sacred visions and levitations, to the consolations and limitations of ritual. Significantly, as works of art, as poetry, they fuse the religious and the aesthetic as different ways or 'shapes' to approach the difficulties humans must face.

The respect Ní Chuilleanáin has for the value of rituals, pilgrimages and other signs of belief in the spiritual can also be seen in a poem like 'Vertigo', from *The Sun-fish* (*S* 40), which depicts a woman and her two daughters who climb the sacred steps along the cliff of an island shrine; *Sceilig Mhichíl* on Ireland's west coast is the setting.[39] 'How did such smart women acquire such a mother?' one of the daughters asks, as she and her sister 'wait and gossip'. They watch their mother, 'shaped like a barrel with asthma', remove her black stockings to climb the steps barefoot, putting the stockings in a bag already filled with 'rosary beads tangled in keys, all the stuff / She's dragged from home'. Observing all the rituals of the shrine, the mother:

> … reaches out in her turn
> To stroke each of five crosses cut in the slab,
> One for the saint, four for his four sisters, named
> In the early *Life* …

Sceilig Mhichíl projects over 700 feet above sea level, with the monastery at the top the steepest part of the climb. Despite the fact that she is afraid of heights and terrified when a puffin lands next to her, however, the mother pushes on to the summit and looks down to see what is there: 'the path to the edge, where everything pours away', a typical Ní Chuilleanáin image of edges bordering an unseen spiritual world.

The action is set before photography exists, when news of the Russian war has reached the island, and what the mother sees is 'The dimensions, the naming. Yes', an affirmation bolstered by faith in a difficult time. Contrasting the attitude and irreligious tone of the daughters, who 'fret' about getting her down, the mother meets her terror head on, armed with a faith which allows her to face the immense frightening and mysterious sea below. Returning here to the sea as symbol of a vast and sometimes dangerous unknown in many of her poems, Ní Chuilleanáin imagines a woman who transcends her fear ('what is there, / The dimensions') with an act of faith demonstrated in her respect for the shrine's sacred rituals. What she feels is some sense of the invisible:

> A broad slick widening, an anachronism,
>
> Ambiguous like a leaf floating where never
> A leaf has blown, like a word, a calque, swimming
> Up into sight through the tides of speech, like a seal
> Who plays on the deep ocean: the gate of her days left open,
> Her daughters like armed angels guarding each side
> Of the path to the edge, where everything pours away.

Ní Chuilleanáin has said that 'Vertigo' is ultimately about death.[40] In a strategy obvious in other poems in *The Sun-fish*, Ní Chuilleanáin compares this moment of revelation to a seal surfacing in the vast sea, much like the sight of the basking sharks the people on Achill Island await yearly in the earlier poems in *The Sun-fish* collection. The seals in 'Vertigo', and ultimately the 'dimensions, the naming', are also compared to 'a word, a calque, swimming / Up into sight through the tides of speech', an image which suggests the search for language, or for words for a poem, rising to the surface. At the edge to which the mother has arrived, a momentary glimpse into what lies beyond, words, 'a calque', translate one world (the secret and mysterious, the world beyond death) into another. Ní Chuilleanáin's fusion here of the sacred and the literary coalesces in the image of the mother, at the top of a cliff looking into a vast abyss, with her two daughters as 'armed angels guarding each side / Of the path'.

These daughters evoke Correggio's painted angels on the dome of Parma Cathedral in Ní Chuilleanáin's 'Fireman's Lift' (*SP* 64) who carry the speaker's dead mother 'to the edge of the cloud'. The convergence of religious ritual and language in each poem suggests that the sacred and the artistic can both give us a sense, a 'naming', of what is beyond the edge. In 'Vertigo' Ní Chuilleanáin imagines the mother with 'the gate of her days left open' having courageously reached the very high 'stony north face of the abbey, the great door', as she confronts 'the edge, where everything pours away'. Her terror, her fear of the unknown, is overcome in this act of faith. The long, narrative lines are framed in seven five-line stanzas, culminating in an eighth six-line stanza that breaks the pattern, a typical Ní Chuilleanáin strategy for undercutting an expected formal pattern. Run-on lines and end-stopping punctuation (period, comma, semi-colon, parenthesis, dash, question mark) at the end of each stanza control the pace of the narrative until the final (one might say 'extra') line, which gives us some sense of the magnitude of the mother's awareness: 'Of the path to the edge, where everything pours away'.

As Jefferson Holdridge explains, Ní Chuilleanáin's poetry is 'one of half-secrets, half-revelations, scrupulously controlled but also continuously startling, using the language of history, religion, landscape, and myth to unlock those categories of experience for which poetry is the proper language'.[41] In drawing her material from the imagery of the sacred, from religious rituals, relics, texts and legends, Ní Chuilleanáin has continuously focused on female figures, on nuns, on saints, on angels. She has also described faithful mothers and female personae who seek comfort and meaning in religious ritual. In the final lines of 'The Cloister of Bones', the speaker describes the value of one sacred space, a women's cloister:

> A runner of garden, the right length
> For taking a prayerbook for a walk,
> A small stitching of cemetery ground,
> Strict festivals, an hour for the tremble
> Of women's laughter, corners for mile-high panics:
>
> And to find the meaning of the Women's Christmas.

This poem suggests that rituals often illustrate the bonds that connect women to one another in social and religious communities. However, the reference to Women's Christmas moves beyond the cloister to other areas as well. In Ireland, *Oíche Nollaig na mBan*, Women's Christmas or Little Christmas, is celebrated on 6 January; it still survives, primarily in Cork, where women get together socially to mark the end of the Christmas season. Alluding to an old Gaelic tradition where women celebrated outside the home with female relatives and friends when the Christmas season was over,[42] the speaker here links *Oíche Nollaig na mBan* to the 'festivals' and the 'tremble / Of women's laughter', which she imagines also within the cloister walls. While the origins ('the meaning') of *Oíche Nollaig na mBan* may not be known, it serves as a demonstration that in the rituals that they celebrate, we can see the links among women, and reinforces Ní Chuilleanáin's assertion that the history of women can be seen in the history of nuns.

CHAPTER 6

Presence and Place

... Questing she roamed
After the windows she loved, and again they showed
The back rooms of bakeries, the clean engine-rooms and all
The floodlit open yards where a van idled by a wall,

A wall as long as life, as long as work.

'The Copious Dark' *The Sun-fish* (*S* 59)

As we can see from the cloisters and chapels and churches described in the previous chapter, we cannot read Ní Chuilleanáin's poems without being struck by her interest in architecture and the ways in which architectural imagery develops the themes of border crossing. We might note, for example, that the title of her early collection, *Acts and Monuments* (1972), is borrowed from John Foxe's sixteenth-century volume *Acts and Monuments of the Latter and Perillous Days*, often called the *Book of Martyrs*, a significant text in Protestant church history.[1] In a typical Ní Chuilleanáin strategy, this becomes the ironic title of a collection that deals with classical and Irish acts and monuments. We read poems about hermits on Ireland's west coast ('Celibates', *SP* 17); the Greeks Odysseus ('The Second Voyage', *SP* 18) or Theseus ('The Retreat', *AM* 23) and the Roman Vercingetorix ('Letter to Pearse Hutchinson', *SP* 27); or we hear a speaker as amazed:

As the mosaic beasts on the chapel floor
When Cromwell had departed, and they saw
The sky growing through the hole in the roof.

('Lucina Schynning in Silence of the Nicht' (*SP* 13).

Ní Chuilleanáin herself has connected her interest in architecture to history; when asked about how she sees history inscribed in Italian architecture, for example, she explains:

> It is an aspect of my preoccupation with history, recent and remote. The architecture especially of the small towns recalls to me the way life in provincial Ireland when I was growing up was organised around the church and the convent … Also, the places that are ruined in Ireland, the medieval monasteries, churches and castles, are alive and functioning to a greater or lesser degree in Umbria.[2]

Not only in the poems about ruins and chapels, but also in the houses, rooms, walls, doors, thresholds, and roofs which appear over and over again in her poetry, Ní Chuilleanáin imagines the cultures which created these buildings as well as the people who inhabited them in what Nicholas Allen calls a 'commitment to the recovery of presence' and what Irene Gilsenan Nordin sees as a dialectic between inner and outer spaces expressed as 'a correlation between contrasting forces of concealment and revelation, or absence and presence'.[3] On another level, much of the search for the absences and presences in places focuses on the lives of women.

As Ní Chuilleanáin's words above illustrate, her interest in architecture is not limited to historical monuments and ruins. Any study of architecture tends to distinguish between structures which embody a more visible public history and a cultural landscape of residences and dwellings which reflects a social life carried on in day-to-day existence. Ní Chuilleanáin in 'The House Remembered' (*AM* 30), for example, suggests the importance of homes for giving us some access to the past: 'The stairs and windows waver but the house stands up; / Peeling away the walls another set shows through'. Her emphasis on both types of architecture serves her many themes well, but much of her imagery reflects the latter of these, a vernacular architecture which records narratives of ordinary life, what the architectural historian Dell Upton calls 'an art of social storytelling'. Upton argues that many architectural historians have turned to other disciplines for interpretation and new perspectives: 'social and economic history, sociology, anthropology, feminism, colonial and post-colonial studies, material culture, cultural landscape studies and literary theory'.[4] Likewise, a poet like Ní Chuilleanáin turns to architecture, as she does to history, folklore and sacred ritual, to suggest a perspective that vernacular architecture reveals. In so doing, she often focuses on the women who inhabit these spaces, and it is worth examining Ní Chuilleanáin's architectural images to consider how these reflect her sense of social history, as well as her feminist interpretation of the roles women have played in Irish and other cultures.

An interesting poem to consider when discussing Ní Chuilleanáin's architectural images is 'Daniel Grose' (*SP* 78), from *The Brazen Serpent*, where the contrast between the scientific and the mythic, which we have seen in 'The Informant', reappears, and where a female figure again plays a central part. Grose, an architect and artist, published a series of drawings of ruins, *Antiquities of Ireland*,[5] in 1792, and the poem imagines him in the act of creating one of these drawings. As in 'The Informant', there is also a contrast between a male and a female. Picturing Grose, a precise military draftsman, drawing an image of a ruin where 'the breach widens at every push', the poem tells us that he:

> Is training his eye
> On the upright of the tower,
> Noting the doors that open on treetops;
> He catches the light in the elder branches
> Rooted in the parapet, captures
> The way the pierced loop keeps exactly
> The dimensions of the first wounding.

As Grose is involved in training his eye for his precise rendering, however, Ní Chuilleanáin suggests that he has missed something that may have occurred at this ruin, ignoring 'the human figure':

> No crowds engaged in rape or killing,
> No marshalling of boy soldiers,
> No cutting the hair of novices.

In discussing this poem, Dillon Johnston suggests that Ní Chuilleanáin's 'Abbey of the Five Wounds', which Grose is drawing in the poem, is 'nowhere explicit' in Grose's text, but represents buildings like Mellifont and Boyle Abbeys which were destroyed when the forces of the Reformation confiscated church properties in Ireland.[6] The opening lines allude to that destruction in their image of a collapsing building:

> The copingstone falls
> To shatter the paved floor.

Then silence for three centuries
While a taste for ruins develops.

Contrasting the figure of Grose in the poem is that of an old woman by an oak tree, the human figure he has 'pressed into service / To occupy the foreground'. However, there is a failure of communication between the artist and this woman because 'He stands too far away / To hear what she is saying'. The woman is a version of the *cailleach* figure that appears in other Ní Chuilleanáin poems. Immersed in his scientific rendering, Grose misses her significance:

How she routinely measures
The verse called the midwife's curse
On all that catches her eye, naming
The scholar's index finger, the piper's hunch,
The squint, the rub, the itch of every trade.

The breach described at the beginning of the poem suggests not only the destruction of the church buildings, which resulted in the split between the newer English and older Gaelic orders, but also the split between two worlds, representative of scientific and folkloric, as well as that between Grose's drawing skills and the old woman's folk wisdom. To ignore the woman, or to 'press' her into service to provide perspective for a foreground in his drawing, is to miss much, just as he has in failing to reflect the rape, killings and boy soldiers also connected to the ruin he is drawing. In Ní Chuilleanáin's poem, the folkloric old woman/*cailleach* becomes as important as the well-known architectural historian Grose. Although she has been ignored or used only to create artistic 'perspective' in Grose's scientific renderings, she represents another perspective that moves beyond the literal and scientific, as well as a symbol of an earlier Gaelic culture which was displaced as these buildings were destroyed. The breach which 'widens at every push' can also be seen as an image of childbirth, reinforcing the importance of the female body here.

In contrast to Daniel Grose, the speaker in 'The Nave', a poem in *The Sun-fish* (*S* 34), presents a different response to an architectural space, one which embodies both human beings and a connection between the place and the person speaking. In the opening lines, the speaker is also drawing, as she becomes more enlightened about spaces:

Learning at last to see, I must begin drawing;
I cast abroad the line
That noses under stones, presses around an instep,
Threads off into distance and forward again
As it pierces and drags. Like a daft graph it shoots
Up, like a weed falls and rises. I am led, I find it
Looped on every hooked corbel …

The speaker here is a typical Ní Chuilleanáin voyager, one we can link to the female figures in other poems. Rather than standing off at a distance surveying a space, as Grose does, the speaker here is 'casting a line'. She is soon pulled into a procession and a carnival, descending into a square and then upwards along curving banisters, darkish stone, a ramp, until crossing the threshold of a church. The church, which Ní Chuilleanáin has said was inspired by a Gothic cathedral in Malaga, is alive and compared to a humming ship where:

… In the rigging clings
A saint whose cure is personal as a song
Performed aloud at a wake by a special call,
Or softly to a patient in her hospital ward.

Integrating people into architectural spaces makes this church not just a sacred place but also the embodiment of energy, belief and pleasure, with its nave that 'Hums like a ship', its uppermost gallery which 'swings and revolves', and its representation of a saint whose cure is 'personal' for those who are ill or mourning. The speaker imagines 'a tall, swaying ship / With wind-filling streamers – / Across the threshold'. The personal, which Grose, with his 'trained eye' ignored in his drawing, is connected not only with the saint known for cures but also with the dead and the sick, like the woman in her hospital bed. Describing this poem as about 'avid presences in places',[7] Ní Chuilleanáin suggests that a person's experience of such a place is often determined by entering and finding a personal perspective, whether it be the image of the saint one relates to personally, or the architecture of nave and gallery. The female speaker here describes a different sense of architectural space from Daniel Grose's, one more clearly connected with active human presence.

The humanised 'I' speaker, is actively 'casting a line' in many senses, not the least of which begins in a line which become a finished poem.

With images suggestive of musical and poetic soundmaking, the speaker's poetic line 'shoots / Up like a weed falls and rises' as she hears the 'four-four beat of the carnival march', leading her to the 'line' that calls her upwards and to the memory of a 'song / Performed aloud at a wake by a special call.' References to music and poetry overlap in the long lines here and the tone and movement is created by energetic action verbs: 'noses', 'presses', 'looped', 'pulls', 'call', 'hums', 'vibrates'. We can see this poem also as a description of a creative process: 'It feels like lifting a tall, swaying ship / With wind-filling streamers – / Across the threshold'. That threshold leads to new insights, which the speaker in the opening lines 'learning at last to see', must begin 'drawing'. In contrast to Daniel Grose, her drawing takes her inside the church, not looking at it from the outside, as Grose does his ruin.

Ní Chuilleanáin's images of more public architectural space are best illustrated in *The Brazen Serpent*, which opens with two poems, 'Fireman's Lift' (*SP* 64) and 'The Architectural Metaphor' (*SP* 66). 'Fireman's Lift', a poem developed with quatrains and tercets, was written after Eilís Dillon died, and Ní Chuilleanáin says that she wrote it because she 'absolutely knew' her mother would want her to write a poem about her dying. The poem describes a scene in the cathedral in Parma which Ní Chuilleanáin had visited with her parents in 1963; the poet explains the background and how her mother disliked the cathedral: 'It was a Romanesque church and they put this vast Renaissance dome on top of it.'[8] Within the cathedral dome, Correggio had painted his 'Assumption of the Virgin', which becomes one of the central images in the poem, with the angels and saints in the painting bending over to lift Mary into heaven. While Ní Chuilleanáin has described this as a 'cheering up poem', the intersection of the church architecture and Correggio's painting of the Virgin's Assumption also emphasises another angle, the dissolution of the human body as one looks up towards the fragments and details of the painting and architecture of the dome:

> We saw the work entire, and how the light
>
> Melted and faded bodies so that
> Loose feet and elbows and staring eyes
> Floated in the wide stone petticoat
> Clear and free as weeds.

Painting, architecture and body merge in the lines of the poem: 'the back making itself a roof / The legs a bridge, the hands / A crane and a cradle'; 'her face a capital leaning into an arch'. The light, which 'melted and faded bodies', suggests the limitations of mortality, as Ní Chuilleanáin imagines her mother's death in a religious sense as an entrance into another world, comparing it to the Assumption of Mary. Typically Ní Chuilleanáin does not try to imagine that other world; she stays grounded as did Correggio, in the material: we see the female figure 'as she came to the edge of the cloud'. We can compare the images in this poem to those in 'Vertigo' (*SP* 40), discussed earlier and described by Ní Chuilleanáin as about death, where two daughters are imagined with their mother on *Sceilig Mhichíl*: 'Her daughters like armed angels guarding each side / Of the path to the edge, where everything pours away'. Both of these images take us to the edge of 'the other side', that something beyond that we cannot know.

Again fusing spiritual and physical, Ní Chuilleanáin has also noted that when she wrote this poem she had in mind the nurses lifting her mother when she was dying.[9] The lines 'We saw them / Lifting her, the pillars of their arms / ... As the muscles clung and shifted' connect the nurses to the cathedral pillars and the angels in the cathedral dome, while highlighting the bodily strength in the nurses' arms. When the speaker views the dome in its entirety, we are told, 'That is what love sees, that angle', referring to the work of the nurses, to a daughter's vision of her mother's completed life, and to the artistic image of Mary's Assumption Correggio created inside the dome. Ní Chuilleanáin's images of the dome's architecture as a 'stone petticoat' which an observer would look up into, and of the 'big tree of the cupola / Where the church splits wide open to admit / Celestial choirs', also highlight the female figures of Virgin and mother in the context of body imagery, another 'angle' suggested by the poem. The observer is in effect looking up under the petticoat of a female. The connection of dead woman and ascending Virgin stresses Ní Chuilleanáin's fusion of material and sacred, of human and spiritual, essential to an understanding of this poem and her work as a whole. Like the poems 'Our Lady of Youghal' and 'A Voice', discussed in an earlier chapter, these images highlight the female body within a sacred architectural space and counteract negative images of the female body prevalent within the church. According to Ní Chuilleanáin, the stone petticoat can also be read as an image of maternity: 'I use the image of a church's cupola resembling a stone petticoat, leading to the idea of churchgoers being enclosed like children under their mothers' skirts.'[10]

In her essay '"Strange Ceremonies": Sacred Space and Bodily Presence in the English Reformation',[11] Ní Chuilleanáin argues that the Reformation attempted, not always successfully, to divorce the sacred from the bodily. She describes how this was illustrated in the use of space in churches and cathedrals where a Protestant emphasis on hearing the Word attempted to undercut the Catholic medieval and traditional linking of body with symbolic meaning. As the Protestant churches de-emphasised the body, as well as bodily gesture and ritual, distinguishing themselves from the medieval church where the intersection of material and sacred was clearer, they reorganised sacred spaces to reflect this. In earlier times, Ní Chuilleanáin maintains, sacred spaces were divided according to a system of pure and impure material states: 'The body was dangerous, more so if female and especially at certain times; the female and bodily were, it has been argued, interlinked categories.'[12] She notes, for example, the traditional women's side (left) of the church, or the ritual of churching, where a woman who had given birth came to the altar veiled to be readmitted to the congregation. While explaining that these rituals had the negative effects of subordinating women to men, or in the case of churching, ritualising the need to cleanse the body after childbirth, they at least made connections between the material and the sacred and acknowledged the physicality of the female body.

The deliberate merging of sacred and bodily in the imagery of 'Fireman's Lift', the integration of human body and action into sacred space to encourage symbolic meaning, grows from Ní Chuilleanáin's feeling that something was lost in the Reformation when emphasis fell on the more abstract. The title image of the poem carries this one level beyond as we are also asked to imagine both the cathedral and the hospital, the angels and the nurses, in terms of the unusual but concrete image of a fireman's lift ('The legs a bridge, the hands / A crane and a cradle'). This is reinforced with a description of the lifters, whether we see them, as in Correggio's painting, as angels assisting the virgin, or as nurses assisting a woman in a hospital bed. The weight and parts of female bodies, human and angelic, are highlighted:

Their heads bowed over to reflect on her
Fair face and hair so like their own
As she passed through their hands.

With this spotlight on female presences, with images of hair, eyes, hands, feet, elbows, jaws, shoulders, legs, face, muscles, Ní Chuilleanáin asks us to see 'the work entire', not only the architecture of the cathedral's dome or the completion of a life but also images of women, be it the assumed Mary or Ní Chuilleanáin's own dead mother, as both body and spirit dwelling within a sacred space.

In the context of Correggio's beautiful painting of the Virgin ascending through the hands of angels, integrated within the architectural lines of the dome, the work of the nurses is acknowledged as the 'church splits wide open' to admit the mother in 'the fall-out of brightness'. For Ní Chuilleanáin, 'what love sees, that angle' becomes a vision of transcendence, one's life, like the completed dome, 'the work entire'. Deliberately highlighting the female body in the context of the cathedral also creates another kind of splitting open, to allow a more realistic and positive image of women within the church. As is typical with Ní Chuilleanáin, there are borders crossed within this architectural space: the mother and the Blessed Mother are linked, angels are humanised, nurses are spiritualised as the poem's subject passes 'through their hands' into another life. As Eamon Grennan says, Ní Chuilleanáin's buildings are 'meeting-places' where 'the world of the spirit and the world of the body – come together'.[13]

In a companion poem in *The Brazen Serpent*, 'The Architectural Metaphor' (*SP* 66), written in three-line unrhymed stanzas with a final quatrain, Ní Chuilleanáin returns to her image of convents and to one 'a good mile on the safe side of the border' where the speaker is part of a group being guided through the remains of the convent. The difference in women's lives is seen in the images of the celibate foundress, who subordinated her body to community vows, and a young barefoot girl, heard laughing when a door opens to reveal her dalliance with a man. Suddenly a hatch flies open and the foundress of the convent, buried with her face turned west, is imagined as searching for a church's rose window and what 'she never saw from any angle but this':

> Herself at fourteen stumbling downhill
> And landing, and crouching to watch
> The sly limbering of the bantam hen
>
> Foraging between gravestones –
>   Help is at hand

Though out of reach:
The world not dead after all.

The convent itself, which still has a cloister, is also 'not dead after all' as it hints at the history of the nuns who have lived there, and is at once a repository of the dead and a place in the present giving us what the opening lines describe as 'the lie of the land'. The shifting lines between past and present, as well as the spiritual life and ascetic life of the nun contrasted to the pleasurable actions of the young girl, are reflected in the architecture of the space: hatch doors opening into an imagined past, real doors allowing the members of the tour to hear the young girl laughing, the cloister that is still there. Attempting to find the human element, the active presence within this space, the speaker notes a faint sound as a 'radio whispers behind the wall':

Since there is nothing that speaks as clearly
As music, no other voice that says
Hold me I'm going … so faintly

The words of the song, '*Hold me I'm going*', while related to the young woman behind the door, also refer to the buried foundress, echoing the end of *Site of Ambush*, where we are told of the young girl who comes back from the dead: 'lay fast hold of her / And do not let her go'. Each poem stresses the importance of imagining active presences within the buildings and landscapes related to the past. The convent in 'The Architectural Metaphor' had a laundry, we are told, evoking the laundries of the Irish Magdalenes described in 'Translation' and noting the importance of places not to be forgotten. In addition, the metaphor of architecture here carries additional weight as it emphasises political borders which are changed, crossed, drawn and redrawn, open and closed: 'The buildings of the convent, founded / Here, a good mile on the safe side of the border / Before the border was changed'. While the guide confidently explains the 'lie of the land', the poem opens up the phrase to the possibility of numerous meanings and ambiguities.

Any discussion of Ní Chuilleanáin's architectural imagery must include the early collection *Cork*, which sets up precedents for much of the poetry to come. Thomas McCarthy maintains that her early childhood in Cork 'presented Ní Chuilleanáin with an entire word-hoard of images and a grammar or world-view that pervade her poetry', and also claims that 'Cork never leaves her consciousness ... it is always there as a restorative psychic architecture'.[14] A series of poems about her native city, *Cork* was commissioned to accompany drawings by Brian Lalor and, though they complement one another, there is no one-to-one correlation between poem and drawing. In 'A Note on the Drawings', Lalor explains that when he returned to Cork in the early 1970s he found 'a city reeling from the cataclysm of urban renewal', and he sought to preserve in his drawings many of the details of a disappearing city. Lalor explains his inspiration:

> This is not Cork seen from its public face but from above and behind, not just observed in its principal role as the second city of the Republic but sought out in all its idiosyncrasies and individuality ... The shock of recognising the invaluable heritage which is now being thoughtlessly annihilated will only come when the area we are concerned with here has been levelled stone by historical stone. To a country lacking the architectural and urban richness of continental Europe it is vitally important to conserve what little there is, before neglect and the developer between them deprive the country of the remnants of its historical and aesthetic past without which the present and the future become incomprehensible.[15]

Though these are Lalor's words, we can assume Ní Chuilleanáin shared his sense of a crumbling city which illustrates the 'idiosyncrasies and individuality' of its multi-faceted past. Her interest in history, as well as her concern for a place in which she spent many happy years, would have influenced Ní Chuilleanáin's collaboration on this project. In 'Home and Places', Ní Chuilleanáin describes the vernacular architecture of Cork, noting its social and historical heritage:

> Much of the city is a haphazard succession of buildings dating from a mixture of periods, still following the medieval pattern of streets and laneways, crammed on their island site, churches, markets and houses. On the hills that surrounded the town suburbs grew up: some respectable, terraces with British Army names recalling Wellington and Waterloo, inhabited by the officers from the barracks higher up again; some grim and filthy with names like Brandy Lane, Spudtown, Cat Lane.[16]

In the opening section of *Cork*, Ní Chuilleanáin sets the tone. Formed where the river Lee splits, Cork is pictured as an island of 'internal spirals / Packed as tight as a ship', full of exiles 'Sheltering against the tide' (*C* 15), recurring images in her early poems in *Acts and Monuments* and *The Rose Geranium*. The spirals, evoking a Celtic past, also represent the winding streets and alleys illustrated in Lalor's drawings. The river reflects the city's quays and roofs, steps and warehouse walls, what Ní Chuilleanáin sees as defences against perennial flooding. Describing the people in Cork, 'their rooms all swamped by dreams' (*SP* 37), Ní Chuilleanáin depicts the ominous destructive force of water seen in many of her poems. Referring to a 'lingua franca of water' (*C* 15) on which this island ship floats, Ní Chuilleanáin alludes to the political history of battles and invasions Cork has endured and to the many cultures and languages the area has assimilated, most notably Gaelic and English. The weeds in the angles of the houses 'flourish and fall in a week' (*SP* 37), symbols not only of Cork's long history but also of the precarious existence of life in the city.

Thomas McCarthy describes the emphasis in Ní Chuilleanáin's images: 'One of the permanent legacies of her Cork, of her entire cloistered childhood, is the very specific architecture of her imagined world ... The house, the kitchen and the sunlit interiors where women wait together are overwhelmingly important constructs in Ní Chuilleanáin's poetry.'[17] In the poems, shelter and protection can be found within buildings, and Ní Chuilleanáin's descriptions of the interiors of these places is central to an understanding of the poems and to the role that women play in sustaining life in the city. Doorways open to reveal life within the home:

> When you pass the doorway
> You are going underground; it is light and warm
> And nothing is as you expected.
> A table laid since breakfast-time,
> Cake and sherry, with whiskey for the men. (*C* 32)

A similar level of comfort defines the pubs:

> A slot of air, the snug
> Just wide enough for the door to open
> And bang the knees of everyone inside;

You face a window blank with dust
Half-inch spider webs
Rounding the squares of glass
And a view on either hand of mirrors
Shining at each other in the gloom.

A woman's head, bowed,
A glint on her forehead
Obliquely seen leaning on the counter
At the end of a vista of glasses
And one damp towel. (*SP* 37–38)

The painterly image here creates an aesthetic vision: the bar is a framed scene closed off from the outside world; light falls from the shining mirrors and the glint on the woman's forehead; the vista is of the woman, bar glasses and a damp towel. The central figure in this pub, we should note, is a female.

Counterpointing these sheltering rooms, however, architectural ruins demonstrate the many tragedies Cork has endured. Several poems in *Cork* portray this destruction; ruined houses show the marks of damp and the tides: 'The crazy houses, walls as soft as cake' (*C* 88). The architecture also demonstrates the ravages of war, the legacy of 'The Duke of Marlborough, the Black and Tans' (*C* 88) which refers to Marborough's siege of Cork in 1690, when Williamite troops breached the walls, and to the Black and Tans who set fire to the city in the War of Independence in 1920. Remnants of the past linger: abandoned limestone houses with no insides, solid chimneys 'venting no smoke or sighs' (*C* 46). The contrast between what these houses were and are now is vividly reflected in the streets:

Geometry of guilt, the windows
Broken or always empty;
Daylight sucked in and lost, a bird astray;

The knife edge of the street, blinded
Fronts of houses like a baconslicer
Dropping to infinity, down

Draughty quays and frozen bridges
And the façades are curves of seeping stone
As damp as a scullery

Or a child's game of windows and doors arranged
Matching the caves of womb and skull.

Inside, nothing but the long drop. (*C* 69)

Ní Chuilleanáin's use of domestic similes and metaphors like cakes, knives, baconslicers and sculleries sharpens her focus on the interiors of homes, particularly of kitchens, a focus we see in later poems like 'The Italian Kitchen' (*SP* 56) and 'In Rome' (*SP* 59). Her Cork is a world of women ('the caves of the womb'); and the source of Ní Chuilleanáin's metaphors is often the home: 'the streets are warm / As a bedroom full of sleeping children'; 'the wheels of a car, a dull / Even sound, as if it drove on a carpet' (*C* 84). As parts of Cork disappear, a woman poet's eyes imagine it from the insides of rooms that have been lost:

Missing from the scene
The many flat surfaces,
Undersides of doors, of doormats
Blank backs of wardrobes
The walls of tunnels in walls
Made by wires of bells, and the shadows of square spaces
Left high on kitchen walls
By the removal of those bells on their boards. (*SP* 38)

Uniquely Ní Chuilleanáin's, these images are not illustrated in Lalor's drawings. Images of the river, of the lizard and salmon, of the winds howling over the hills, appear in the poems as well, but it is the insides of the city, including the architectural remnants of those rooms and houses which have disappeared but are re-imagined, which tell the human story of Ní Chuilleanáin's native city.

After *Cork*, house interiors and vernacular domestic architecture continued to play a significant role in developing Ní Chuilleanáin's themes. In this sense she distinguishes between a building and a home, between monument and residence, and in so doing emphasises the cultural significance of spaces where the work and achievements of women have often been underrated. 'An Alcove' in *The Girl who Married the Reindeer* (*GMR* 31) describes a home in which the 'walls / Hunched over'; the speaker and the rooms reflect the life within. Pictured is a tense time while a caretaker waits for a medical diagnosis of a sick woman:

> In these rooms every stitch, step and
> Edge of a tile is the same age, is wearing
> Away at the same rate, like an old lady
> Who brings out the sherry because tea means trouble
> But has not barred her door.

This home also has 'porched crannies' where a speaker shelters, waiting for news of the sick woman 'while the doctor is with her'; a cranny becomes 'one safe place, an alcove in the wind'.

A companion poem, 'The Crevasse' (*GMR* 30), presents a different architectural angle, a house which begins to break apart as a man sits drinking in a beanbag chair:

> … He reached for the bottle again,
> And all the vertical lines of the house moved
>
> A little forward, and left. They dangled and waltzed,
> Hanging brittle, ready to crash and split
> Every straight chair in the room, leaving the halves
>
> To hop away two-legged, leaving
> The walls of the house wedged open
> To the four winds and the polar light.

On a literal level, the excessive drinking may create a drunken vision of dangling and waltzing rooms, but the poem also hints at other consequences of the situation, where the walls might crash and split, leaving the home and its inhabitants open to the chaos of the wind and the polar light. 'The Alcove' and 'The Crevasse' are linked not only by images of walls and rooms but also by these concluding images, metaphors for potential tragedy. The difference between the protective, sheltering alcove in the first poem and the walls 'ready to crash' described in 'The Crevasse' illustrates the way in which Ní Chuilleanáin uses architectural elements for different purposes.

'The Party Wall' (*SP* 84) from *The Brazen Serpent* portrays other issues, including the secrecy which is a hallmark of some family relationships. Ní Chuilleanáin has said that as she grew older she became increasingly aware of the ways in which families fail to talk about quarrels which divide them, or about traumatic experiences they have gone through.[18] The house's party wall symbolises the barriers in communications among the family members. The speaker in 'The Party Wall' remembers a home whose inhabitants came and went through gates, 'gliding to business and back at night' for tea, oblivious to the neighbours in a connecting house until an aerial photograph reveals not only their own garden filled with white feathers but also the roof and courtyards of the adjacent house. The speaker recalls a puzzling revelation: 'The tenants had my grandfather's name', but a visit to the parish priest fails to provide the full story: 'he had never been told my aunt's story / About all the trouble over building the party wall'. Comparing this poem to another, 'The Secret' (*SP* 86), Ní Chuilleanáin has said that both are about families made up of women and are about the 'interchange between the outside world and the home which is defined by boundaries'.[19] In typical Ní Chuilleanáin fashion, the reader of 'The Party Wall' is not told the story either, though the wall represents both the conflict in the family and the lack of access to the many secrets families hide.

'The interchange between the outside world and the home' is also the focus of another poem, where both political and gender boundaries are illustrated by divisions inside and outside a home. In 'In Her Other House' (*SP* 97), Ní Chuilleanáin pictures a man returning to his home, contrasting that to the more public place from which he has come, where 'You turn out your pockets every time a door is opened'. The background for the image here is the family house where Ní Chuilleanáin's father ('The only boy with six sisters') and aunts lived. Ní Chuilleanáin describes her early memories of such spaces: 'My aunts' house lives in my mind as a feeling of calm and affection, a view of the enamel kitchen table and, beyond, of the small window lighting the scrubbed back kitchen, and the sound of an aunt chopping kindling wood in a tiny yard.'[20]

Looking back through memory, and maintaining that 'it is the dead who serve us', the speaker sees the inside of the home divided by gender roles, with a man leaving each day to work outside the home and his sisters busy at work inside. The speaker describes a home where a 'glass and the bottle of sour stout' are 'Guarding his place', but says that the man never learned 'To set a table, though books lined up at his command'. This man finds comfort and shelter in the house that is kept for him by his sisters, in a room with a 'fire, books, a meal and a minute / When everyone is out of sight washing their hands'. The invisible hands of his sisters, not necessarily acknowledged, have on one level made this man's public life possible. The final lines of the poem, 'In this house there is no need to wait for the verdict of history / And each page lies open to the version of every other', make it clear that 'In Her Other House' comments on a neglected social history of women who established comfort and stability in the home.

In poems like 'The Door', 'The Cure' and 'The Copious Dark' from the collection *The Sun-fish*, Ní Chuilleanáin again uses images of homes, windows and doors to present a glimpse into the past, or into secret lives. 'The Cure' (*S* 37), with alternating long and short lines, sets two dramatic conversations within a sequence of quatrains. One depicts a young female servant's letters to her mother describing a situation where '*The lady of this house / Keeps to her room*'. In the other, the servant overhears a conversation between a group in another room who have temporarily opened their door because the fire is too hot: 'She hears them settling the great questions: / How treat a case / Of green-sickness or, again, one of unrequited love?' The door on this conversation closes again and the servant returns to her letter, warning her mother not to seek help from a fraudulent healer:

… Don't think
Of consulting that fraudulent woman. Her sister, who
Died, had the gift.

… I understand, it must be hard for her,
So long, no news.

When she again hears voices, the servant rises to guide a guest at the home's door to bed and then returns to her letter, explaining to her mother:

… The lady of this house
Keeps to her room.
The master sighs as he locks the heavy street door.
There is no cure.

In this short narrative, the doors of the home, and the clearly marked boundaries of the rooms, are central images as they shut people off from one another, male doctors in one room talking about their female patients in clinical terms contrasted to the servant in another room dealing with the same issue, green sickness, in her own family. The opening and closing doors represent a glimpse into the past, as well as into the secret ways in which such illnesses are often discussed. In the history of medicine, the green sickness was identified with an ailment specific to young women (it was also known as the maid's disease) that supposedly involved their skin turning green and a host of other symptoms, including lack of menstruation, and general malaise.

The green sickness has a long medical history, including Hippocrates' treatise on the Disease of Virgins, one of the earliest recorded discussions, and Johannes Lange's 1554 medical description of the disorder. Eventually the disease was given a more scientific name, chlorosis, which still appears occasionally but, in effect, earlier diagnoses of green sickness disappeared in the twentieth century as medicine became more science-based and attempts were made to connect the symptoms to anaemia. Helen King, in her 2003 book *The Disease of Virgins*, suggests that green sickness may have been a series of ailments classified under one name and applied exclusively to women, rather than a single disease. King explains that in the 1550s the disease was thought to be caused by thick blood becoming trapped in the body of a virgin and that, by implication, the cure involved marriage and the loss of virginity. King also notes that the symptoms described for this disease were similar to those for love sickness, in this case 'a love sickness without a clear love object'.[21] Ní Chuilleanáin's poem also mentions the latter, in the reference to 'unrequited love'. Ian Maclean notes that identifying and naming such a disease played a role in regulating the sexual conduct of young women and, Maclean argues, became a way to justify women's relegation to marriage and home.[22]

The overheard conversation between the master and his colleagues on 'How treat a case / Of green-sickness or, again, one of unrequited love?' involves a medical quandary about what to do with women suffering from these vaguely defined diseases. In the letters the daughter writes to her mother, the focus is on the servant's sister, a victim of green sickness, and on her mother's desire to consult a local healer, whom the servant considers 'fraudulent' because it was the woman's sister who 'had the gift'.[23] Another snippet of the letter mentions the ill sister struggling over her illness ('*it must be hard for her*'). In counterpointing the medical doctors with the more folk-based healer, the poem highlights the approaches to issues of women's suffering – and how causes could be assigned to love sickness or blood trapped in a virgin's body – and cures sought from the local healers.

The young servant also writes that she sympathises with the lady of the house who keeps to her room, isolated with another undisclosed ailment. The final line, '*There is no cure*', sums up the situation of many 'female diseases' in the course of history, like green sickness or hysteria, where medical diagnoses tended to depend on myths and stereotypes about women for their identification. As imagined by the opening and closing doors, most of the discussions of these problems were secret, carried on in letters or in conversations behind closed doors. In the poem the emphasis is on female lives, the young servant who cannot go to bed until the master's friends are come and gone, the young woman suffering from an ill-defined ailment, or indeed the lady of the house who keeps to her room, a sign perhaps of depression. This house contains a number of separate rooms, cut off from one another by closed doors, in which issues of class and gender are reflected in the separate and lonely lives of those who live within. The life of the lady here is no better than that of the servant girl.

In the poem 'The Copious Dark' (*S* 59), architectural images of rooms, walls and doors again focus on what lies beyond the surfaces we see. As the last poem in *The Sun-fish*, 'The Copious Dark' imagines points of light within an all-encompassing darkness, and describes lit windows enclosing secrets. The subject of the poem is a woman moving through the streets:

> After the windows she loved, and again they showed
> The back rooms of bakeries, the clean engine-rooms and all
> The floodlit open yards where a van idled by a wall,
>
> A wall as long as life, as long as work.

The copious dark becomes the source of small points of light, moments of sight or revelation through the windows and doors. However, there are so many shuttered doors, 'too many to scan' we are told, that there is no time to see them all. The final lines of this poem move from images of buildings, walls and windows to more philosophical and meditative questions:

> ... Who can explain
> Why the wasps are asleep in the dark in their numbered holes
> And the lights shine all night in the hospital corridors?

As in some of Ní Chuilleanáin's other poems, we are left here with a question with no answer, but one that again involves enclosures and the insides of spaces, the wasps asleep in the nest, the hospital lights reflecting the illnesses and suffering which continue in the dark. For the female subject/quester in this poem, older now than when she 'used to love the darkness', the journey is more taxing, the shuttered doors 'blighted', the questions more difficult to answer, and the dark increasingly more copious. However, it is important to notice how this female figure gives the dark, and the buildings, windows, and walls within it, a human dimension – the sick in the hospital, for example. This is the dimension that Daniel Grose, in his images of architectural ruin, had ignored, but it is the final image noted by the speaker in 'The Nave' who imagines a song sung 'softly to a patient in her hospital bed'. As we have seen in her many descriptions of architectural spaces, it is avid presences that Ní Chuilleanáin is always seeking, and the buildings, windows and doors behind which they lived or still live represent an entry into their lives. At the same time, the images also suggest our exclusion from those lives in the copious dark, where a wall 'as long as life, as long as work' has shuttered doors 'too many to scan'.

CHAPTER 7

Transformation and Translation

I listen to their accents, they are not all
From this island, not all old,
Not even, I think, all masculine.

'Studying the Language' (*SP* 89)

The copious dark in the final poem of *The Sun-fish*, discussed at the end of the last chapter, has applications not only to space and place but also to language. In discussing the value of Renaissance rhetoric, Ní Chuilleanáin notes the many alternative ways of expressing an idea, what she defines as 'copiousness': 'I find that when I write something – when I write a line – I sometimes look at it and say what could I change about that? What could be different?'[1] The issue of difference and the ways in which language both insists upon and allows for diversity underpin many of Ní Chuilleanáin's poetic strategies; she chooses from the multiple meanings inherent in words, creating what Irene Gilsenan Nordin has described as other 'meanings hiding in the shadows struggling to be set free'.[2] This strategy, which can be applied not only to words but also to images, is illustrated in her own original poems as well as in both what we can loosely call adaptations of poems by other writers, and her translations from other languages.

In all three of these categories, issues of gender surface as Ní Chuilleanáin focuses on established views and beliefs, particularly as these involve female figures as subjects and speakers. In the poems 'Gloss/*Clós*/*Glas*' and 'Studying the Language', for example, the relationship between language and gender, as these reflect the lives of women and men, are central to an understanding of both poems. Likewise, in her 'rewritings' or adaptations of some well-known poems by male poets, Ní Chuilleanáin creates female figures where there are none in the original texts, in so doing giving us a new and different way to view the settings and themes of the poems. Finally, in her translations of a female poet like the Romanian Ileana Mălăncioiu, the abundance of female figures in the original poems allows Ní Chuilleanáin to demonstrate another side of 'copiousness', the translator's many options to express the similarities and differences between poets writing in different languages.

'Gloss/*Clós*/*Glas*' (*SP* 119), the last of her *Selected Poems*, shows us that Ní Chuilleanáin's attitudes towards poetic voices and potential meanings embedded in words are also connected to issues of gender. Placed before two translations in the 'Coda' in the collection *The Girl who Married the Reindeer*, this poem explores not only the variety of meanings implicit in words but also how words may be related to one another yet distinct in themselves. Finally, the poem comments on the ways in which words in one language have no equivalents in another. One of the central themes in the poem revolves around the adjectives 'his' and 'hers' and the ways in which different languages use, or do not use, such terms.

The poem focuses on a male language scholar late at night, searching to unlock the meaning of words. When asked whether there was a model for this figure, Ní Chuilleanáin answered: 'I suppose it could be my father in that he was a scholar, but I think I wanted more to have a male figure and a female figure meeting each other in that poem.'[3] The scholar's work is complicated by the alternative and multiple meanings words can have, which Ní Chuilleanáin glosses in her choice of images in carefully worked alliterative and assonantal lines, and repeated consonantal words like '*clós*' and 'close'. The scholar, 'stiff as a shelf', is seeking in his dictionaries 'the price of his release', searching for:

> Two words, as opposite as *his* and *hers*
> Which yet must be as close
> As the word *clós* to its meaning in a Scots courtyard
> Close to the spailpín ships, or as close as the note
> On the uilleann pipe to the same note on the fiddle –
> As close as the grain in the polished wood, as the finger
> Bitten by the string, as the hairs of the bow
> Bent by the repeated note –

From English to Scots to Irish, from courtyards to ships, from uilleann pipe to fiddle notes, from woodgrain to bitten fingers and bow hairs, Ní

Chuilleanáin glosses similarity and difference, 'opposite' but 'close', with valuable images which parallel the close but opposite gender pronouns 'his' and 'hers'.

Helen Emmitt, in a review of *The Girl who Married the Reindeer*, gives a very good reading of the above lines in relation to the poem's title:

> Glossing a 'gloss' means, for the poet, coming close but never really arriving. '*Clós*' in Irish means 'yard', though not necessarily the stillness (another meaning of '*clós*' in Scots Gaelic) of the enclosed passage of the Scots courtyard, which may itself be close to an itinerant ship, but the courtyard is nonetheless cut off from exactly the open sea that the ship was made for. As the simile of the pipe and fiddle suggests, words, like instruments, may be tuned to a single note, but they retain their own timbre, their own character.[4]

Such glossing does not make the scholar's, or the translator's, job an easy one. Examining both the fluidity and limitations of words and language, Ní Chuilleanáin also portrays the obstacles and difficulties one faces in attempting to understand the meanings a word might have.

In 'Gloss/*Clós*/*Glas*', a scholar in his library, 'still not gone to bed', pours through 'the rags of language', frustrated in his attempts to find the exact words he needs for the concept he wants to express: 'his' and 'hers'. Eventually he reaches the language that has no words for 'his' or 'hers'. Ní Chuilleanáin notes that 'the language that does arrive at the end is Irish', but she says, 'I don't necessarily have to say that. Because in Irish the word for 'his', 'hers', and 'theirs' is all the same.'[5] Ní Chuilleanáin emphasises the problems with fixed meanings for words; 'opposite' but 'close' is the best one can arrive at when language is 'Pouring and slippery'. 'The rags of language are streaming like weathervanes, / Like weeds in water they turn with the tide', the poem tells us, using an image (weeds turning in the tide) which in Ní Chuilleanáin's poems like 'St Mary Magdalene Preaching at Marseilles' represents fluidity and change.

By extension, we might apply this to issues of gender as well. Having reached the conclusion that one language has no word 'for *his*, / No word for *hers*', one can question whether gender constructs defined by these words are also fixed, since they do not appear in every language. Are the concepts and meanings often associated with them, like the words themselves, open to different interpretations? Are we able to apply single meanings to these possessive adjectives, 'his' always means one thing, 'hers' always another, or are they 'pouring' and 'slippery' as well? From other poems, in which males and females ignore the boundaries of these definitions, we can see that Ní Chuilleanáin is attempting to get beyond narrow definitions of 'his' and 'hers'.

When the scholar reaches his linguistic conclusion, he is confronted with a dilemma beyond his locked door. Counterpointing his cerebral work is another life suggested by bodily images and sensual words ironically used to describe his linguistic search: 'the silk thighs of the tomcat / Pouring through the slit in the fence'. On the other side of the door, the scholar hears a woman 'panting', the 'steam of her breath … turning the locked lock green'. In this final line, Ní Chuilleanáin alludes to the Irish *clós* which can mean both 'lock' and 'green'. Nicholas Allen suggests that the scribe in the final lines 'approaches a point where language is silence, meaning a blank that registers presence without form. The surprise of this insight prompts the subject to use other senses, listening now, not reading … The realisation of the limits of language is a first step to freedom.'[6] At the same time, this freedom allows for a view of the human as both mind and sense, one part of which the scholar ignores.

Never one to leave the body out of the picture, Ní Chuilleanáin here highlights the danger of too much emphasis on striving for verbal exactness, while neglecting other aspects of life. For all the scholar's 'raking the dictionaries' and 'hunting for keys', he is in the end 'brought up sudden / Like a boy in a story faced with a small locked door', on the other side of which is a mystery. The pattern of words created by 'silken thighs', 'embrace', 'release', panting', 'twining of bone and flesh' suggestive of a sexual 'nightwork', which the scholar is missing, also contrasts with the scholar's linguistic search, highlighting the close but different realms of mind and body, logic and sense. Ní Chuilleanáin has said that the scholar does not know what is outside the door,[7] connecting this poem with others in which closed doors hide secrets, thus denying the reader, like the scholar, the complete story.

From another angle, this poem repeats a pattern we have seen in poems like 'Daniel Grose' (*SP* 78) or 'The Informant' (*SP* 62), where a male and female figure are juxtaposed. In the former poem, the old woman/*cailleach* offsets Grose's more scientific approach for a 'human' prespective; in the latter, the old woman/informant continues to speak, to tell her folklore story, as the young man's tape recorder, on which he is dependent, breaks down. In using these figures, as she does with the woman beyond the locked door in 'Gloss/*Clós*/*Glas*', Ní Chuilleanáin emphasises the value of folk wisdom as much as the logical 'raking of dictionaries', or of the senses as much as of the mind. The images of locking are another iteration of the borders and barriers Ní Chuilleanáin's subjects continually confront. We can compare the scholar, who is 'like a boy in a story faced with a small locked door', to the male in 'Permafrost Woman' who encounters a female who unfolds 'among peaks of / Frozen sea', as the 'body opens its locks'. The mysterious panting behind the door, like 'the wide mouth' the man stares at in 'Permafrost Woman' or the musical sound in 'A Voice' (both related to the image of the sexually explicit *sheela-na-gig*), gives these female figures importance, not the least of which is sexual. The locks and borders in all of these poems resonate on several levels.

In 'Studying the Language' (*SP* 89), the final poem in *The Brazen Serpent*, Ní Chuilleanáin presents a different perspective on the issue of language and gender as the speaker hears male and female voices while watching a group of hermits come out of their beehive huts: 'I listen to their accents, they are not all / From this island, not all old, / Not even, I think, all masculine'. The setting here, as it is in the poems 'Vertigo' (*S* 40) and 'Celibates' (*SP* 17),[8] is *Sceilig Mhichíl*, on Ireland's west coast; by imagining the hermits are neither all Irish nor all male, Ní Chuilleanáin is broadening the context of a community usually associated with older Irish monks. The speaker describes the hermits gathered on the warm rocks, walking past them to drink from the pools of melted snow from which they drink. The mingling of languages within this diverse group of people creates a sense of community in which the speaker can participate. The hermits talking to one another cut across categories, from different cultures, speaking different languages, of different ages and sexes.

Interestingly, in the collection *The Brazen Serpent*, which highlights women, 'Studying the Language' has an indeterminate speaker, reinforcing the thematic emphasis on placing the hermits here in a broader context which includes both men and women. Ní Chuilleanáin explains that in writing 'Studying the Language' she was thinking about 'listening for the signs of gender which are so different in languages'. 'For example,' she says, 'in Irish and English, you never have to learn to refer to yourself in the feminine. In Romance languages, you must',[9] thus pointing out another way in which, as she did in 'Gloss/*Clós*/*Glas*', signifiers of gender like 'his' and 'hers' do not exist in every language. The use of a non-gendered speaker, as well as the multiple voices described in 'Studying the Language', is reinforced in the final couplet of the poem, where the speaker borrows words from the preface to Thomas More's *Utopia*: 'I call this my work, these decades and stations – / Because, without these, I would be a stranger here'.

The source for the allusion to More is a prefatory letter to Peter Giles in *Utopia*, where More stresses the importance of his family life and the need to interact with his wife and children.[10] Ní Chuilleanáin explains her use of the allusion to More and what she describes as a writer's usual complaint of lack of time and the distractions that hold a book up:

> That was lifted from Sir Thomas More's Preface to *Utopia* where he is writing to a friend, and he says I haven't really been able to write my book because I have been having to go to work, and when I come home I must talk to my children and my wife and my servants and all these people who live in my house, and that is work too because it must be done. If you don't talk to the people who live in your house, you are a stranger. I thought, this is a good one. It corresponds to the working mother.[11]

Ní Chuilleanáin adds another dimension to this side of More when she notes:

> Evidence, along with his affectionate letters, that More had at least noticed his family's existence, that he had felt their claims and experienced that essentially modern anxiety of wondering what the loved ones are up to when a parent is far away. More has to count as a feminist, with due allowance being made for the standards of his time: we know not only the names of his wives, daughters, and adopted daughters and some of their women servants; we know their characters, their talents and interest. Theirs do not form part of their age's large body of lost women's lives.[12]

This is not the way most people think of Sir Thomas More but, in using his own words or alluding to his writing, Ní Chuilleanáin has placed him in a new light, a new context, transforming him into someone who acknowledged and wrote about the women with whom he lived so that they are not part of the large 'body of lost women's lives'. By comparing him to a working mother who needs to balance time between work and family and, by extension, to a writer where lack of time has held up his book, Ní Chuilleanáin is calling attention to the multiple roles and tensions which affect many women as well. In the context of the poem, we need to connect this image to the speaker's view of the hermits, imagining them also as not part of the 'body of lost women's lives', and not 'all masculine', or all Irish, but as a family of sorts, a community 'who come out of their holes' on Sundays and 'crowd together on warm shoulders of rock'.

Echoing the integration of multiple languages within the community of hermits, 'Studying the Language' is a fourteen-line variation of a sonnet in the English literary tradition but focused on different speakers and languages in the Irish-speaking *Gaeltacht* on the western coast of Ireland. John Kerrigan notes the influences of different languages in this poem as Ní Chuilleanáin 'produces a verse movement which is Anglophone but not quite English', and maintains that the poem 'realizes a home-place which doesn't cohere linguistically but traffics between Latin, Italian, Gaelic and English',[13] a home place which we might almost see, given the allusion to More, as utopian. In appropriating the words of Thomas More for her poetic speaker, Ní Chuilleanáin incorporates words translated into English from a Latin text, written by a man, into a contemporary Irish poem, written in English by a woman, who is herself a working mother. The words in the final lines, 'I call this my work', can be applied to Ní Chuilleanáin's own poetry, a good example of the *lingua franca* she uses in describing the multiple cultures embedded in her native Cork.

Themes involving the complexity of language and gender, similarity and difference, are developed in other Ní Chuilleanáin poems as well. Eamon Grennan suggests that Ní Chuilleanáin has a gift for transforming, but one that 'never seems to do violence to its subject'. Although Grennan is specifically relating this to the ways in which Ní Chuilleanáin sees 'through matter into mystery',[14] there are other transformations, especially as this applies to her 'rewriting' of images by male poets. Reworking some well-known Irish poems to include or substitute female figures or female speakers, Ní Chuilleanáin responds to the abundance of male figures and perspectives in Irish poetry by transforming a text into a poem of her own which both acknowledges the value of the original but suggests the limits of its vision.

The major Irish poets dominating the literary landscape in the first half of the twentieth century included Yeats, Pádraic Colum and Patrick Kavanagh. In the case of Yeats, in particular, his work often became the standard against which other poets were judged, a point Kavanagh raised in explaining what his own poetry represented as he challenged some of Yeats's assumptions and images. Ní Chuilleanáin, who knew and appreciated the work of these poets, and who dedicated *The Magdalene Sermon* to the memory of Kavanagh's wife Katherine,[15] sees some of her own work as presenting a different angle from these poets, sometimes keeping the same narrative but changing the character or speaker. Ní Chuilleanáin has commented on the difference between her work and that of some well-known Irish poets, not only in terms of gender but also of class. In an interview with Inés Praga, Ní Chuilleanáin explains:

> From the start it was clear to me that I couldn't imitate the male writer. This was particularly so in Ireland because there was a stereotype of the male writer who was also the rural writer, for instance, Patrick Kavanagh and, later, Seamus Heaney. The main fact was that the poet sees himself as speaking for the inarticulate members of his peasant clan. My father was a University professor and my mother was a writer and I could see from a very early stage that this option was not open to me. I don't think I ever imitated male writers although I certainly studied them and learnt from them and I tried to find an oblique approach.[16]

Part of this 'oblique approach' involves poems which respond in different ways to poems written by male poets. Like her poems in which saints, nuns or women in folklore are foregrounded, Ní Chuilleanáin adapts some well-known poetic narratives to change the central figure from male to female, in the process often presenting different perspectives on the settings or themes of the original poems. Her poems are not attacks on the original poem or poet; in fact, one could argue that Ní Chuilleanáin's attempt to provide a different context or perspective underlines the success of the original.

Ní Chuilleanáin's 'Following' (*SP* 76) borrows from Pádraic Colum's 'She Moved through the Faire'. Colum based this poem on an Irish song,

'Our Wedding Day', in which a young man describes his last glimpse of his wife-to-be walking through a fair before she dies and subsequently appears to him in a dream. Colum's poem reads:

> Then she stepped away from me, and she moved thru the Faire,
> And so fondly I watched her move here and move there;
> At last she turned homeward, with one star awake,
> As the Swan in the evening moves over the lake.
> Last night she came to me, my dead love came in,
> And so soft did she move that her feet made no din;
> She put her arms 'round me; these words she did say:
> It will not be long, love, 'til our wedding day![17]

Borrowing from the *aisling* or dream vision tradition, the poem presents an image of a beautiful woman who, compared to a swan when he last saw her, returns in the speaker's dream to embrace her bridegroom and imagine their promised wedding day.

In Ní Chuilleanáin's poem 'Following', a girl follows her father through a fair, a very conventionally male scene of livestock and traders, shirt-cuffs, handkerchiefs and hats, but her poem creates a figure different from Colums's dead woman. Ní Chuilleanáin's speaker, a female, imagining the woman crossing a bog, replaces Colum's dead bride-to-be with a risen corpse who '[glides] before her in a white habit'. The figure in this dream vision is neither a bride-to-be nor linked to a male, and given Ní Chuilleanáin's interest in nuns, could be imagined as one, with her white habit. In Ní Chuilleanáin's vision, the 'ground is forested with gesturing trunks, / Hands of women dragging needles' and the landscape is terrifying. Instead of Colum's image of the peaceful swan moving across the lake, Ní Chuilleanáin's poem presents 'Half-choked heads in the water of cuttings, / Mouths that roar like the noise of the fair day', ironically reminding one also of the beasts at the fair.

In the final stanza of the poem, the speaker comes to a place where her father is seated, and the lines repeat a familiar image from other Ní Chuilleanáin poems, including 'Gloss/*Clós*/*Glas*'. A man sits in a library 'where the light is clean' and 'His clothes all finely laundered, / Ironed facings and linings', work done by women in the background in the home.[18] The natural life at the fair is ironically echoed in metaphors for his books: 'foxed leaf' and 'forest of fine shufflings'. The father's handkerchief glimpsed at the fair is replaced here with another:

The square of white linen
That held three drops
Of her heart's blood is shelved
Between the gatherings
That go to make a book –

This image is an allusion to a line in Colum's story *The King of Ireland's Son*, where a woman is asked to give seven drops of her heart's blood so that the King of Ireland's son can be reunited with his mother, which the woman refuses to do. Like the scenario in 'Gloss/*Clós*/*Glas*', where the man is detached from the panting woman in the next room, the father in 'Following' is also in his library where the story of the sacrifice asked of the woman in *The King of Ireland's Son* is shelved between the covers of a book.

The sense of control and order symbolised by the lighted library, juxtaposed with the images of the fair and the sacrifice of the woman's heart's blood, suggests the difference not only between two different kinds of life but also between the physical (the men at the fair are described as 'A block of a belly, a back like a mountain, / A shifting elbow like a plumber's bend') and the mental life of the man in the library. Dillon Johnston has commented on 'Following' that in transforming Colum's slow air, Ní Chuilleanáin 'reassigns gender roles', but she also 'gestures towards the "Real", towards something of bestial and human nature beyond the margins of the father's books and order'.[19] In doing this, Ní Chuilleanáin also challenges a cultural image, the *aisling* figure in Colum's dream vision, with a female subject whose terrifying vision counterpoints Colum's more sentimental one. 'Following' borrows from Colum's narrative but changes the context, creating a different poem with a different vision, replacing the idealised *aisling* female with a more haunting one and highlighting the privileged scholar's library work, made more comfortable by the women who provide him with finely laundered clothes. The title is, on one level, ironic, because in 'following' Colum's poem Ní Chuilleanáin is using his narrative, which he based on an old Irish song, to present a new point of view and a different female figure.

Ní Chuilleanáin once suggested that her poem 'Pygmalion's Image' (*SP* 49), where the female body as landscape undulates as it comes to life, was in some way responding to the 'suspicion of women' illustrated in Patrick Kavanagh's poetry,[20] and we might look at 'Pygmalion's Image', the first poem in *The Magdalene Sermon*, as a response to Kavanagh's poem 'Pygmalion'. In Ovid's *Metamorphosis*, Pygmalion, a sculptor from Cyprus, creates an ivory statue. Vowing not to marry, he nevertheless falls in love with the statue, dressing it and offering it presents. Eventually, with the help of Aphrodite, the statue comes alive and Pygmalion marries her.

Working from the classical image of the stone figure, in 'Pygmalion's Image' Ní Chuilleanáin presents the statue arising from the landscape as the valley in which she lies begins to move, and the 'wind knifes under her skin and ruffles it like a book'. The final quatrain creates an assertive figure, an amalgam of Galatea, the Earth Mother and Medusa, who rises speaking:

> The crisp hair is real, wriggling like snakes;
> A rustle of veins, tick of blood in the throat;
> The lines of the face tangle and catch, and
> A green leaf of language comes twisting out of her mouth.

In Ní Chuilleanáin's poem, the female figure, removed from the control, artistic and otherwise, of Pygmalion, is brought out of her original mythic silence. In another form, as Medusa, who turned people to stone, she ironically contrasts with Pygmalion, who created a woman who then came to life. The references to language, to books, to women speaking, shift the focus from the male creator of Ovid's mythology to female figures and a woman writer. The metamorphosis here is from the silent Galatea, the passive image Pygmalion created, and from the frightening negative image of Medusa, to a female figure who has her own language and her own voice. Likewise we move from a male poet, author of *Metamorphosis*, to a female poet and, noting the word 'image' in the poem's title, understand that Ní Chuilleanáin seeks to revise the classical images to create a more active and speaking female character.

When we juxtapose Ní Chuilleanáin's 'Pygmalion's Image' with Kavanagh's 'Pygmalion', we see a similar contrast. Kavanagh's intention no doubt was to create a more realistic rural Irish figure rather than an ideal classical female: we find Kavanagh's figure in a field, 'a stone-proud woman … engirdled by the ditches of Roscommon', with a 'twisted face, like Hardship's, to me'. Incorporating a version of Mother Ireland, the metaphoric land as suffering female, she embodies stereotypical female characteristics: the mother 'hugging the monster passion's granite child' with lips 'frozen in the signature / Of Lust', her hair 'set eternally'. The speaker asks 'every man from Balladreen to grassy Boyle' who this woman is and all reply that she is 'a stone pygmalion / Once lipped to grey terrific smile'.

However, we should notice how Kavanagh's poem differs from Ní Chuilleanáin's: there is a male poet, a presumed male speaker who asks his fellow males about the woman, and who, even though he maintains that he will make her 'Clay sensuous' and turn abstract into real woman, never allows her to speak. No 'rustle of veins', 'tick of blood in the throat' or 'green leaf of language comes twisting out of her mouth', as in Ní Chuilleanáin's poem. Kavanagh did indeed see himself speaking, as Ní Chuilleanáin has said, for the 'inarticulate members of his peasant clan', and he is expressing the hardship endured by poor women in rural Ireland. In the context of his poems, however, as 'Pygmalion' illustrates, Kavanagh is often a man speaking to a man, or a poet speaking to men.

The most obvious example of changing the narrative to include women, however, can be seen in Ní Chuilleanáin's early poem 'The Lady's Tower' (*SP* 29), which she has described as a 'feminist riposte' to Yeats.[21] In his later poetry, Yeats's tower became a symbol with many meanings. As part of a series of poems which deal with the struggle between Self and Soul, the real and ideal worlds, his tower represents a space where the poet tries to unify the two. Ní Chuilleanáin has suggested that Yeats's poem 'Blood and the Moon'[22] lies in the background of 'The Lady's Tower'. In this poem Yeats describes both real and imagined towers, those of Alexandria and of Babylon, as well as those of Shelley: 'thought's crowned powers he called them once'. Yeats's own tower, at Ballylee, is described as 'blessed' and he alludes to four Irish literary ancestors – Swift, Goldsmith, Berkeley and Burke – in defining his conflict between ideal and real:

> I declare this tower is my symbol; I declare
> This winding, gyring, spiring treadmill of a stair is my ancestral stair;
> That Goldsmith and the Dean, Berkeley and Burke have travelled
>   there.

His tower, Yeats writes, sits on 'blood-saturated ground', an allusion to its use as a fortification in the past. In Part III, Yeats turns to the 'purity of the unclouded moon' as opposed to the earth below where 'soldier, assassin, executioner' have stood. In the final stanza, butterflies cling to the tower windows as the speaker meditates on wisdom and power, asking whether 'every modern nation like the tower' is 'half dead at the top', but ends with the idealistic image of 'no stain … upon the visage of the moon'.

Certainly many poets have responded both to Yeats and a Yeatsian vision but the point of view in this poem is decidedly male, as are the literary ancestors. Yeats places himself in a specific context, that of the male writer, and also within the context of specific philosophical issues which these writers, particularly Shelley, address. As a modernist, he is on one level grappling with a symbolic inheritance but also struggling to move away from the romanticism Shelley represents. For a woman poet to place herself within such contexts, especially in terms of Irish writers, is not easy. However, in writing 'A Lady's Tower', Ní Chuilleanáin accepts the challenge.

As an alternative to the poet in a tower, whose voice laments his plight in a difficult world, Ní Chuilleanáin's poem celebrates a female speaker's integration with the natural world, rather than isolation from it, and the tone of the poem, very different from Yeats's, illustrates her delight in creative powers. Rather than Yeats's winding (and descending) stair and a tower separating ground and sky, the lady's tower merges with nature: it 'leans / Back to the cliff … The grey wall slices downward and meets / A sliding flooded stream' and downstairs, the 'cellars plumb'. The lady is at the stove in the kitchen, where quarry brambles rise as high as the door. The sycamore roots are 'even' with the upstairs bed, providing what Ní Chuilleanáin describes as a shifting angle and a tower different from Yeats's. In the final stanza, evoking Yeats's butterflies clinging outside the tower windows, Ní Chuilleanáin imagines a woman asleep while the cats climb the tower and the spiders dance:

> All night I lie sheeted, my broom chases down treads
> Delighted spirals of dust: the yellow duster glides
> Over shelves, around knobs: bristle stroking flagstone
> Dancing with the spiders around the kitchen in the dark
> While cats climb the tower and the river fills
> A spoonful of light on the cellar walls below.

The 'spoonful' of light on the cellar walls is provided by the moon. In Yeats's poem the moon flings its 'arrowy shaft upon the floor' – the difference in metaphors is important as it distinguishes an arrow connected with combat, which is central to Yeats's stanza in 'Blood and the Moon', to a spoon connected with domestic daily life which Ní Chuilleanáin's poem celebrates.

Ní Chuilleanáin's images of the 'hollow' tower leaning back and the 'thatch' conversing 'with spread sky' give an additional dimension to this poem in their suggestion of female body imagery. Other images suggest a sexual life: the 'grey wall' which 'slices downward and meets / A sliding flooded stream'. Juxtaposing images of female genitalia with kitchens and spoons represents another direction in poetic towermaking, and a way for a female poet to create a female speaker who presents a different vision of the world from Yeats's. Ní Chuilleanáin has said, referring to 'The Lady's Tower', that 'anything hollowed or enclosed can suggest the feminine, a body that contains and then reveals'.[23] Like many of the other poems in which Ní Chuilleanáin focuses on women's body imagery, her imagery here puts more stress on a physical life as a woman might experience and imagine it.

'The Lady's Tower', while responding to Yeats, also connects to the title poem in her volume, 'The Second Voyage' (*SP* 18), where the warrior Odysseus chooses to turn away from home to go back to his battles with the sea. He looks down to 'the simmering sea where scribbles of weed defined / Uncertain depth, and the slim fishes progressed / In fatal formation'. In Ní Chuilleanáin's alternative vision, the lady in her tower looks out of her kitchen window to see a peaceful scene on water that Odysseus would reject, where 'the punt is now floating freely / Bobs square-ended, the rope dead-level'. In this early volume, Ní Chuilleanáin established herself as a poet ready to bring different kinds of female figures and images into a canon of poetry long dominated by male poets, and certain male perspectives and images.

While the three poems above respond to works by Irish poets, in the volume *The Girl who Married the Reindeer*, Ní Chuilleanáin's poem 'After Leopardi's Storm' (*SP* 110) represents a response to a poem by a male Italian poet. Although the title of the poem suggests that this is closer to translation than the poems discussed above, there are interesting changes made in Ní Chuilleanáin's poem. Like the title 'Following' in the poem which alludes to Colum's poem noted above, the word 'after' here might be seen as leading us to a different and later version of Leopardi's imagery. 'The Calm after the Storm', written by Leopardi in 1829,[24] describes how the beauty of the natural world is appreciated after a storm, how the light crossing the landscape lifts an individual's spirits. Leopardi's opening lines create a pastoral scene as the storm ends: a hen is 'giving out her litany', sounds can be heard across the landscape, and light illuminates all. Leopardi suggests that nature provides this bounty, an escape from pain so that one can carry on, providing a respite from grief. The poem was written at a time when Leopardi himself was suffering from both ill health and a family situation that forced him to move throughout Italy, seeking work. Ní Chuilleanáin's poem follows 'Crossing the Loire' (*SP* 108), in which her sister's death is mentioned, and the storm can certainly refer to the grief involved in that death.

Ní Chuilleanáin begins with imagery similar to Leopardi's: 'the hen giving out her litany, / The stream rattling down the slope'. However, she moves away from his poem in a significant way and again there is an emphasis on women. Leopardi pictures a workman standing in a doorway singing while his wife goes out to gather rainwater; later images present men working: a man selling his wares in the lanes and a labourer driving his wagon on the highway. In Ní Chuilleanáin's poem, we see instead a woman at work and she is pictured at a window, framed like some of the women in other Ní Chuilleanáin poems:

> ... The lacemaker now
> Stands at her window singing,
> Her hand clutching her work, a cloudy ruffle
> Wavering its fins in the watery breeze.

The use of the word 'now' is telling; in one sense it refers literally to the time after the storm, but in another it suggests a new vision in which a female image centres the poem.[25] Ní Chuilleanáin's descriptions are painterly:

> Her pale face like the sky
> Slowly fills up with light, and spokes of light
> Burst from the deep hooded clump of thunder, departing.

Later lines describe an unexpected festival highlighting the woman's art of lacemaking in artistic terms which echo the storm: 'now dark, now bright, an overlapping of wonders / Each one confounding the last'.

In highlighting lacemaking, Ní Chuilleanáin is also alluding to the importance of this work for women in Ireland in the nineteenth century.

In 'Irish Lace and Irish Crochet', an essay in Ní Chuilleanáin's collection *Irish Women: Image and Achievement*, Mary Coleman explains that the development of this art among Irish women marked an interaction between different classes where ascendency patrons collaborated with the daughters of their tenants. At the time Leopardi's poem was written, many schools of lacemaking, including one run by nuns at a Youghal convent, produced different kinds of Irish lace. As Coleman notes: 'This flourishing industry made an important contribution to the lives of the poor in the severe depression of post-Famine years, and the prestige of the lace gained it many followers in other convents throughout the country.'[26] The woman in the window, then, fits into the pattern of working women whom Ní Chuilleanáin continually highlights.

Another departure from Leopardi's imagery occurs in the last stanza where Ní Chuilleanáin's speaker repeats Leopardi's theme that the light after the storm represents a kind of salvation which 'claims / Our whole attention, like grief'. However, at the end of Ní Chuilleanáin's poem, the focus is again on the lacemaker: 'on this side of the mountain / Where the single life is lived, the backbone / Upright, bracing for the next surprise'. As opposed to Leopardi's poem, where the wife of the man in the doorway is the only female figure and subordinated to the male figures, Ní Chuilleanáin focuses on a woman as the major figure in the scene. In so doing, she also replaces the wife with a single woman, one earning her living in lacemaking. Given that many of the poems in *The Girl who Married the Reindeer* deal with grief and responses to the deaths of loved ones, we can see that Ní Chuilleanáin has borrowed Leopardi's imagery to describe how the beauty of the natural world, specifically the sun appearing after a stormy time, can give respite while one waits for the 'next surprise'. However, in adapting and changing Leoparadi's imagery, Ní Chuilleanáin has also made this poem her own, and her message is quite clear: she focuses on the female lacemaker as an active presence, as a worker to be acknowledged.

When we move from adaptation of works by other poets to translation, the issues become more complex; in translating poetry, especially when one poet translates another, a new poem is created, affected by the translator's access to a treasury of potential choices. However, Ní Chuilleanáin, actively involved both in publishing translation as an editor of the journal *Cyphers* and in her own translation of the work of poets like Nuala Ní Dhomhnaill and Michelle Ranchetti, defines translation in very broad terms. In a collection of essays, *Translation and Censorship: Patterns of Communication and Interference*, which Ní Chuilleanáin edited with David Parris and her brother Cormac Ó Cuilleanáin, the introduction states that while 'translators may be constrained, and these constraints may be external, often it is the translator her/himself who modifies the text in the course of "rewriting" – for that is what a translation necessarily is – and the borderline between translation and adaptation is fluctuating and uncertain'.[27] Stressing again fluctuating and uncertain borderlines, Ní Chuilleanáin continues to emphasise the crossed borders and barriers we see in poems like 'Gloss/*Clós*/*Glas*' and 'Studying the Language' described above.

While the collection specifically covers translation from one language to another, it deals with broad questions of how translators can use texts as political weapons, negotiate with what is socially acceptable, and self-censor when audience and reception are factors in translation. As her poem 'Translation', discussed in an earlier chapter, suggests, Ní Chuilleanáin's broad definition of the term would include finding words for the silent and the unspoken.[28] The poet Nuala Ní Dhomhnaill, describing Ní Chuilleanáin's 'Fireman's Lift' (*SP* 64) as a classic poem about a mother/daughter relationship and 'an immense act of grieving', notes also that the 'poem itself is perhaps a translation of the mother's image in the older, medieval, and religious sense of the word as transformation, or removal from earth into heaven'.[29]

In regard to Ní Chuilleanáin's translation of poems from other languages, Aidan O'Malley raises the issue of whether one should simply 'arrogate these poems to Ní Chuilleanáin' or evaluate their 'approximation to the foreign-language texts on which they are based', an ongoing contemporary debate especially relevant to translations of poetry. Arguing for an approach that sees Ní Chuilleanáin's translations as 'foreign bodies in her *corpus*', O'Malley also warns against any straightforward association between the original and the translation.[30] Having made this distinction, however, O'Malley points out some connections between the themes and subjects in Ní Chuilleanáin's translation of Michelle Ranchetti's collection *Verbale* (translated with her brother Cormac Ó Cuilleanáin and Gabriel Rosenstock),[31] which deals with the deaths of Ranchetti's father and mother and illustrates a focus on mourning similar to what we have seen in Ní Chuilleanáin's work.

Ní Chuilleanáin's familiarity with Italian made the process involved in translating Ranchetti different from her later translation of *After the Raising of Lazarus* by the Romanian poet Ileana Mălăncioiu.[32] The translation of Mălăncioiu's poetry stems from an increase in collaboration among poets in European countries, which Ní Chuilleanáin has been involved in, and a transnational interest in making poetry available to larger audiences. For the Mălăncioiu translation, Ní Chuilleanáin explained that its source was the PEN Irish Poets Foundation – and a collaboration established through PEN Romanian Poets. Ní Chuilleanáin explains that while she once believed that the job of the translator was to write a new poem, she later felt that a translation of this type must stay as true as possible to the original text.[33] Given, however, what Raluca Rădulescu, who worked with Ní Chuilleanáin on the translations and on the Romanian language, describes as Mălăncioiu's archaisms, old-fashioned folkstyle and use of rhyme and archaic rhythm, this may be easier said than done. Rădulescu believes that Ní Chuilleanáin's translations are 'neither time- nor space-dependent and in this respect they become universal rather than particular to the place, language and time where they were originally composed'.[34]

The complicated process of translation for *After the Raising of Lazarus* actually involved four people – the two poets, Raluca Rădulescu and a friend of Mălăncioiu's – and four languages – Romanian, English, French and Italian. Ní Chuilleanáin explains that when she first met with Mălăncioiu they worked through French as Mălăncioiu had no English; this initial work was supplemented with help from a friend of Mălăncioiu's who spoke French and Italian. Rădulescu says: 'I think Eiléan's translation is a very personal one, which reflects, as I said in my introduction to the edition, her empathetic style of engagement with the original texts. As such the translations are, to a large extent, reflections of Eiléan's feelings towards the Romanian original.'[35] Evidence of a 'personal' translation is illustrated in a poem like Mălăncioiu's 'A Request' (*ARL* 12), where we hear echoes of Ní Chuilleanáin's own imagery, use of folktales and conversational poetic voices:

> I'm asking you, fearless lad,
> Who conquered the wall of death at the children's fair,
> Don't come to rescue me from the seven-headed giant
> In hopes of half the kingdom for your reward.

Likewise, 'the chapel made out of bones' in Mălăncioiu's 'The World' (*ARL* 28) reminds us of Ní Chuilleanáin's 'The Cloister of Bones' (*SP* 95). The angels and saints who appear in some of Ní Chuilleanáin's poems show up in her translation of Mălăncioiu's 'From the Bluish-Green sky': 'The tree in the middle of the field begins to bud, / From the bluish-green sky come angels and saints' (*ARL* 63).

One can often trace elements of the translator's own work in the translation, leading to the debate over literal versus freer translating, as well as to the point Aidan O'Malley makes about seeing Ní Chuilleanáin's translations as 'foreign bodies in her *corpus*'. With Mălăncioiu and Ní Chuilleanáin, however, we need to see the ways in which the shared experiences and perspectives of two women poets lead to similarities of image, subject and voice, even though the poems are written in different languages by poets from different cultures. Most of Mălăncioiu's poems are spoken in the first person, with an identifiable female voice, and poems like 'Antigone' (*ARL* 60) and 'Samson's Hair' (*ARL* 48) illustrate her revising of the images of iconic females, a characteristic of Ní Chuilleanáin's work as well.

Even though Mălăncioiu's poetry reflects the recent upheaval in a country marked by political violence and repression, she still shares much with Ní Chuilleanáin, as Rădulescu's introduction to *After the Raising of Lazarus* illustrates. Both poets exhibit an interest in life and death as 'consubstantial', where the emphasis falls on life and salvation and where, as the introduction states, 'communication between the two worlds, of the living and the dead, is established through the poetic persona'. Rădulescu sees Mălăncioiu as writing about a 'common poetic state … of seclusion, the margin where a heroine is … "listening by the bolted door / To the trampling and the struggle"',[36] the type of setting we see in Ní Chuilleanáin's poems such as 'Gloss/*Clós*/*Glas*'. Mălăncioiu shares an interest in fairy tales with Ní Chuilleanáin, and a fascination with the mystical and the religious, which for Mălăncioiu provides solace for the suffering experienced under totalitarian rule.

However, the most significant similarity between the two poets involves their emphasis on female figures. Both create female speakers and subjects and both accept the challenge to write poetry in a female voice about unspeakable violence. Mălăncioiu's 'It Snowed on the Body' (*ARL* 25), for example, has similarities to Ní Chuilleanáin's 'Passing Over in Silence' (*SP* 71). The former describes following a trail of blood 'thickening sharp on snow' to find a dead body; the latter describes discovering in the wood, 'the woman lying / In darkness breathing hard, / A hooked foot holding her down'. In both poems the landscape reflects the horror of the scene, but we know few of the narrative details, a characteristic we see in many of Ní Chuilleanáin's other poems. We can conclude also, as does Rădulescu, that Ní Chuilleanáin's translations 'reflect her views of the themes tackled by Ileana'.[37]

When we compare poems written by both poets about the deaths of their respective sisters, the similarities are most striking. Ní Chuilleanáin's poems in *The Brazen Serpent* and *The Girl who Married the Reindeer*, including 'An Alcove' (*GMR* 31), 'Autun' (*SP* 106) – which is set at the shrine of Lazarus, the subject of Mălăncioiu's 'After the Raising of Lazarus' (*ARL* 67) – 'Crossing the Loire' (*SP* 108), 'A Note' (*BS* 28), 'A Posting' (*BS* 45) and 'A Hand, A Wood' (*SP* 88), illustrate details about a sister's final days and about the role of the poet in responding to such experiences. Mălăncioiu's poetry reveals similar figures, settings and themes, as Rădulescu notes:

> The one deeply moving point of Mălăncioiu's poetry comes with the painful recollection of her sister's last moments … she recounts moments spent beside her (departed) sister, whose promised return from the beyond cannot be accepted even in a fairytale scenario ('My sister as Empress'), while every step of her suffering, as well as that brought by the performance of traditional rituals accompanying death and burial are relived ('The doctor on duty', 'The clock', 'Your pink dress', 'Your hair had grown', 'Laid beside you', and so on).
>
> The last poems in this collection reflect Mălăncioiu's self-analysis, her view of the poetic mission and the self-imposed isolation of creativity …[38]

In Ní Chuilleanáin's translation of Mălăncioiu's *After the Raising of Lazarus*, a sister who is dead but not lost appears in 'You Have Not Absolutely Left' (*ARL* 37):

> You have not utterly gone, not utterly
> gone. My brain in fever holds you
> in its most secret inner cell
> where you are well again.

. . . .
Last night you got away for a few instants,
I saw you clearly as you came out of the flame
how you trod lightly over my left temple
and went back willingly to your place.

There are similarities here to Ní Chuilleanáin's poem 'A Posting' (*BS* 45), in its opening lines suggesting a voice from another world, another kind of translation: 'You are reaching me in translation, / A voice with no taste or weight', and in the poem 'A Hand, A Wood', where the speaker describes the days after her sister's death:

I am wearing your shape
Like a light shirt of flame;
My hair is full of shadows.

For the female speakers in both poems, the identification with the dead sister is through body imagery ('I am prising you from under my nails', Ní Chuilleanáin's speaker says), or through similar metaphors like flame, as their personae try to come to terms with the material loss. Because neither poet was familiar with the other's poems when her own was written, the influence is not direct. However, Ní Chuilleanáin explains that she found Mălăncioiu to be a very 'strong' poet with 'striking' images. The clearly identified female personae and the numerous women who populate Mălăncioiu's poems were no doubt a significant factor in this judgment. As opposed to her adaptations of poems by male poets, where she changed a central figure or speaker from male to female, Ní Chuilleanáin found in the poetry of Mălăncioiu speakers and themes similar to those of her own poems and to some of the experiences of her own life. The similarities between these women poets are significant, and Ní Chuilleanáin's translations are important in this regard.

In this chapter, I have taken liberties with the definition and concept of translation to include translation as a type of revising, transforming and adapting which I see in Ní Chuilleanáin's work. I have done this, however, because I believe in some ways it reflects both the ideas and the strategies she uses in her poetry. We can see how Ní Chuilleanáin has adapted the words, settings, and ideas of other writers in her own language and other languages to say both different and similar things, especially as this relates to the images and roles of women past and present. There is both communication and interference (as the subtitle of *Translation and Censorship* defines it) in her work, words that present barriers but also provide the possibility for new contexts, new perspectives, new meanings.

In 'Gloss/*Clós*/*Glas*' Ní Chuilleanáin stresses the numerous meanings words can have and the comcomitant idea that too much focus on the mental task of searching for exact meaning ('darting at locked presses') can lead to ignoring other aspects of life, especially the physical. In 'Studying the Language', she highlights the possibilities of similarities and differences among cultures and languages and suggests that words have limitless potential. In her adaptations of poems by male poets, she borrows a narrative to present new speakers and characters and this leads to new ideas; in her translation of a poet like Mălăncioiu, she finds in the words from another language female figures similar to those in her own poems. In all of the images discussed in this chapter, whether the woman behind the locked door in 'Gloss/*Clós*/*Glas*', the hermits in 'Studying the Language', the lacemaker, the lady in her tower, the new Pygmalion image or the female subject in 'Following', the most unique characteristic of her work is her addition of the female subject or speaker. Ní Chuilleanáin has said 'that to move through different languages seemed important to me, not as an Irish writer but as a woman writer, to exist in a sort of macaronic dimension in which the meanings of words were not too fixed'.[39] One could say that the same applies to her images, especially of females, where an iconic cultural image is challenged by her creation of an alternative, or reinforced by her translations of female figures in the work of another woman poet.

Ultimately poetry by definition involves imaginative transformations and translations; 'close' but 'opposite' and similar but different are the foundation on which metaphor rests. Providing a variety of ways of saying things, poetry allows Ní Chuilleanáin to ask and to answer the questions 'What could I change about that? What could be different?' In her images of the female, whether in her original poems, in her loose adaptations of other poets, or in her translations, she demonstrates the ways in which 'copiousness' – 'being able to choose from a variety of ways of saying things' – serves her well.

CHAPTER 8

Conclusion

Thin as a wash, does it get any deeper
At all, or could we see its depth, since we catch
Only the gleam when the flipped blade
Rewards the light, like a silk flash of hair in the water.

'The Water' (*S* 38)

Eiléan Ní Chuilleanáin's ability to tease many associations and meanings from images and what she calls 'slippery' words is a key to her work, as well as to how she views human experience. Hers is a world of questions, ambiguities and complexities, where we get glances and limited revelations, but also confront secrets and obstacles to understanding. Words are open to different meanings and different translations. There is always the 'other side', whether that is a shore across water, a spiritual world behind the material world, a scene seen from another angle, or a different point of view. Open to the possibility that meaning is rarely fixed, Ní Chuilleanáin, as was noted in Chapter 1, is like the speaker in 'Early Recollections' (*SP* 24) who tells us: 'I know how things begin to happen / But never expect an end'. Nevertheless, Ní Chuilleanáin has said 'what attracts me is that which I do not know', and her poetry is a quest to continue to search.

The poem 'The Water' from *The Sun-fish* (*S* 38) illustrates some of the major images and themes that Ní Chuilleanáin has developed throughout her career. Water, a central symbol from her earliest volumes, is used again to suggest the limits of our vision and understanding, but also to evoke the glimpses we get of an immaterial world. This sonnet, like many of Ní Chuilleanáin's poems, is an extended question which asks whether water gets any deeper or 'could we see its depth?' when we can only catch 'the gleam when the flipped blade / Rewards the light'. The difficulty of certainty is reinforced in this poem by the images of light and shadow which both reveal and hide. Nevertheless, the poem maintains that, despite the mystery that water represents, 'floating shards of light are really there' and the material world gives us hints and guesses of what lies beneath the surface. This is the major theme in Ní Chuilleanáin's poetry, and the image in the final line of a 'lighthouse searching the dark, scraping the sea with its beam' also highlights, as it has in other poems, the related theme of the destructive power of water, dark oceans and floods symbols for disaster and violence. In an early poem from *Acts and Monuments*, 'Wash' (*SP* 15), for example, the ordinary task of washing water from a fish is juxtaposed with a 'deeper' but undefined image of violence: 'Wash the man out of the woman: / The strange sweat from her skin, the ashes from her hair. / Stretch her to dry in the sun / The blue marks on her breast will fade'.

More than any other element of her poetry, it is Ní Chuilleanáin's images that reinforce her belief that the material world gives us only hints of what lies behind, what is below the surface, what is on the other side. Water is part of a pattern of images of nature, including sunlight, shadow, ocean, land, mists, clouds, mountains and floods, which reinforces the idea of 'now you see it, now you don't', which Ní Chuilleanáin has used to describe her view of history, but applies to other aspects of her work as well. The architectural details of walls, doors, windows, houses and churches, which appear over and over again in her poetry, represent both openings and barriers, and bridges suggest a movement from one realm to another. The spaces of convents, cloisters and cathedrals illustrate enclosures which both satisfy and mystify, material spaces which embody spiritual rituals, values and meaning. The recurring images of angles reinforce her belief that seeing something from a different viewpoint can provide new insight.

Such images demonstrate a vision that influences every aspect of Ní Chuilleanáin's work. She has created a unique collection of unusual and often unexpected female figures who illustrate many aspects of human character and behaviour. In dealing with iconic females, Ní Chuilleanáin does not necessarily reject all the attributes embodied in a conventional image, but rather shows us the figure from a new angle. St Mary Magdalene, for example, is imagined preaching at the end of her life, and nuns, often perceived as removed from the world and under the control of a patriarchal church, are shown living in vital female communities where their lives are more under their own control than would first appear. Significantly, these figures are often presented as maintaining, or trying to maintain, their own livelihood, like Rosa O'Doherty struggling to establish a residence in Rome after having left Ireland, or Ní Chuilleanáin's sister and mother who had their own careers. At the same time, Ní Chuilleanáin's female figures are not one-dimensional and she sometimes maintains negative characteristics associated with traditional mythic and folkloric images. The witch of C.S Lewis's stories is still identified in Ní Chuilleanáin's poem 'The Witch in the Wardrobe' (*S* 11) with limiting the pleasures of the senses; the old queen who betrays the girl who married the reindeer tries to prevent her from returning to the husband she loves. Likewise, the remorseful woman in 'On Lacking the Killer Instinct' (*S* 14) runs away when her father is dying; and two daughters 'wait and gossip' as their mother climbs the steps of a cliffside shrine in 'Vertigo' (*SP* 40).

In working against stereotypes, Ní Chuilleanáin takes advantage of the possibility for renewing an image. Not only does she undercut gender constructions as she portrays confident women working both in and outside the home, she also gives importance to domestic work, challenging the division of private and public realms and action which gives less importance to work inside the home. Likewise, her male figures do not always fit the Irish stereotypes of the powerful man of action or manly soldier-warrior. 'Brother Felix Fabri' (*S* 53), for example, uses an 'old bone-handled knife / His grand-aunt kept and used / to pare her afternoon apples' to cut the squares of paper containing the names of all he prayed for, 'forgetting / Nobody who wanted prayers'. Like the cloistered nuns whose lives are devoted to praying for others, Brother Felix is a male version of the 'Anchoress' (*SP* 93) who would sit behind the 'mossgrown window beside the church porch' to listen to requests: 'Yes she knew who was there, / She still prayed for them all by name'. By questioning and 'opening up' some conventional images of male and female, Ní Chuilleanáin imagines men and women, their lives and roles, not fixed, but fluid and flexible.

This openness carries over into the formal elements of her poetry as well. As noted throughout this book, it is difficult to categorise Ní Chuilleanáin's work because she uses many genres, moving from lyric to narrative to dramatic, retelling myths and folktales, using all kinds of voices, including her own as woman poet, to create the speakers in her poems. She adapts, she translates, and she rewrites and revises traditional poems, maintaining elements of the original while changing a speaker, a figure, a form to create a different emphasis. While many of her poems, especially those in her later books, are written in stanzas or conventional forms like sonnets, there is almost always an unexpected irregularity to enhance or develop a poem. Variations of accentual and syllabic verse merge English and Gaelic conventions, illustrating how the rhythms and sounds of one poetic language might find new life in another.

Perhaps the most significant value of Ní Chuilleanáin's work, especially as it relates to female figures, is how she has used these to create poems with universal relevance and profound ideas on the human condition. Looking over the body of her work, we can trace the same images and words from *Acts and Monuments* through *The Sun-fish*, in poems that focus on the passage of time, on death and absence, on rituals and the value of memory, on oppression, on grief, and on the complexity of family and political relationships. We can also follow the development of a woman poet who uses the art of poetry to express the trajectory of her own life, from poems about her parents and her early childhood in her native Cork to those which express grief over the death of loved ones and the eventual acceptance of the inevitability of absence and the value of memory. While one of Ní Chuilleanáin's objectives was no doubt to create more poems with female subjects and speakers, another was, as noted above, to get beyond narrow male/female boundaries illustrated in earlier Irish poetry and concentrate on shared human concerns. In this, Ní Chuilleanáin has succeeded. From her earliest work, Ní Chuilleanáin has written poems with specific female subjects; however, *The Magdalene Sermon*, *The Brazen Serpent* and *The Girl who Married the Reindeer* are the collections most focused on females, as they are also the volumes where the woman poet's voice and details from Ní Chuilleanáin's own personal life begin to be more apparent. Having established a more visible place for the woman poet and the female figure, she has also illustrated how women's lives, while unique and different in some ways, involve shared experiences, which have application to all lives.

In *The Sun-fish*, while the emphasis on female figures continues in poems like 'Vertigo', 'The Sister', 'Inscribed', 'The Married Women' and 'In the Desert', there are also more poems focused on males: her father in 'On Lacking the Killer Instinct'; her grandfathers and the sculptors Séamus Murphy and Ken Thompson in 'Ballinascarthy'; and the males imagined in 'A Revelation, for Eddie Linden', 'Michael and the Angel',

'Update for Paul Cahill' and 'Brother Felix Fabri'. In this volume, where the predominant theme is remembering and the benefits of memory in stitching together the present and the past, both female and male figures are highlighted, given equal weight as it were. The earlier collections might be seen as a preparation for this.

With the relatively recent emergence and publication of many excellent women poets in Ireland, acknowledgement has been made of both the achievements of Irish women and the talents of women poets, changing popular perceptions of the nature and history of Irish writing. Ní Chuilleanáin's contribution to this as poet, academic, and translator cannot be overestimated, and the theme of her early edited collection of essays, *Irish Women: Image and Achievement*, has been illustrated quite well in her poetry collections. An innovative poet, she has taken it upon herself, over several decades, to demonstrate that the Irish poet can 'be male or female, nomadic without losing tribal identity'. Her interests in Irish history and culture have influenced her work, and combined with her knowledge of languages, folklore, and Irish and English literary traditions, have led to some of the most impressive poetry in recent Irish literature. While she admits that her poems can sometimes be obscure and difficult, the complexity of her vision and her skill as a poet demand that the reader spend some time engaging with her words and images. She is asking us to look at our world in new ways, encouraging us to accept both the mystery and the enlightenment of the 'copious dark'.

In a poem in *The Sun-fish*, Ní Chuilleanáin writes:

> As every new day waking finds its pitch
> Selecting a fresh angle, so the sun
> Hangs down its veil, so the old verbs
> Change their invocation and their mood.

Entitled 'The Litany' (*S* 42), this poem refers to the traditional prayer of invocation and response, alluding to a ritual that acknowledges the limits of our knowledge and our power, while it asks for divine understanding. At the same time, in modern English the word 'litany' can suggest a list of problems and the poem is also about the difficult effects of change, the mysteries of presence and absence, with waves arriving and then withdrawing as 'The soaking tears of centuries drill down / Low passages in between the stones'. The poem includes references to history and religious ritual, to angels, music, veils, water – typical Ní Chuilleanáin images – and also to language, to the 'old verbs' of the litanies which can 'Change their invocation and their mood'.

Encapsulating much of what and how Ní Chuilleanáin writes, 'The Litany' develops themes related to time, death, change, and to language, which, like a tide, 'sucks back down as deep / As it rode high'. The wave is compared to a 'gap', to the liminal 'pause' in a litany between invocation and response, which suggests not only how words interrelate but also how they can appear and disappear in different times, interpretations and languages. In 'Vertigo' (*S* 40), a poem which precedes 'The Litany' in *The Sun-fish*, a word is both 'ambiguous' and 'a calque' imagined as 'swimming / Up into sight through the tides of speech'. This image takes us back to the very early volume *Cork*, where the phrase *lingua franca* suggests the different languages embedded in the watery and tidal history of Ní Chuilleanáin's native city. The many potential meanings of images, words, translations and transformations are, for Ní Chuilleanáin, like 'every new day waking finds its pitch / 'Selecting a fresh angle' – a good description for her female figures, her poetic process and her finished poems.

Endnotes

CHAPTER 1. Beginnings

1. Where possible, I have given the page numbers from Ní Chuilleanáin's *Selected Poems* (*SP*) published by Gallery Press in 2008. When poems are not included in the *Selected Poems*, I have given page numbers from the Gallery Press collections in which they were published, using the following abbreviations: *AM*, *Acts and Monuments* (1972); *C*, *Cork* (1977); *RG*, *Rose Geranium* (1981); *SV*, *The Second Voyage* (1986); *MS*, *The Magdalene Sermon* (1989); *BS*, *The Brazen Serpent* (1994); *GMR*, *The Girl who Married the Reindeer* (2001); *S*, *The Sun-fish* (2009). The poems are also available in the Wake Forest University Press editions of Ní Chuilleanáin's poems, in some cases in combined volumes like *The Magdalene Sermon and Earlier Poems* (1991).
2. Deborah McWilliams Consalvo, 'An Interview with Eiléan Ní Chuilleanáin', *Irish Literary Supplement*, vol. 12, no. 1 (1993), p. 16.
3. Eiléan Ní Chuilleanáin, 'Introduction', *Irish Women, Image and Achievement* (Dublin: Arlen House, 1985), pp. 3, 8.
4. Ibid., p. 2.
5. Maria Luddy and Cliona Murphy (eds), *Women Surviving: Studies in Irish Women's History in the 19th & 20th Centuries* (Dublin: Poolbeg, 1989), pp. 4–5.
6. Pilar Villar-Argáiz, '"The Text of It": A Conversation with Eavan Boland', *New Hibernia Review*, vol. 10, no. 2 (2006), pp. 52–67, at pp. 53–4. Boland has written extensively about the place of women in Irish culture; see especially her poetry collection, *Outside History* (Manchester: Carcanet, 1990), and her essay collection, *Object Lessons* (Manchester: Carcanet, 1995).
7. Patricia Boyle Haberstroh, 'An Interview with Eiléan Ní Chuilleanáin', *Canadian Journal of Irish Studies*, vol. 20, no. 2 (1994), pp. 63–74, at p. 65.
8. Seamus Deane et al. (eds), *The Field Day Anthology of Irish Writing*, vols I–III (Derry: Field Day Publications, 1992).
9. For information on the development and reception of the Field Day volumes on women's writing, see Margaret Kelleher, '*The Field Day Anthology* and Irish Women's Literary Studies', *Irish Review*, vol. 30 (2003), pp. 82–94; Gerardine Meaney's essay, 'Engendering the Postmodern Canon? *The Field Day Anthology of Irish Writing, Volumes IV and V: Women's Writing and Traditions*', in Patricia Boyle Haberstroh and Christine St Peter (eds), *Opening the Field: Irish Women, Texts and Contexts* (Cork University Press, 2007); and Helen Thompson (ed.), *The Current Debate about the Irish Literary Canon* (Lampeter,

UK and Lewiston, NY: Edwin Mellen Press, 2006). In the latter, Rebecca Pelan's essay 'Literally Loose Cannon or Loosening the Canon' discusses the judgment of *The Irish Times* literary editor Eileen Battersby that the new volumes had a 'sociological agenda' and were more 'sociological than textual and scholarly', as well as Patricia Coughlan's response to Battersby.

10. A.A. Kelly's *Wildish Things: An Anthology of Verse by Irish Women* (Dublin: Wolfhound, 1988) and *Voices on the Wind: Women Poets of the Celtic Twilight*, edited by Eilís Ní Dhuibhne (Dublin: New Island, 1995) are also significant anthologies of women's verse. By the late 1960s writing by women began to appear more frequently in poetry journals and from some of the smaller presses like Arlen House, Attic Press and Salmon Publishing, whose missions involved publishing women poets. Ní Chuilleanáin's *Acts and Monuments* was issued by Gallery Press in 1972, though she was the only woman on the Gallery list at that time, a typical situation at other presses also. Not until Joan McBreen's and Peggy O'Brien's anthologies in 1999 were comprehensive collections of modern women poets available in an anthology of Irish poetry. In her introduction, McBreen points out the need for such a collection, noting that while more women poets were slowly finding their way into print in Ireland, anthologies were often failing to acknowledge their work, citing the *Oxford Book of Irish Verse* whose 1958 collection featured seventeen women poets, while the later 1986 version had none. A review of other poetry anthologies reveals similar small representation.
11. Gerardine Meaney, *Gender, Ireland, and Cultural Change* (New York: Routledge, 2010), p. xviii.
12. Inés Praga, 'Eiléan Ní Chuilleanáin', in Jacqueline Hurtley, Rosa Gonzáles, Inés Praga and Esther Aliaga (eds), *Ireland in Writing: Interviews with Writers and Academics* (Amsterdam: Rodopi, 1998), pp. 83–93, at p. 83. It must be said that Ireland was not alone in this phenomenon of women poets gradually disappearing from view. Jane Dowson, in '"Older Sisters are Very Sobering Things": Contemporary Women Poets and the Female Affiliation Complex', *Feminist Review*, vol. 62, no. 1 (1999), pp. 6–20, points out the ways in which English women poets were also eclipsed, ascribing this to a pattern over the last three centuries of women publishing, gaining recognition and then dropped from literary records, mainly because they have not received enough attention from male-dominated literary criticism. In this she agrees with Ní Chuilleanáin's concept of the need to recuperate women in history and literature, what Ní Chuilleanáin called a 'spiral progression'. There are, however, unique cultural factors influencing the situation for women poets in Ireland which the following pages will explore.
13. David Gardiner, 'The Other Irish Renaissance: The Maunsel Poets', *New Hibernia Review*, vol. 8, no. 1 (2004), pp. 54–79, at p. 67. See also Katherine Parr, 'Integrating Women's Writing into the Canon: Women Poets of Young Ireland', in Helen Thompson (ed.), *The Current Debate about the Literary Canon:*

Essays Reassessing The Field Day Anthology of Irish Writing (Lampeter, UK and Lewiston, NY: Edwin Mellen Press, 2006). A good selection of these poets can be found in Eilís Ní Dhuibhne's *Voices on the Wind: Women Poets of the Celtic Twilight* (Dublin: New Island, 1995).
14. Eiléan Ní Chuilleanáin (ed.), *The Wilde Legacy* (Dublin: Four Courts Press, 2003).
15. Eiléan Ní Chuilleanáin, 'Borderlands of Irish Poetry', in Elmer Andrews (ed.), *Contemporary Irish Poetry: A Collection of Critical Essays* (Basingstoke: Macmillan, 1992), pp. 25–40, at p. 37.
16. Ibid., p. 38.
17. 'Eiléan Ní Chuilleanáin', Special Issue, *Irish University Review*, vol. 37, no. 1 (2007), edited by Anne Fogarty.
18. Irene Gilsenan Nordin, *Reading Eiléan Ní Chuilleanáin, A Contemporary Irish Poet* (Lewiston, NY: Edwin Mellen Press, 2009).
19. Geraldine Plunkett, *All in the Blood*, edited by Honor Ó Brolcháin (Dublin: A&A Farmar, 2009).
20. Eilís Dillon, 'In the Honan Hostel', in *The Cork Anthology*, edited by Sean Dunne (Cork: Cork University Press, 1993), pp. 107–14, at p. 114.
21. Thomas McCarthy, '"We Could be in any City": Eiléan Ní Chuilleanáin and Cork', *Irish University Review*, vol. 37, no. 1, pp. 230–43, at p.
22. Mary Leland, *The Lie of the Land: Journeys through Literary Cork* (Cork: Cork University Press, 1999), p. 246.
23. Eiléan Ní Chuilleanáin, 'Nuns: A Subject for a Woman Writer', in Patricia Boyle Haberstroh (ed.), *My Self, My Muse* (Syracuse, NY: Syracuse University Press, 2001), p. 21.
24. Cormac Ó Cuilleanáin, 'Introduction' in Eilís Dillon, *Death at Crane's Court* (Boulder, CO: The Rue Morgue Press, 2009), p. 8.
25. Eiléan Ní Chuilleanáin, '*Cyphers*: Threescore and Ten', *Poetry Ireland News* (January/February 2001).
26. Ibid.
27. Ní Chuilleanáin, 'Nuns', p. 19.
28. Ibid., pp. 20–1.
29. 'A Brief Interview by Wake Forest University Press Interns' (November 2009), available at http://wfu.edu/wfupress/an%20interviewchuilleanain1.html. [accessed 5 January 2010].
30. Ibid.
31. Helen Lojek, '"Man, Woman, Soldier": Heaney's "In Memoriam Francis Ledwidge" and Boland's "Heroic"', *New Hibernia Review*, vol. 10, no. 1 (2006), pp. 123–38.
32. J. Watson Doering, 'Sacred Enclosures: Eiléan Ní Chuilleanáin talks to J. Watson Doering about *The Brazen Serpent*', *Cascando*, vol. 5, no. 6 (1996), pp. 25–33, at p. 32.
33. Leslie Williams. '"The stone recalls its quarry": An Interview with Eiléan Ní Chuilleanáin', in Susan Shaw Sailer (ed.), *Representing Ireland: Gender, Class,*

Nationality (Gainesville, FL: University Press of Florida, 1997), pp. 29–44, at p. 36.

34. Nuala O'Faoláin in Eiléan Ní Chuilleanáin, *Irish Women: Image and Achievement*, p. 130.
35. Praga, 'Eiléan Ní Chuilleanáin', p. 85.
36. Tom Dunne, 'Subaltern Voices? Poetry in Irish, Popular Insurgency and the 1798 Rebellion', *Eighteenth-Century Life*, vol. 22, no. 3 (1998), pp. 31–44, at p. 34.
37. Patrick Pearse, 'Roisin Dubh', in Thomas Kinsella and Sean Ó Tuama (eds), *Duanaire, 1600–1900: Poems of the Dispossessed* (Dublin: Dolmen Press, 1981).
38. Written with Maud Gonne in mind.
39. David Cairns and Shaun Richards, 'Tropes and Traps: Aspects of "Woman" and Nationality in Twentieth-Century Irish Drama', in Toni O'Brien Johnson and David Cairns (eds), *Gender in Irish Writing* (Buckingham: Open University Press, 1991), pp. 128–37, at p. 130.
40. Sarah E. McKibben, 'Speaking the Unspeakable: Male Humiliation and Female National Allegory after Kinsale', *Éire-Ireland*, vol. 43, nos 3–4 (2008), pp. 11–30, at p. 22.
41. Ibid., p. 23.
42. Gerardine Meaney, *Gender, Ireland, and Cultural Change* (London: Routledge, 2010), p. xviii; and Ailbhe Smyth, '"Staged Quaintness": Subalternity, Gender, and Popular Identity', in Colin Graham (ed.), *Deconstructing Ireland: Identity, Theory, Culture* (Edinburgh: Edinburgh University Press, 2001), pp. 102–31, at pp. 107, 113.
43. Síghle Bhreathnach-Lynch, *Ireland's Art and Ireland's History: Representing Ireland, 1845 to Present* (Omaha, NE: Creighton University Press, 2007), p. 89.
44. Claire Connolly, *Theorising Ireland* (London: Macmillan, 2003), p. 4.
45. Eiléan Ní Chuilleanáin, 'Acts and monuments of an unelected nation: The *Cailleach* writes about the Renaissance', *The Southern Review*, vol. 31, no. 3 (1995), pp. 570–80, at p. 576.
46. Ibid.
47. Mary Montague, 'The Art of the Body: poem as female self-portrait', in Joan McBreen (ed.), *The Watchful Heart: A New Generation of Irish Poets* (Co. Clare: Salmon Poetry, 2009), pp. 125–8, at pp. 126–7.
48. Nuala Ní Dhomhnaill, *Selected Poems/Rogha Dánta*, translated by Michael Hartnett (Dublin: Raven Arts Press, 1988), p. 45.
49. Leanne O'Sullivan, *Cailleach, The Hag of Bear*a (Northumberland: Broadaxe, 2009), p. 12; Eavan Boland, *In a Time of Violence* (Manchester: Carcanet, 1994), pp. 41–6; Mary O'Malley, *The Knife in the* Wave (Co. Clare: Salmon Poetry, 1997), pp. 57–76.
50. Catherine Phil MacCarthy, 'Sand Goddess', in *The White Page/An Bhileog Bhán*, edited by Joan McBreen (Co. Clare: Salmon Poetry, 1999), p. 130; Paula Meehan, *Painting Rain* (Manchester: Carcanet, 2009), p. 45.
51. Theo Dorgan, *Irish Poetry Since Kavanagh* (Dublin: Four Courts Press, 1996).

CHAPTER 2. Female Figures and Poetic Strategies

1. Borbála Faragó, '"Alcove in the Wind": Silence and Space in Ní Chuilleanáin's Poetry', *Irish University Review*, vol. 37, no. 1 (2007), pp. 68–83, at p. 70. Maintaining that women often write to 'provoke an ethical discourse' about care and justice, Faragó sees Ní Chuilleanáin as creating silences in her poetry: 'Situated at the threshold of speech as a simultaneous absence and presence of expression, silence endorses an ethics of linguistic care towards issues of morality.' Given that Ní Chuilleanáin says that she always starts from a moral position, this is a valuable approach to her poems.
2. Butler's theories are developed in *Gender Trouble: Feminism and the Subversion of Identity* (London: Routledge, 1990), and *Undoing Gender* (London: Routledge, 2004).
3. The different approaches of Butler and Benhabib are examined by Fiona Webster in 'The Politics of Sex and Gender', *Hypatia*, vol 15, no. 1 (2000), pp. 1–22. Kathy Dow Manus, in 'The Unaccountable Subject: Judith Butler and the Social Conditions of Intersubjective Agency', *Hypatia*, vol. 21, no. 2 (2006), pp. 81–103, explains the way in which Butler's ideas have evolved.
4. Irene Gilsenan Nordin, *Reading Eiléan Ní Chuilleanáin, a Contemporary Irish Poet* (Lewiston, NY: Edwin Mellen Press, 2009), pp. 2, 5, 17.
5. Ibid., pp. 24, 2.
6. Eiléan Ní Chuilleanáin, 'Acts and monuments of an unelected nation: The *Cailleach* writes about the Renaissance', *The Southern Review*, vol. 31, no. 3 (1995), pp. 570–80, at p. 572.
7. Ibid., p. 573.
8. For more on the *cailleach*, especially as the figure has come down in Irish legend, see Gearóid Ó Crualaoich, *The Book of the Cailleach: Stories of the Wise Woman Healer* (Cork: Cork University Press, 2003), and Ó Crualaoich's RTÉ Radio 1 series 'Hags, Queens and Wise Women: Supernatural Females of the Irish Otherworld'. Patricia Coughlan in '"Bog Queens": The Representation of Women in the Poetry of John Montague and Seamus Heaney', in Toni O'Brien Johnson and David Cairns (eds), *Gender in Irish Writing* (Buckingham: Open University Press, 1991), pp. 88–111 discusses the construction of this figure by both poets. See also Helen Kidd, '*Cailleachs*, Keens and Queens: Refiguring Gender and Nationality in the Poetry of Eiléan Ní Chuilleanáin, Nuala Ní Dhomhnaill and Eavan Boland', *Critical Quarterly*, vol. 15, no. 1 (2003), pp. 34–47.
9. Eiléan Ní Chuilleanáin (ed.), *The Wilde Legacy* (Dublin: Four Courts Press, 2003), p. 43.
10. In an interview with me in May 2010.
11. Ní Chuilleanáin says that she wants to create multidimensional females and, although she often portrays the domestic life which women have shared, she thinks it also important to show women working in other ways, outside a stereotypical framework. Every Irish poet, she claims, has probably written

a poem about her or his mother in the kitchen, and Ní Chuilleanáin says she wants to avoid the trap of sentimentalising women's domestic work, while still acknowledging their importance in the home (interview with me in April 2009).

12. J. Watson Doering, 'Sacred Enclosures: Eiléan Ní Chuilleanáin talks to J. Watson Doering about *The Brazen Serpent*', *Cascando*, vol. 5, no. 6 (1996), pp. 25–33, at p. 29.
13. Eddie Linden, *A Thorn in the Flesh: Selected Poems* (London: Hearing Eye, 2011). In a review of this book in *The Irish Times* on 24 December 2011, Gerry Harrison writes: 'The mention of Linden can raise an eyebrow from those who know him well, but the proud self-confession that he is an "illegitimate, illiterate, working-class, Communist, homosexual, Catholic, pacifist poet" always insures that his readings are worth attending.' Linden's collection *The City of Razors* was published by J. Landesman in 1980.
14. Christian Michener, 'Saints and Sisters: The Sacred Chorus in the Poetry of Eiléan Ní Chuilleanáin', *New Hibernia Review*, vol. 14, no. 2 (2010), pp. 118–32.
15. Leslie Williams, '"The stone recalls its quarry": An Interview with Eiléan Ní Chuilleanáin', in Susan Shaw Sailer (ed.), *Representing Ireland: Gender, Class, Nationality* (Gainesville, FL: University Press of Florida, 1997), pp. 29–44, at p. 39.
16. Irene Gilsenan Nordin, 'The Weight of Words: An Interview with Eiléan Ní Chuilleanáin', *Canadian Journal of Irish Studies*, vols 28–29, nos 1–2 (2002–2003), pp. 75–83, at p. 76. For an analysis of different approaches to self-representation, see Catriona Clutterbuck, 'Gender and Self-Representation in Irish Poetry: The Critical Debate', *Bullán*, vol. 4, no. 1 (1998), pp. 43–58.
17. In an interview with me in April 2009.
18. Doering, 'Sacred Enclosures', p. 28.
19. Peter Sirr, '"How things begin to happen": notes on Eiléan Ní Chuilleanáin and Medbh McGuckian', *The Southern Review*, vol. 31, no. 1 (1995), pp. 450–67, at p. 450.
20. Kevin Ray, 'An Interview with Eiléan Ní Chuilleanáin', *Éire–Ireland*, vol. 31, nos 1–2 (1996), pp. 62–73, at p. 66.

CHAPTER 3. Imagining History

1. Helen Emmitt, '"The One Free Foot Kicking under the White Sheet of History": Eiléan Ní Chuilleanáin's Uncanny Landscapes', *Women's Studies: An Interdisciplinary Journal*, vol. 29 (2000), pp. 477–94, at p. 480.
2. Eiléan Ní Chuilleanáin, *Acts and Monuments* (Dublin: Gallery Press, 1972). The title alludes to John Foxe's *The Acts and Monuments of the Christian Church*, also known as the *Book of Martyrs*, published in 1563.
3. Kevin Ray, 'Interview: Eiléan Ní Chuilleanáin', *Éire-Ireland*, vol. 31, nos 1–2 (1996), pp. 62–73, at p. 73.

4. Patricia Boyle Haberstroh, 'Interview with Eiléan Ní Chuilleanáin', *Irish University Review*, vol. 37, no. 1 (2007), pp. 36–49, at p. 41.
5. J. Watson Doering, 'Sacred Enclosures: Interview with Eiléan Ní Chuilleanáin', *Cascando*, vol. 5, no. 6 (1996), pp. 25–32, at p. 27.
6 Nícholas Allen, '"Each Page Lies Open to the Version of Every Other": History in the Poetry of Eiléan Ní Chuilleanáin', *Irish University Review*, vol. 37, no. 1 (2007), pp. 22–35, at p. 22.
7. Ibid., p. 26.
8. Joan Hoff, 'The Impact and Implications of Women's History', in Maryann Gialanella Valiulis and Mary O'Dowd (eds), *Women and Irish History: Essays in Honour of Margaret MacCurtain* (Dublin: Wolfhound, 1997), pp. 15–38, at pp. 24–5.
9. Eiléan Ní Chuilleanáin, 'Acts and monuments of an unelected nation: The *Cailleach* writes about the Renaissance', *The Southern Review*, vol. 31, no. 3 (1995), pp. 570–80, at p. 573.
10. Irene Gilsenan Nordin, 'The Weight of Words: An Interview with Eiléan Ní Chuilleanáin', *Canadian Journal of Irish Studies*, vols 28–9, nos 1–2 (2002–3), pp. 75–83, at p. 77.
11. Ní Chuilleanáin, 'Acts and monuments of an unelected nation', p. 574.
12. Her mother, Eilís Dillon, was the daughter of Geraldine Plunkett, sister of Joseph Mary Plunkett; both maternal and paternal families were involved in the republican cause.
13. Ní Chuilleanáin described him to me in an interview in Dublin in April 2009.
14. Eiléan Ní Chuilleanáin, 'Borderlands of Irish Poetry', in Elmer Andrews (ed.), *Contemporary Irish Poetry: A Collection of Critical Essays* (Basingstoke: Macmillan, 1992), pp. 25–40, at p. 25.
15. This story is the subject of one of Thomas Moore's *Irish Melodies*, which also has political overtones as 'Erin lies sleeping'.
16. Patricia Coughlan, '"No Lasting Fruit at All": Containment, Recognition and Relinquishing in *The Girl who Married the Reindeer*', *Irish University Review*, vol. 37, no. 1 (2007), pp. 157–77, at p. 160.
17. Ní Chuilleanáin, 'Acts and monuments of an unelected nation', p. 570.
18. Thomas McCarthy, '"We Could Be in Any City": Eiléan Ní Chuilleanáin and Cork', *Irish University Review*, vol. 37, no. 1 (2007), pp. 230–43, at p. 237.
19. I discuss this poem in more detail in Chapter 5.
20. The contrast between garden and battleground is developed throughout the imagery of the poem. An allusion to St Ciarán imagines him as holding up a bird's nest.
21. Maurice Craig, *The Architecture of Ireland: From the Earliest Times to 1880* (London: Batsford, 1983).
22. *The Irish Times* article is available at http://www.irishtimes.com/newspaper/property/2009/1015/1224256675017.html [accessed 23 February 2012]
23. Haberstroh, 'Interview with Eiléan Ní Chuilleanáin', p. 44.

24. An exception to this is the poem 'Rosa O'Doherty' by Frank McGuinness in his collection *The Sea with No Ships* (Dublin: Gallery Press, 1999), where Rosa O'Doherty is pictured in Louvain, Belgium.
25. Inés Praga, 'Eiléan Ní Chuilleanáin', in Jacqueline Hurtley, Rosa González, Inés Praga and Esther Aliaga (eds), *Ireland in Writing: Interviews with Writers and Academics* (Amsterdam: Rodopi, 1998), pp. 83–92, at p. 87.
26. John Flood and Phil Flood, *Kilcash: A History, 1190–1801* (Dublin: Geography Publications, 1999).
27. Leslie Williams, '"The stone recalls its quarry": An Interview with Eiléan Ní Chuilleanáin', in Susan Shaw Sailer (ed.), *Representing Ireland: Gender, Class, Nationality* (Gainesville, FL: University Press of Florida, 1970), pp. 29–44, at pp. 37–8.
28. Deborah Sarbin, '"Out of Myth into History": The Poetry of Eavan Boland and Eiléan Ní Chuilleanáin', *Canadian Journal of Irish Studies*, vol. 9, no. 1 (1993), pp. 86–96, at p. 87.
29. Allen, '"Each Page Lies Open to the Version of Every Other"', p. 22.

CHAPTER 4. Fictive Women: Myth and Folklore

1. Peter Heehs, 'Myth, History and Theory', *History and Theory*, vol. 33, no. 1 (1994), pp. 1–49, at p. 5.
2. Ibid., pp. 5,16.
3. Angela Bourke, 'Language, Stories, Healing', in Anthony Bradley and Maryann Gialanella Valiulis (eds), *Gender and Sexuality in Modern Ireland* (Amherst, MA: University of Massachusetts Press, 1997), pp. 299–314, at p. 313.
4. Diarmuid Ó Giolláin, *Locating Irish Folklore: Tradition, Modernity, Identity* (Cork: Cork University Press, 2000).
5. Irene Gilsenan Nordin, 'The Weight of Words: An Interview with Eiléan Ní Chuilleanáin', *Canadian Journal of Irish Studies*, vols 28–9, nos 1–2 (2002–3), pp. 73–83, at p. 80.
6. Gerardine Meaney, 'History Gasps: Myth in Contemporary Irish Women's Poetry', in Michael Kenneally (ed.), *Poetry in Contemporary Irish Literature* (Gerrards Cross, Buckinghamshire: Colin Smythe, 1995), pp. 99–113, at p. 109. Meaney's essay is focused on Sara Berkeley's *Penn* (Dublin: Raven Arts Press, 1986) and *Home Night Movies* (Dublin: Raven Arts Press, 1989), and Ní Chuilleanáin's *The Second Voyage*.
7. Eavan Boland has written several poems based on this section of the *Odyssey*.
8. Eiléan Ní Chuilleanáin, 'Acts and monuments of an unelected nation: The *Cailleach* writes about the Renaissance', *The Southern Review*, vol. 31, no. 3 (1995), pp. 570–80, at p. 575.
9. W.B. Yeats, 'Leda and the Swan', in Augustine Martin (ed.), *W.B. Yeats: Collected Poems* (London: Arena, 1990), p. 221.

10. The images in 'The Married Women' bring to mind the traditional image of the Virgin Mary and the 'protective wing' of the Angel Gabriel whose 'manteled oxter' also covered 'a girl's hesitant body' as the angel announced that she was to be the mother of the saviour. This reading is enhanced by the recurring images of angels who appear in *The Sun-fish*, like 'Michael and the Angel' or 'Vertigo'. As in other poems, like 'Fireman's Lift', which stress the materiality of the angels and of the Virgin Mary in Correggio's 'Assumption', Ní Chuilleanáin highlights the importance of acknowledging and valuing the female body rather than, as the child and young woman in 'The Married Women' had, running from it.
11. Patricia Boyle Haberstroh, 'Interview with Eiléan Ní Chuilleanáin', *Irish University Review*, vol. 37, no. 1 (2007), pp. 36–49, at p. 39.
12. References to Munster, to 'northern', to Fenian men and to troops, ruined houses and welcoming islands also encourage a political reading where the conflicts in Ireland might eventually be over and a new model of the world constructed, another way Ní Chuilleanáin imagines 'alternative systems'.
13. For more on the *sheela-na-gig*, see Joanne McMahon and Jack Roberts (eds), *The Sheela-na-Gigs of Ireland and Britain* (Dublin: Mercier Press, 2000). With specific reference to Irish art and poetry, see Luz Mar González Arias, '"Wide Open to Myth and Wonder": Twentieth-Century Sheela-Na-Gigs as Multiple Signifiers of the Female Body in Ireland', in Patricia Boyle Haberstroh and Christine St Peter (eds), *Opening the Field: Irish Women, Texts and Contexts* (Cork: Cork University Press, 2007), pp. 102–18, which examines the paintings of Carmel Benson and the poetry of Susan Connolly.
14. Patricia Boyle Haberstroh, 'An Interview with Eiléan Ní Chuilleanáin', *Canadian Journal of Irish Studies*, vol. 20, no. 2 (1994), pp. 63–74, at p. 63.
15. Carmen Zamorano Llena, '(Re)membering the Disembodied Verse: Constructs of Identity in Contemporary Irish Women's Poetry', in Mereta Falck Borch, Eva Rask Knudsen and Martin Leer (eds), *Bodies and Voices: the Force-Field of Representation and Discourse in Colonial and Postcolonial Studies* (Amsterdam/New York: Rodopi, 2008), pp. 349–62, at p. 357.
16. Catriona Clutterbuck, 'Gender and Self-Representation in Irish Poetry: the Critical Debate', *Bullán*, vol. 4, no. 1 (1998), pp. 43–58.
17. Patricia Coughlan, '"Bog Queens": The Representation of Women in the Poetry of John Montague and Seamus Heaney', in Toni O'Brien Johnson and David Cairns (eds), *Gender in Irish Writing* (Buckingham: Open University Press, 1991), pp. 88–111, at p. 108.
18. Ibid., p. 89.
19. Haberstroh, 'An Interview with Eiléan Ní Chuilleanáin', *Canadian Journal of Irish Studies*, p. 64.
20. Joyce Carol Oates, 'When Wishing Was Having ... Classic and Contemporary Fairy Tales', *The Kenyon Review*, vol. 19, nos 3, 4 (1997), pp. 98–110, at p. 98.
21. Ibid., p. 110.
22. Ibid.

23. Irene Gilsenan Nordin, *Reading Eiléan Ní Chuilleanáin, A Contemporary Poet* (Lampeter, UK, and Lewiston, NY: The Edwin Mellen Press, 2008), p. 62.
24. In an interview with me in May 2009.
25. Helen Emmitt, 'Through the Looking Glass (*The Girl who Married the Reindeer*)', *Irish Literary Supplement*, 22 September 2002.
26. Lucy McDiarmid, 'Ritual Encounters', *The New York Times*, 14 April 1996, p. 11.
27. Nordin, *Reading Eiléan Ní Chuilleanáin*, p. 49.
28. Haberstroh, 'An Interview with Eiléan Ní Chuilleanáin', *Canadian Journal of Irish Studies*, p. 71.
29. Nordin, 'The Weight of Words', p. 80.
30. Ní Chuilleanáin, 'Acts and monuments of an unelected nation', p. 576.
31. Carla de Petris, 'Italian Dialogues: An Interview with Eiléan Ní Chuilleanáin', *Irish University Review*, vol. 37, no. 1 (2007), pp. 197–201, at p. 200.
32. Leslie Williams, '"The stone recalls its quarry": An Interview with Eiléan Ní Chuilleanáin', in Susan Shaw Sailer (ed.), *Representing Ireland: Gender, Class, Nationality* (Gainesville, FL: University Press of Florida, 1997), pp. 29–44, at p. 41.
33. Ibid.
34. Nordin, 'The Weight of Words', p. 80.
35. Padraic Colum, *The King of Ireland's Son* (New York: Henry Holt, 1916).
36. Moynagh Sullivan, 'Raising the Veil: Myth and Melancholia in Irish Studies', in Patricia Coughlan and Tina O'Toole (eds), *Irish Literature: Feminist Perspectives* (Dublin: Carysfort Press, 2008), pp. 245–77, at p. 252.
37. Angela Bourke, 'The Virtual Reality of the Irish Fairy Legend', in Claire Connolly (ed.), *Theorising Ireland* (Dublin: Lilliput Press, 2003), pp. 27–40, at pp. 31–2.
38. Eiléan Ní Chuilleanáin, 'Acts and monuments of an unelected nation', p. 574.
39. Seamus Heaney, 'Meaning Business', in Pat Boran (ed.), *Flowing, Still: Irish Poets on Irish Poetry* (Dublin: The Dedalus Press, 2009), pp. 57–62, at p. 62.

CHAPTER 5. Women and the Sacred

1. Eiléan Ní Chuilleanáin, 'Acts and monuments of an unelected nation: The *Cailleach* writes about the Renaissance', *The Southern Review*, vol. 31, no. 3 (1995), pp. 570–80, at p. 579.
2. See, for example, Eiléan Ní Chuilleanáin, 'Time, Place and the Congregation in Donne's Sermons', in John Scattergood (ed.), *Literature and Learning in Medieval and Renaissance England: Essays Presented to Fitzroy Pyle* (Blackrock: Irish Academic Press, 1984), pp. 197–215.
3. *The Journal of Ecclesiastical History*, vol. 39, no. 3 (1988), pp. 382–411.
4. Deborah Hunter McWilliams, 'Eiléan Ní Chuilleanáin: Interviewed by Deborah Hunter McWilliams', in James P. Myers, Jr (ed.), *Writing Irish:*

Selected Interviews with Irish Writers from the Irish Literary Supplement (Syracuse, NY: Syracuse University Press, 1999), pp. 201–9, at p. 207.

5. Catriona Clutterbuck, 'Good Faith in Religion and Art: The Later Poetry of Eiléan Ní Chuilleanáin', *Irish University Review*, vol. 37, no. 1 (2007), pp. 131–56, at p. 132.
6. Ibid., p. 131.
7. Ibid.
8. Ibid.
9. Patricia Coughlan, '"No Lasting Fruit at All": Containment, Recognition and Relinquishing in *The Girl who Married the Reindeer*', *Irish University Review*, vol. 37, no. 1 (2007), pp. 157–77, at p. 161.
10. Ibid.
11. Patricia Boyle Haberstroh, 'Interview with Eiléan Ní Chuilleanáin', *Irish University Review*, vol. 37, no. 1 (2007), pp. 36–49, at p. 38.
12. John Donne, *Complete English Poems*, ed. A.J. Smith (London: Penguin, 1977), p. 305. The poem 'To the Lady Magdalen Herbert: Of St Mary Magdalen' was dedicated by Donne to George Herbert's mother.
13. See, for example, Ann Graham Brock, *Mary Magdalene, The First Apostle: The Struggle for Authority* (Cambridge, MA: Harvard University Press, 2003); Jane Schaberg, *The Resurrection of Mary Magdalene* (New York: Continuum Publishing, 2002); and Marina Warner, *Alone of All Her Sex: The Myth and Cult of the Virgin Mary* (New York: Knopf, 1976).
14. Inés Praga, 'Eiléan Ní Chuilleanáin', in Jacqueline Hurtley, Rosa González, Inés Praga and Esther Aliaga (eds), *Ireland in Writing: Interviews with Writers and Academics* (Amsterdam: Rodopi, 1998), pp. 83–92, at p. 91.
15. Haberstroh, 'Interview with Eiléan Ní Chuilleanáin', p. 40.
16. Interview with me in April 2009.
17. Praga, 'Eiléan Ní Chuilleanáin', p. 91.
18. Irene Gilsenan Nordin, 'The Weight of Words: An Interview with Eiléan Ní Chuilleanáin', *Canadian Journal of Irish Studies*, vols 28–9, nos 1–2 (2002–3), pp. 73–83, at p. 79. The reference to hair refers to Ní Chuilleanáin's own hair. Ní Chuilleanáin has also said that she began the poem in Philadelphia, after having seen an image of Magdalene in the Philadelphia Museum of Art.
19. Coughlan, '"No Lasting Fruit at All"', pp. 162–3.
20. James Smith's *Ireland's Magdalene Laundries and the Nation's Architecture of Containment* (Notre Dame, IN: University of Notre Dame Press, 2007) is a good study of the laundries. The Magdalene Homes were not exclusive to Ireland, nor were they run only by the Catholic Church. Frances Finnegan, in *Do Penance or Perish: Magdalene Asylums in Ireland* (Piltown, Kilkenny: Congrave, 2001), examines those that were established in England in the nineteenth century for helping prostitutes to leave the streets. From 1800 to 1907, there was a Magdalene Home in Philadelphia, first established by a group comprised of Quakers, Episcopalians and Presbyterians. The Irish

Laundries, however, lasted well into the twentieth century, with harsher conditions and an emphasis on punishment and penance.

21. Available at *www.childabusecommission.ie/rpt* [accessed 24 February 2012].
22. Quoted in Brian Titley, 'Magdalene Asylums and Moral Regulation in Ireland', in Anthony Potts and Tom O'Donoghue (eds), *Schools as Dangerous Places: A Historical Perspective* (Youngstown, NY: Cambria Press, 2007), pp. 119–44, at p. 131.
23. Ibid., p. 132.
24. Available at http://historical-debates.oireachtas.ie/D/0352/D.0352.19840 6280267.html [accessed 24 February 2012].
25. Clutterbuck, 'Good Faith in Religion and Art', p. 153.
26. Eiléan Ní Chuilleanáin, 'Nuns: A Subject for a Woman Writer', in Patricia Boyle Haberstroh (ed.), *My Self, My Muse* (Syracuse, NY: Syracuse University Press, 2001), pp. 17–31, at pp. 21–2.
27. Ibid.
28. In an interview with me in April 2009, Ní Chuilleanáin said that her aunt had written the words 'J'ai mal à nos dents' in a letter to her.
29. Eiléan Ní Chuilleanáin, 'Introduction', in Eiléan Ní Chuilleanáin (ed.), *Irish Women: Image and Achievement* (Dublin: Arlen House, 1985), p. 1.
30. An early history of the statue and the Dominican priory at Youghal can be found in James A. Dwyer, *The Dominicans of Cork City and County* (Cork: Guy & Company, 1896).
31. Jefferson Holdridge, '"A Snake Pouring Over the Ground": Nature and the Sacred in Eiléan Ní Chuilleanáin's Poetry', *Irish University Review*, vol. 37, no. 1 (2007), pp. 115–30, at p. 116.
32 Haberstroh, 'Interview', p. 42
33. Nordin, 'The Weight of Words', p. 78.
34. Helen Emmitt, '"One Free Foot Kicking Under the White Sheet of History": Eiléan Ní Chuilleanáin's Uncanny Landscapes', *Women's Studies: An Interdisciplinary Journal*, vol. 29 (2000), pp. 477–94, at p. 482.
35. Dillon Johnston '"Our Bodies' Eyes and Writing Hands": Secrecy and Sensuality in Ní Chuilleanáin's Baroque Art', in Anthony Bradley and Maryann Gialanella Valiulis (eds), *Gender and Sexuality in Modern Ireland* (Amherst, MA: University of Massachusetts Press, 1997), pp. 187–211, at p. 200.
36. Nordin, 'The Weight of Words', p. 78.
37. I discuss 'Fireman's Lift' in more detail in Chapter 6.
38. Giorgio Vasari, *Lives of the Artists*, translated by Julia Conway Bondanella and Peter Bondanella (Oxford: Oxford University Press, 2007), pp. 414–48.
39. On *Sceilig Mhichíl*, the ruins of a seventh-century monastery and a chapel built around AD 1000 are about 700 feet above sea level, with 600 steps to the shrine. The shrine is known for its beehive huts.
40. In an interview with me in May 2010.
41. Holdridge, '"A Snake Pouring Over the Ground"', p. 115.

42. The holiday is the subject of a poem in Irish by Seán Ó Riordáin entitled '*Oíche Nollaig na mBan*'.

CHAPTER 6. **Presence and Place**

1. Joseph Foxe, *The Acts and Monuments of the Latter and Perilous Days*, published in 1563; online variorum edition available at http://www.hrionline.ac.uk/johnfoxe [accessed 24 February 2012].
2. Carla de Petris, 'Italian Dialogues: An Interview with Eiléan Ní Chuilleanáin', *Irish University Review*, vol. 37, no. 1 (2007), pp. 197–201, at p. 200.
3. Nícholas Allen, '"Each Page Lies Open to the Version of Every Other": History in the Poetry of Eiléan Ní Chuilleanáin', *Irish University Review*, vol. 37, no. 1 (2007), pp. 22–35, at p. 29; and Irene Gilsenan Nordin, *Reading Eiléan Ní Chuilleanáin, A Contemporary Poet* (Lampeter, UK and Lewiston, NY: The Edwin Mellen Press, 2008), p. 24.
4. Dell Upton, *Architecture in the United States* (Oxford: Oxford University Press, 1998), pp. 11–12.
5. Daniel Grose, *Antiquities of Ireland* (Dublin: Irish Architectural Archive, 1991).
6. Dillon Johnston, '"Our Bodies' Eyes and Writing Hands": Secrecy and Sensuality in Ní Chuilleanáin's Baroque Art', in Anthony Bradley and Maryann Gialanella Valiulis (eds), *Gender and Sexuality in Modern Ireland* (Amherst, MA: University of Massachusetts Press, 1997), pp. 187–211, at p. 201.
7. In an interview with me in May 2010.
8. Patricia Boyle Haberstroh, 'Interview with Eiléan Ní Chuilleanáin', *Irish University Review*, vol. 37, no. 1 (2007), pp. 36–49, at p. 47.
9. Leslie Williams, '"The stone recalls its quarry": An Interview with Eiléan Ní Chuilleanáin', in Susan Shaw Sailer (ed.), *Representing Ireland: Gender, Class, Nationality* (Gainesville, FL: University Press of Florida, 1997), pp. 29–43, at p. 37.
10. J. Watson Doering, 'Sacred Enclosures: Interview with Eiléan Ní Chuilleanáin', *Cascando*, vol. 5, no. 6 (1996), pp. 25–32, at p. 27.
11. Eiléan Ní Chuilleanáin, '"Strange ceremonies": sacred space and bodily presence in the English Reformation', in Amanda Piesse (ed.), *The Making of Sixteenth-Century Identity* (Manchester: Manchester University Press, 2001), pp. 133–52.
12. Ibid., p. 138.
13. Eamon Grennan, 'Real Things', *Poetry Ireland Review*, vol. 46, no. 2 (1995), pp. 44–52, at p. 45.
14. Thomas McCarthy, '"We Could Be in Any City": Eiléan Ní Chuilleanáin and Cork', *Irish University Review*, vol. 37, no. 1 (2007), pp. 230–43, at p. 232.
15. Brian Lalor, *Cork* (Dublin: Gallery Press, 1977), p. 99.

16. Eiléan Ní Chuilleanáin, 'Home and Places', available at http://uiowa.edu/paros/2008/paros/chuilleanáin [accessed 10 November 2008].
17. McCarthy, '"We Could Be in Any City"', p. 239.
18. In an interview with me in May 2009.
19. Williams, '"The stone recalls its quarry"', p. 40.
20. Eiléan Ní Chuilleanáin, 'Nuns: A Subject for a Woman Writer', in Patricia Boyle Haberstroh (ed.), *My Self, My* Muse (Syracuse, NY: Syracuse University Press, 2001), pp. 17–32, at p. 19.
21. Helen King, *The Disease of Virgins* (London: Taylor & Francis, 2003), p. 3.
22. Ian Maclean, *The Renaissance Notion of Women* (Cambridge: Cambridge University Press, 1980).
23. Ní Chuilleanáin told me that she had in mind the healer Biddy Early described in Lady Gregory's *Visions and Beliefs in the West of Ireland* (Gerrards Cross, Buckinghamshire: Colin Smythe, 1992).

CHAPTER 7. **Transformation and Translation**

1. Kevin Ray, 'An Interview with Eiléan Ní Chuilleanáin', *Éire-Ireland*, vol.31, nos 1–2 (1996), pp. 62–73, at p. 67.
2. Irene Gilsenan Nordin, *Reading Eiléan Ní Chuilleanáin, A Contemporary Poet* (Lampeter, UK and Lewiston, NY: Edwin Mellen Press, 2008), p. 123.
3. Patricia Boyle Haberstroh, 'Interview with Eiléan Ní Chuilleanáin', *Irish University Review*, vol. 37, no. 1 (2007), pp. 36–49, at p. 42.
4. Helen Emmitt, 'Through the looking glass (*The Girl who Married the Reindeer*)', *Irish Literary Supplement*, 22 September 2002.
5. Haberstroh, 'Interview with Eiléan Ní Chuilleanáin', p. 42.
6. Nícholas Allen, '"Each Page Lies Open to the Version of Every Other": History in the Poetry of Eiléan Ní Chuilleanáin', *Irish University Review*, vol. 37, no. 1 (2007), pp. 22–35, at pp. 33–4.
7. In an interview with me in May 2010.
8. Guinn Batten in '"The World Not Dead after All": Eiléan Ní Chuilleanáin's Work of Revival', *Irish University Review*, vol. 37, no. 1 (2007), pp. 1–21, says: '"Studying the Language" allows the poet to revive these celibates, and it also permits her to situate the speaker, without irony, as a follower rather than detached scholar of their ways, or archaeologist of their remains' (p. 17).
9. Haberstroh, 'Interview with Eiléan Ní Chuilleanáin', p. 46.
10. Thomas More, *Utopia*, ed. George M. Logan and Robert M. Adams (Cambridge: Cambridge University Press, 2002).
11. Haberstroh, 'Interview with Eiléan Ní Chuilleanáin', pp. 46–7.
12. Eiléan Ní Chuilleanáin, 'Acts and monuments of an unelected nation: The *Cailleach* writes about the Renaissance', *The Southern Review*, vol. 31, no. 3 (1995), pp. 570–80, at p. 573.
13. John Kerrigan, 'Hidden Ireland: Eiléan Ní Chuilleanáin and Munster Poetry', *Critical Quarterly*, vol. 40, no. 4 (1998), pp. 76–100, at p. 95.

14. Eamon Grennan, 'Real Things: The Work of Eiléan Ní Chuilleanáin', in Eamon Grennan (ed.), *Facing the Music: Irish Poetry in the Twentieth Century* (Omaha, NE: Creighton University Press, 1999), pp. 283–95, at pp. 285–6.
15. Ní Chuilleanáin had met Patrick Kavanagh only once because he had died shortly after she arrived back in Dublin from Oxford. Her relationship with Katherine developed after Patrick Kavanagh's death.
16. Inés Praga, 'Eiléan Ní Chuilleanáin', in Jacqueline Hurtley, Rosa González, Inés Praga and Esther Aliaga (eds), *Ireland in Writing: Interviews with Writers and Academics* (Amsterdam: Rodopi, 1998), pp. 83–92, at p. 84.
17. Padraic Colum, 'She Moved Through the Faire', *Wild Earth and Other Poems* (New York: Henry Holt & Co., 1922), p. 26.
18. For example, another poem, 'Macmoransbridge' (*SP* 53), describes a setting where several sisters 'never / All resting at once' kept house for a man.
19. Dylan Johnston, '"Our Bodies' Eyes and Writing Hands": Secrecy and Sensuality in Ní Chuilleanáin's Baroque Art', in Anthony Bradley and Maryann Gialanella Valiulis (eds), *Gender and Sexuality in Modern Ireland* (Amherst, MA: University of Massachusetts Press, 1997), pp. 187–211, at p. 206.
20. In an interview with me in May 2010.
21. In an interview with me in 1992.
22. W.B. Yeats, 'Blood and the Moon,' in Augustine Martin (ed.), *W.B. Yeats Collected Poems* (London: Arena, 1989), p. 244.
23. Haberstroh, 'Interview with Eiléan Ní Chuilleanáin', p. 37.
24. Giocomo Leopardi, *Selected Poems*, trans. Eamon Grennan (Princeton, NJ: Princeton University Press, 1997), p. 49.
25. We might see this as similar to reading the title of Ní Chuilleanáin's poem 'Following' as suggesting that the poem extends (or follows from) the vision in Colum's 'She Moved Through the Faire', a point I have made earlier in this chapter.
26. Mary Coleman, 'Irish Lace and Irish Crochet', in Eiléan Ní Chuilleanáin (ed.), *Irish Women: Image and Achievement* (Dublin: Arlen House, 1985), pp. 85–94, at p. 90.
27. Eiléan Ní Chuilleanáin, Cormac Ó Cuilleanáin and David Parris (eds), *Translation and Censorship: Patterns of Communication and Interference* (Dublin: Four Courts Press, 2009), p. 17.
28. Borbála Faragó describes Ní Chuilleanáin's emphasis on silence in her essay '"Alcove in the Wind": Silence and Space in Ní Chuilleanáin's Poetry', *Irish University Review*, vol. 37, no. 1 (2007), pp. 68–83.
29. Nuala Ní Dhomhnaill, 'Tidal Surge (1909–1999)', in Pat Boran (ed.), *Flowing, Still: Irish Poets on Irish Poetry* (Dublin: Dedalus Press, 2009), pp. 71–82, at p. 76.
30. Aidan O'Malley, '*Praeteritio*: (Non-) Possession and the Translational Impulse in Ní Chuilleanáin's Work', *Irish University Review*, vol. 37, no. 1 (2007), pp. 178–96, at p. 179.

31. Michele Ranchetti, *Verbale/Minutes/Tuairisc*, trans. Eiléan Ní Chuilleanáin, Cormac Ó Cuilleanáin and Gabriel Rosenstock (Dublin: Instituto Italiano di Cultura, 2003).
32. Ileana Mălăncioiu, *After the Raising of Lazarus*, trans. Eiléan Ní Chuilleanáin (Cork: Southword Editions, 2005).
33. Ray, 'An Interview with Eiléan Ní Chuilleanáin', p. 72.
34. In correspondence with me in August 2009.
35. Ibid.
36. Rădulescu, in the introduction to Mălăncioiu's *After the Raising of Lazarus*, p. 7.
37. In correspondence with me in August 2009.
38. Rădulescu, in the introduction to Mălăncioiu's *After the Raising of Lazarus*, p. 10.
39. Praga, 'Eiléan Ní Chuilleanáin', p. 85.

Select Bibliography

Allen, Nicholas, '"Each Page Lies Open to the Version of Every Other": History in the Poetry of Eiléan Ní Chuilleanáin', *Irish University Review*, vol. 37, no. 1 (2007), pp. 22–35

Allison, Jonathan, 'Poetry from the Irish', *Irish Literary Supplement* (Spring 1991), p. 14

Batten, Guinn, '"The World Not Dead after All": Eiléan Ní Chuilleanáin's Work of Revival', *Irish University Review*, vol. 37, no. 1 (2007), pp. 1–21

Batten, Guinn, 'Boland, McGuckian, Ní Chuilleanáin and the Body of the Nation', in Matthew Campbell (ed.), *The Cambridge Companion to Contemporary Irish Poetry* (Cambridge: Cambridge University Press, 2003), pp. 169–88

Benhabib, Seyla, Judith Butler, Nancy Fraser and Drucilla Cornel (eds), *Feminist Contentions: A Philosophical Exchange* (London: Routledge, 1996)

Bhreathnach-Lynch, Síghle, *Ireland's Art and Ireland's History: Representing Ireland, 1845 to Present* (Omaha, NE: Creighton University Press, 2007)

Boland, Eavan (ed.), *Irish Writers on Writing* (San Antonio, TX: Trinity University Press, 2007)

Boland, Eavan, *Object Lessons* (Manchester: Carcanet, 1995)

Boland, Eavan, *Outside History* (Manchester: Carcanet, 1990)

Boran, Pat (ed.), *Flowing, Still: Irish Poets on Irish Poetry* (Dublin: The Dedalus Press, 2009)

Borch, Merete Falck and Anna Rutherford (eds), *Bodies and Voices: The Force-Field of Representation and Discourse in Colonial and Postcolonial Studies* (Amsterdam and New York: Rodopi, 2008)

Bourke, Angela, 'The Virtual Reality of the Irish Fairy Legend', in Claire Connolly (ed.), *Theorising Ireland* (Dublin: Lilliput Press, 2003), pp. 27–40

Bourke, Angela, 'Language, Stories, Healing', in Anthony Bradley and Maryann Gialanella Valiulis (eds), *Gender and Sexuality in Modern Ireland* (Amherst, MA: University of Massachusetts Press, 1997), pp. 299–314

Bourke, Angela, et al. (eds), *The Field Day Anthology of Irish Writing: Women's Writing and Traditions, Vols. IV and V* (Cork: Cork University Press, 2002)

Bradley, Anthony and Maryann Gialanella Valiulis (eds) *Gender and Sexuality in Modern Ireland* (Amherst, MA: University of Massachusetts Press, 1997)

Brock, Ann Graham, *Mary Magdalene, The First Apostle: The Struggle for Authority* (Cambridge, MA: Harvard University Press, 2003)

Burt, Stephen, 'Poetry Chronicle', *The New York Times Book Review*, 2 August 2009, p. 16

Butler, Judith, *Undoing Gender* (London: Routledge, 2004)

Butler, Judith, *Gender Trouble: Feminism and the Subversion of Identity* (London: Routledge, 1990)

Caldecott, Moyra, *Women in Celtic Myth* (Rochester, VT: Destiny Books, 1988)

Cairns, David and Shaun Richards, 'Tropes and Traps: Aspects of "Woman" and Nationality in Twentieth-Century Irish Drama', in Toni O'Brien Johnson and David Cairns (eds), *Gender in Irish Writing* (Buckingham: Open University Press, 1991), pp. 128–37

Cairns, David and Shaun Richards, *Writing Ireland: Colonialism, Nationalism and Culture* (Manchester: Manchester University Press, 1988)

Clutterbuck, Catriona, 'Good Faith in Religion and Art: The Later Poetry of Eiléan Ní Chuilleanáin', *Irish University Review*, vol. 37, no. 1 (2007), pp. 131–56

Clutterbuck, Catriona, 'Gender and Self-Representation in Irish Poetry: The Critical Debate', *Bullán*, vol. 41 (1998), pp. 43–58

Coleman, Mary, 'Irish Lace and Irish Crochet', in Eiléan Ní Chuilleanáin (ed.), *Irish Women: Image and Achievement* (Dublin: Arlen House, 1985), pp. 85–94

Collins, Lucy, '"Why Didn't They Ask the Others?" Resisting Disclosure in the Poetry of Eiléan Ní Chuilleanáin', in Michael Böss and Eamon Maher (eds), *Engaging Modernity: Readings of Irish Politics, Culture and Literature at the Turn of the Century* (Dublin: Veritas, 2003), pp. 169–80

Colum, Pádraic, 'She Moved Through the Faire', *Wild Earth and Other Poems* (New York: Henry Holt & Co., 1922)

Colum, Pádraic, *The King of Ireland's Son* (New York: Henry Holt & Co., 1916)

Conboy, Sheila C. '"What You Have Seen is Beyond Speech": Female Journeys in the Poetry of Eavan Boland and Eiléan Ní Chuilleanáin', *The Canadian Journal of Irish Studies*, vol. 16, no. 1, (1990), pp. 65–72

Condren, Mary, *The Serpent and the Goddess: Women, Religion and Power in Celtic Ireland* (New York: Harper & Row, 1989)

Connolly, Claire, *Theorizing Ireland* (London: Macmillan, 2003)

Connolly, Linda, *The Irish Women's Movement: From Revolution to Devolution* (Dublin: Lilliput Press, 2003)

Consalvo, Deborah McWilliams, 'An Interview with Eiléan Ní Chuilleanáin', *Irish Literary Supplement*, vol. 12, no. 1, (1993), pp. 15–17

Coughlan, Patricia, '"No Lasting Fruit at All": Containment, Recognition and Relinquishing in *The Girl who Married the Reindeer*', *Irish University Review*, vol. 37, no. 1 (2007), pp. 157–77

Coughlan, Patricia, '"Bog Queens": The Representation of Women in the Poetry of John Montague and Seamus Heaney', in Toni O'Brien Johnson and David Cairns (eds), *Gender in Irish Writing* (Buckingham: Open University Press, 1991), pp. 88–111

Coughlan, Patricia and Tina O'Toole (eds), *Irish Literature: Feminist Perspectives* (Dublin: Carysfort Press, 2008)

Coulter, Carol, *The Hidden Tradition: Feminism, Women and Nationalism in Ireland* (Cork: Cork University Press, 1993)

Craig, Maurice, *The Architecture of Ireland: From the Earliest Times to 1880* (London: Batsford, 1983)

Craig, Patricia, 'The Field Day Anthology of Irish Writing, volumes IV and V: Irish Women's Writing and Traditions', *Irish Independent*, 28 December 2002

Cullinan, Emma, 'Maurice Craig – Ireland's First Conservation Warrior', *The Irish Times*, 15 October 2009

Cullingford, Elizabeth Butler, *Gender and History in Yeats's Love Poetry* (Cambridge: Cambridge University Press, 1993)

Curtin, Chris, Pauline Jackson and Barbara O'Connor, *Gender in Irish Society* (Galway: Galway University Press, 1987)

Dáil Éireann, 'Written Answers – Mother and Baby Homes', Proceedings, vol. 352, 8 June 1984

Deane, Seamus, et al. (eds), *The Field Day Anthology of Irish Writing*, vols I–III (Derry: Field Day Publications, 1992)

de Petris, Carla, 'Italian Dialogues: An Interview with Eiléan Ní Chuilleanáin', *Irish University Review*, vol. 37, no. 1 (2007), pp. 197–201

Dillon, Eilís, *Death at Crane's Court* (Boulder, CO: The Rue Morgue Press, 2009)

Dillon, Eilís, 'In the Honan Hostel', in Seamus Deane (ed.), *The Cork Anthology* (Cork: Cork University Press, 1993)

Doering, J. Watson, 'Sacred Enclosures: Eiléan Ní Chuilleanáin talks to J. Watson Doering about *The Brazen Serpent*', *Cascando*, vol. 5, no. 6 (1996), pp. 25–33

Donne, John, *The Complete English Poems*, ed. A.J. Smith (London: Penguin, 1977), p. 305

Donovan, Katie, A. Norman Jeffares and Brendan Kennelly, *Ireland's Women: Writings Past and Present* (Dublin: Gill & Macmillan, 1994)

Dorgan, Theo (ed.), *Irish Poetry Since Kavanagh* (Dublin: Four Courts Press, 1995)

Dowson, Jane, '"Older Sisters Are Very Sobering Things": Contemporary Women Poets and the Female Affiliation Complex', *Feminist Review*, vol. 62, no. 1 (1999), pp. 6–20

Dunne, Tom, 'Subaltern Voices? Poetry in Irish, Popular Insurgency and the 1798 Rebellion', *Eighteenth-Century Life*, vol. 22, no. 3 (1998), pp. 31–44

Dwyer, James A. *The Dominicans of Cork City and County* (Cork: Guy & Company, 1896)

Emmitt, Helen, 'Through the looking glass (*The Girl who Married the Reindeer*)', *Irish Literary Supplement*, 22 September 2002

Emmitt, Helen, '"The One Free Foot Kicking Under the White Sheet of History": Eiléan Ní Chuilleanáin's Uncanny Landscapes', *Women's Studies: An Interdisciplinary Journal*, vol. 29 (2000). pp. 477–94

Faragó, Borbála, '"Alcove in the Wind": Silence and Space in Ní Chuilleanáin's Poetry', *Irish University Review*, vol. 37, no. 1 (2007), pp. 68–83

Faragó, Borbála, 'Origin and Oblivion: Representations of Death in the Poetry of Medbh McGuckian and Eiléan Ní Chuilleanáin', in Liam Harte, Yvonne Whelan and Patrick Crotty (eds), *Ireland: Space, Text, Time* (Dublin: Liffey Press, 2005), pp. 67–76

Felski, Rita, *The Gender of Modernity* (Cambridge, MA: Harvard University Press, 1995)

Finnegan, Frances, *Do Penance or Perish: Magdalene Asylums in Ireland* (Piltown, Kilkenny: Congrave, 2001)

Flood, John and Phil Flood, *Kilcash: A History, 1190–1801* (Dublin: Geography Publications, 1999)

Fogarty, Anne (ed.), 'Eiléan Ní Chuilleanáin: Special Issue', *Irish University Review*, vol. 31, no. 7 (2007)

Foster, John Wilson, *Between the Shadows: Modern Irish Writing and Culture* (Dublin: Irish Academic Press, 2009)

Foxe, Joseph, *The Acts and Monuments of the Latter and Perilous Days*, published in 1563; online variorum edition available at http://www.hrionline.ac.uk/johnfoxe

Fulford, Susan, *Gendered Spaces in Contemporary Irish Poetry* (Oxford: Peter Lang, 2002)

Gardiner, David, 'The Other Irish Renaissance: The Maunsel Poets', *New Hibernia Review*, vol. 8, no. 1 (2004), pp. 54–79

Gonzalez, Alex, *Contemporary Irish Women Poets: Some Male Perspectives* (Westport, CT: Greenwood Press, 1997)

González Arias, Luz Mar, '"Wide Open to Myth and Wonder": Twentieth-Century Sheela-na-Gigs as Multiple Signifiers of the Female Body in Ireland', in Patricia Boyle Haberstroh and Christine St Peter (eds), *Opening the Field: Irish Women, Texts and Contexts* (Cork: Cork University Press, 2007), pp. 102–18

Graham, Colin, *Deconstructing Ireland: Identity, Theory, Culture* (Edinburgh: Edinburgh University Press, 2001)

Gregory, Lady Augusta, *Visions and Beliefs in the West of Ireland* (Gerrards Cross, Buckinghamshire: Colin Smythe, 1992)

Grennan, Eamon, *Facing the Music: Irish Poetry in the Twentieth Century* (Omaha, NE: Creighton University Press, 1999)

Grennan, Eamon, 'Real Things', *Poetry Ireland Review*, vol. 46, no. 1 (1995), pp. 44–52

Grose, Daniel, *Antiquities of Ireland* (Dublin: Irish Architectural Archive, 1991)

Haberstroh, Patricia Boyle, 'Interview with Eiléan Ní Chuilleanáin', *Irish University Review*, vol. 37, no. 1 (2007), pp. 36–49

Haberstroh, Patricia Boyle, 'The Architectural Metaphor in the Poetry of Eiléan Ní Chuilleanáin', *Irish University Review*, vol. 37, no. 1 (2007), pp. 84–97

Haberstroh, Patricia Boyle, *Women Creating Women: Contemporary Irish Women Poets* (Syracuse, NY: Syracuse University Press, 1996)

Haberstroh, Patricia Boyle, 'An Interview with Eiléan Ní Chuilleanáin', *Canadian Journal of Irish Studies*, vol. 20, no. 2 (1994), pp. 63–74

Haberstroh, Patricia Boyle and Christine St Peter (eds), *Opening the Field: Irish Women, Texts and Contexts* (Cork: Cork University Press, 2007)

Haberstroh, Patricia Boyle (ed.), *My Self, My Muse: Irish Women Poets Reflect on Life and Art* (Syracuse, NY: Syracuse University Press, 2001)

Hartigan, Anne Le Marquand, *Clearing the Space: A Why of Writing* (Co. Clare: Salmon Poetry, 1996)

Hayes, Allen and Diane Urquhart (eds), *Irish Women's History Reader* (London: Routledge, 2000)

Heaney, Seamus, 'Sheelagh na Gig', *Station Island* (London: Faber & Faber, 1984), pp. 49–50

Heaney, Seamus, 'Meaning Business', in Pat Boran (ed.), *Flowing, Still: Irish Poets on Irish Poetry* (Dublin: The Dedalus Press, 2009), pp. 57–62

Heehs, Peter, 'Myth, History and Theory', *History and Theory*, vol. 33, no. 1 (1994), pp. 1–19

Herr, Cheryl, 'The Erotics of Irishness', *Critical Inquiry*, vol. 17 (1990), pp. 1–34

Hoff, Joan, 'The Impact and Implications of Women's History', in Maryann Gialanella Valiulis and Mary O'Dowd (eds), *Women and Irish History: Essays in Honour of Margaret MacCurtain* (Dublin: Wolfhound, 1997), pp. 24–5

Holdridge, Jefferson, '"A Snake Pouring Over the Ground": Nature and the Sacred in Eiléan Ní Chuilleanáin's Poetry', *Irish University Review*, vol. 37, no. 1 (2007), pp. 115–30

Hooley, Ruth (ed.), *The Female Line: Northern Irish Women Writers* (Belfast: Northern Ireland Women's Rights Movement, 1985)

Hooper, Glenn and Colin Graham (eds), *Irish and Postcolonial Writing: History, Theory, Practice* (Basingstoke: Macmillan, 2002)

Hurtley, Jacqueline, Rosa Gonzáles, Inés Praga and Esther Aliaga (eds), *Ireland in Writing: Interviews with Writers and Academics* (Amsterdam: Rodopi, 1998)

Innes, Catherine, *Woman and Nation in Irish Literature and Society, 1880–1935* (Athens, GA: University of Georgia Press, 1993)

Johnson, Toni O'Brien and David Cairns (eds), *Gender in Irish Writing* (Buckingham: Open University Press, 1991)

Johnston, Dillon '"Our Bodies' Eyes and Writing Hands": Secrecy and Sensuality in Ní Chuilleanáin's Baroque Art', in Anthony Bradley and Maryann Gialanella Valiulis (eds), *Gender and Sexuality in Modern Ireland* (Amherst MA: University of Massachusetts Press, 1997), pp. 187–211

Kelleher, Margaret, '*The Field Day Anthology* and Irish Women's Literary Studies', *Irish Review*, vol. 30 (2003), pp. 82–94

Kelleher, Margaret, 'Writing Irish Women's Literary History', *Irish Studies Review*, vol. 9, no. 1 (2001), pp. 5–14

Kelly, A.A. *Pillars of the House: An Anthology of Irish Verse by Women from 1690 to the Present* (Dublin: Wolfhound Press, 1987)

Kerrigan, John, 'Hidden Ireland: Eiléan Ní Chuilleanáin and Munster Poetry', *Critical Quarterly*, vol. 40, no. 4 (1995), pp. 76–100

Kidd, Helen, '*Cailleachs*, Keens and Queens: Refiguring Gender and Nationality in the Poetry of Eiléan Ní Chuilleanáin, Nuala Ní Dhomhnaill and Eavan Boland', *Critical Quarterly*, vol. 15, no. 1 (2003), pp. 34–47

Kilfeather, Siobhán, 'Irish Feminism', in Joe Cleary and Claire Connolly (eds), *The Cambridge Companion to Irish Culture* (Cambridge: Cambridge University Press, 2005), pp. 96–116

King, Helen, *The Disease of Virgins* (London: Taylor & Francis, 2003)

Kinsella, Thomas and Sean Ó Tuama (eds), *Duanaire, 1600–1900: Poems of the Dispossessed* (Dublin: Dolmen Press, 1981)

Kirkpatrick, Kathryn (ed.), *Border Crossings: Irish Women Writers and National Identities* (Tuscaloosa, AL: University of Alabama Press, 2000)

Leland, Mary, *The Lie of the Land: Journeys through Literary Cork* (Cork: Cork University Press, 1999)

Leopardi, Giacomo, *Selected Poems*, trans. Eamon Grennan (Princeton, NJ: Princeton University Press, 1997), p. 49

Linden, Eddie, *A Thorn in the Flesh: Selected Poems* (London: Hearing Eye, 2011)

Lloyd, David, *Anomalous States: Irish Writing and the Post-Colonial Movement* (Durham, NC: Duke University Press, 1993)

Lojek, Helen, 'Man, Woman, Soldier: Heaney's "In Memoriam Francis Ledwidge" and Boland's "Heroic"', *New Hibernia Review*, vol. 10, no. 1 (2006), pp. 123–38

Longley, Edna, *The Living Stream: Literature and Revisionism in Ireland* (Newcastle upon Tyne: Bloodaxe Books, 1994)

Luddy, Maria and Cliona Murphy, *Women Surviving: Studies in Irish Women's History in the 19th & 20th Centuries* (Dublin: Poolbeg Press, 1989)

Maclean, Ian, *The Renaissance Notion of Woman* (Cambridge: Cambridge University Press, 1980)

MacCurtain, Margaret, *Ariadne's Thread: Writing Women into Irish History* (Dublin: Arlen House; Syracuse, NY: Syracuse University Press, 2009)

Mahony, Christina Hunt, *Contemporary Irish Literature: Transforming Tradition* (New York: St Martin's Press, 1998)

Mălăncioiu, Ileana, *After the Raising of Lazarus*, trans. Eiléan Ní Chuilleanáin (Cork: Southword Editions, 2005)

Manus, Kathy Dow, 'The Unaccountable Subject: Judith Butler and the Social Conditions of Intersubjective Agency', *Hypatia*, vol. 21, no. 2 (2006), pp. 81–103

McBreen, Joan, *The White Page/An Bhileog Bhán: Twentieth-Century Irish Women Poets* (Co. Clare: Salmon Poetry, 1999)

McCarthy, Conor, *Modernization, Crisis and Culture in Ireland, 1969–92* (Dublin: Four Courts Press, 2000)

McCarthy, Thomas, '"We Could Be in Any City": Eiléan Ní Chuilleanáin in Cork', *Irish University Review*, vol. 37, no. 1 (2007), pp. 230–43

McDiarmid, Lucy, 'Ritual Encounters', *The New York Times*, 14 April 1996, p. 11

McGuiness, Frank, *The Sea with No Ships* (Co. Meath: Gallery Press, 1999)

McKibben, Sarah E. 'Speaking the Unspeakable: Male Humiliation and Female National Allegory after Kinsale', *Éire-Ireland*, vol. 43, nos 3–4 (2008), pp. 11–30

McMahon, Joanne and Jack Roberts, *The Sheela-na-Gigs of Ireland and Britain* (Dublin: Mercier Press, 2000)

Meaney, Gerardine, *Gender, Ireland and Cultural Change* (London: Routledge, 2010)

Meaney, Gerardine, 'Engendering the Postmodern Canon: The Field Day Anthology of Irish Writing, Volumes IV & V: Women's Writing and

Traditions', in Patricia Boyle Haberstroh and Christine St Peter (eds), *Opening the Field: Irish Women, Texts and Contexts* (Cork: Cork University Press, 2007), pp. 15–30

Meaney, Gerardine, 'History Gasps: Myth in Contemporary Irish Women's Poetry', in Michael Kenneally (ed.), *Poetry in Contemporary Irish Literature* (Gerrards Cross, Buckinghamshire: Colin Smythe, 1995), pp. 99–113

Meaney, Gerardine, 'Myth, History and the Politics of Subjectivity', *Women: A Cultural Review*, vol. 4, no. 2 (1993), pp. 136–53

Meaney, Gerardine and Maria Luddy (eds), *Women in Modern Irish Culture, 1800–2005*, database available at http://www.arts-humanities.net/projects/women_modern_irish_culture [accessed 24 February 2012]

Michener, Christian, 'Saints and Sisters: The Sacred Chorus in the Poetry of Eiléan Ní Chuilleanáin', *New Hibernia Review*, vol. 14, no. 2 (2010), pp. 118–32

Montague, John, *Mount Eagle* (Co. Meath: Gallery Press, 1988)

Montague, Mary, 'The art of the body: poem as female self-portrait', in Joan McBreen (ed.), *The Watchful Heart: A New Generation of Irish Poets* (Co. Clare: Salmon Poetry, 2009), pp. 125–8

More, Thomas, *Utopia*, ed. George M. Logan and Robert M. Adams (Cambridge: Cambridge University Press, 2002)

Murphy, Richard, *The Mirror Wall* (Winston-Salem, NC: Wake Forest University Press, 1989)

Myers, James P. Jr, *Writing Irish: Selected Interviews with Irish Writers from the Irish Literary Supplement* (Syracuse, NY: Syracuse University Press, 1999)

Ní Chuilleanáin, Eiléan, *The Sun-fish* (Co. Meath: Gallery Press, 2009)

Ní Chuilleanáin, Eiléan, *Selected Poems* (Co. Meath: Gallery Press, 2008; London: Faber & Faber, 2008; Winston-Salem, NC: Wake Forest University Press, 2009)

Ní Chuilleanáin, Eiléan, 'Home and Places', *Home/Lands* (University of Iowa, 2008), available at http://iwp.uiowa.edu/paros/2008paros/Chuilleanáin_Home_and_Places.pdf [accessed 10 November 2008]

Ní Chuilleanáin, Eiléan, 'Vivian Mercier', *New Hibernia Review*, vol. 8, no. 4 (2004), pp. 146–7

Ní Chuilleanáin, Eiléan, 'Becoming the Patriarch: Masculinity in Maria Edgeworth's *Ormond*', in Patricia Boyle Haberstroh and Christine St Peter (eds), *Opening the Field: Irish Women, Text and Context* (Cork: Cork University Press, 2007), pp. 31–42

Ní Chuilleanáin, Eiléan, 'Speranza, an Ancestor for a Woman Poet in 2000', in Eiléan Ní Chuilleanáin (ed.), *The Wilde Legacy* (Dublin: Four Courts Press, 2003), pp. 17–34

Ní Chuilleanáin, Eiléan, *The Girl who Married the Reindeer* (Dublin: Gallery Press, 2001; Winston-Salem, NC: Wake Forest University Press, 2002)

Ní Chuilleanáin, Eiléan, 'Nuns: A Subject for a Woman Writer', in Patricia Boyle Haberstroh (ed.), *My Self, My Muse* (Syracuse, NY: Syracuse University Press, 2001), pp. 17–32

Ní Chuilleanáin, Eiléan, '*Cyphers*: Threescore and Ten', *Poetry Ireland News* (January/February 2001)

Ní Chuilleanáin, Eiléan, 'Strange ceremonies: sacred space and bodily presence in the English Reformation', in Amanda Piesse (ed.), *The Making of Sixteenth-Century Identity* (Manchester: Manchester University Press, 2000), pp. 133–54

Ní Chuilleanáin, Eiléan, 'Acts and monuments of an unelected nation: The *Cailleach* writes about the Renaissance', *The Southern Review*, vol. 31, no. 3 (1995), pp. 570–80

Ní Chuilleanáin, Eiléan, *The Brazen Serpent* (Dublin: Gallery Press, 1994; Winston-Salem, NC: Wake Forest University Press, 1995)

Ní Chuilleanáin, Eiléan, 'Borderlands of Irish Poetry', in Elmer Andrews (ed.), *Contemporary Irish Poetry: A Collection of Critical Essays* (Basingstoke: Macmillan, 1992), pp. 25–40

Ní Chuilleanáin, Eiléan, *The Magdalene Sermon and Earlier Poems* (Winston-Salem, NC: Wake Forest University Press, 1991)

Ní Chuilleanáin, Eiléan, *The Magdalene Sermon* (Co. Meath: Gallery Press, 1989)

Ní Chuilleanáin, Eiléan, 'The Debate Between Thomas More and William Tyndale, 1528–33: Ideas on Religion and Literature', *The Journal of Ecclesiastical History*, vol. 39, no. 3 (1988), pp. 382–411

Ní Chuilleanáin, Eiléan, *The Second Voyage* (Dublin: Gallery Press, 1986; Winston-Salem, NC: Wake Forest University Press, 1977; Revised Edition, Winston-Salem, NC: Wake Forest University Press, 1991)

Ní Chuilleanáin, Eiléan, 'Women as Writers: Dánta Grá to Maria Edgeworth', in Eiléan Ní Chuilleanáin (ed.), *Irish Women: Image and Achievement* (Dublin: Arlen House, 1985), pp. 111–26

Ní Chuilleanáin, Eiléan, 'Time, Place and the Congregation in Donne's Sermons', in John Scattergood (ed.), *Literature and Learning in Medieval and Renaissance England: Essays Presented to Fitzroy Pyle* (Dublin: Irish Academic Press, 1984), pp. 197–215

Ní Chuilleanáin, Eiléan, *The Rose Geranium* (Dublin: Gallery Press, 1981)

Ní Chuilleanáin, Eiléan, *Cork* (Dublin: Gallery Press, 1977)

Ní Chuilleanáin, Eiléan, *Site of Ambush* (Dublin: Gallery Press, 1975)

Ní Chuilleanáin, Eiléan, *Acts and Monuments* (Dublin: Gallery Press, 1972)

Ní Chuilleanáin, Eiléan, Cormac Ó Cuilleanáin and David Parris (eds), *Translation and Censorship: Patterns of Communication and Interference* (Dublin: Four Courts Press, 2009)

Ní Chuilleanáin, Eiléan, translation of Ileana Mălăncioiu's *After the Raising of Lazarus* (Cork: Southword Editions, 2005)

Ní Chuilleanáin, Eiléan, Cormac Ó Cuilleanáin and Gabriel Rosenstock, translation of Michele Ranchetti's *Verbale/Minutes/Tuairisc* (Dublin: Instituto Italiano di Cultura, 2002)

Ní Chuilleanáin, Eiléan and Medbh McGuckian, translation of Nuala Ní Dhomhnaill's *The Water Horse: Poems in Irish* (Co. Meath: Gallery Press, 1999)

Ní Chuilleanáin, Eiléan (ed.), *The Wilde Legacy* (Dublin: Four Courts Press, 2003)

Ní Chuilleanáin, Eiléan (ed.), Joseph Campbell, *As I Was Among the Captives: The Prison Diary of Joseph Campbell, 1922–23* (Cork: Cork University Press, 2001)

Ní Chuilleanáin, Eiléan (ed.), Maria Edgeworth, *Belinda* (London: Dent, 1993)

Ní Chuilleanáin, Eiléan and J.D. Pheifer (eds), *Noble and Joyous Histories: English Romances 1375–1650* (Dublin: Irish Academic Press, 1993)

Ní Chuilleanáin (ed.), *Irish Women: Image and Achievement* (Dublin: Arlen House, 1985)

Ní Dhomhnaill, Nuala, 'Tidal Surge (1909–1999)', in Pat Boran (ed.), *Flowing, Still: Irish Poets on Irish Poetry* (Dublin: The Dedalus Press, 2009), pp. 71–82

Ní Dhuibhne, Eilís, *Voices on the Wind: Women Poets of the Celtic Twilight* (Dublin: New Island Books, 1995)

Nolan, Emer, 'Postcolonial Literary Studies, Nationalism and Feminist Critique in Contemporary Ireland', *Éire-Ireland*, vol. 42, nos 1–2 (2007), pp. 336–61

Nordin, Irene Gilsenan, *Reading Eiléan Ní Chuilleanáin, A Contemporary Poet: The Element of the Spiritual* (Lampeter, UK and Lewiston, NY: The Edwin Mellen Press, 2008)

Nordin, Irene Gilsenan, 'Green Leaf of Language', *Irish University Review*, vol. 31, no. 2 (2001), pp. 420–30

Nordin, Irene Gilsenan, 'The Weight of Words: An Interview with Eiléan Ní Chuilleanáin', *Canadian Journal of Irish Studies*, vols 28–9, nos 1–2 (2002–3), pp. 73–83

Oates, Joyce Carol, 'When Wishing Was Having … Classic and Contemporary Fairy Tales', *The Kenyon Review*, vol. 19, nos 3–4 (1997), pp. 98–110

O'Brien, Peggy, *The Wake Forest Book of Irish Women's Poetry: 1967–2000* (Winston-Salem, NC: Wake Forest University Press, 1999; 2011)

O'Brien, Sean, '*The Sun-fish* by Eiléan Ní Chuilleanáin', *The Guardian*, 6 February 2010

O'Connor, Pat, *Emerging Voices: Women in Contemporary Irish Society* (Dublin: Institute of Public Administration, 1998)

Ó Crualaoich, Gearóid, *The Book of the Cailleach: Stories of the Wise Woman Healer* (Cork: Cork University Press, 2003)

Ó Crualaoich, Gearóid, 'Hags, Queens and Wise Women: Supernatural Females of the Irish Otherworld', RTÉ Radio 1 series.

O'Dowd, Mary, *A History of Women in Ireland* (London: Longmans, 2004)

Ó Giolláin, Diarmuid, *Locating Irish Folklore: Tradition, Modernity, Identity* (Cork: Cork University Press, 2000)

Ó Giolláin, Diarmuid, 'Revisiting Holy Wells', *Éire-Ireland*, vol. 40, nos 1–2 (2005), pp. 11–41

O'Malley, Aidan, '*Praeteritio*: (Non-) Possession and the Translational Impulse in Ní Chuilleanáin's Work', *Irish University Review*, vol. 37, no. 1 (2007), pp. 178–96

O'Toole, Shane, 'Ireland: Maurice Craig', *The Times*, 25 June 2006

Pearse, Patrick, 'Roisin Dubh', in Thomas Kinsella and Sean Ó Tuama (eds), *Duanaire, 1600–1900: Poems of the Dispossessed* (Dublin: Dolmen Press, 1981)

Pelan, Rebecca, 'Literally Loose Cannon or Loosening the Canon', in Helen Thompson (ed.), *The Current Debate about the Literary Canon: Essays Reassessing the Field Day Anthology of Irish Writing* (Lampeter, UK and Lewiston, NY: The Edward Mellen Press, 2006)

Pelan, Rebecca, *Two Irelands: Literary Feminisms North and South* (Syracuse, NY: Syracuse University Press, 2005)

Potts, Anthony and Tom O'Donoghue (eds), *Schools as Dangerous Places: A Historical Perspective* (Youngstown, NY: Cambria Press, 2007)

Plunkett, Geraldine, *All in the Blood*, ed. Honor Ó Brolcháin (Dublin: A&A Farmar, 2006)

Praga, Inés, 'Eiléan Ní Chuilleanáin', in Jacqueline Hurtley, Rosa Gonzáles, Inés Praga and Esther Aliaga (eds), *Ireland in Writing: Interviews with Writers and Academics* (Amsterdam: Rodopi, 1998), pp. 83–93

Quinn, Deirdre, Sharon Tishe-Mooney and Moynagh Sullivan, *Essays in Literary Criticism: Themes of Gender, Sexuality and Corporeality* (Lampeter, UK and Lewiston, NY: The Edwin Mellen Press, 2009)

Quinn, Justin, (ed.) *The Cambridge Introduction to Modern Irish Poetry* (Cambridge: Cambridge University Press, 2008)

Ranchetti, Michele, *Verbale/Minutes/Tuairisc*, trans. Eiléan Ní Chuilleanáin, Cormac Ó Cuilleanáin and Gabriel Rosenstock (Dublin: Instituto Italiano di Cultura, 2003)

Ray, Kevin, 'An Interview with Eiléan Ní Chuilleanáin', *Éire-Ireland*, vol. 31, nos 1–2 (1996), pp. 62–73

Report of the Commission to Inquire into Child Abuse (Dublin: Government Publications Office, 2009)

Ryan, Louise and Margaret Ward (eds), *Irish Women and Nationalism: Soldiers, New Women and Wicked Hags* (Dublin: Irish Academic Press, 2004)

Sailer, Susan Shaw (ed.), *Representing Ireland: Gender, Class, Nationality* (Gainesville, FL: University Press of Florida, 1997)

Sarbin, Deborah, '"Out of Myth Into History": The Poetry of Eavan Boland and Eiléan Ní Chuilleanáin', *The Canadian Journal of Irish Studies*, vol. 19, no. 1 (1993), pp. 86–96

Scattergood, John, *Literature and Learning in Medieval and Renaissance England: Essays Presented to Fitzroy Pyle* (Blackrock: Irish Academic Press, 1984)

Schaberg, Jane, *The Resurrection of Mary Magdalene* (New York: Continuum Publishing, 2002)

Simic, Charles, 'Notes on Poetry and History', *The Uncertain Certainty: Interviews, Essays and Notes on Poetry* (Ann Arbor, MI: University of Michigan Press, 1985), pp. 124–44

Sirr, Peter '"How things begin to happen": Notes on Eiléan Ní Chuilleanáin and Medbh McGuckian', *The Southern Review*, vol. 31, no. 1 (1995), pp. 450–67

Smith, James, *Ireland's Magdalene Laundries and the Nation's Architecture of Containment* (Notre Dame, IN: University of Notre Dame Press, 2007)

Smyth, Ailbhe, '"Staged Quaintness": Subalternity, Gender and Popular Identity', in Colin Graham (ed.), *Deconstructing Ireland: Identity, Theory, Culture* (Edinburgh: Edinburgh University Press, 2001)

Smyth, Ailbhe, *Wildish Things: An Anthology of New Irish Women's Writing* (Dublin: Attic Press, 1989)

Sullivan, Moynagh, 'Feminism, Postmodernism and the Subjects of Irish and Women's Studies', in P.J. Mathews (ed.), *New Voices in Irish Criticism* (Dublin: Four Courts Press, 2000) pp. 243–51

Sullivan, Moynagh, 'Raising the Veil: Myth and Melancholia in Irish Studies', in Patricia Coughlan and Tina O'Toole (eds), *Irish Literature: Feminist Perspectives* (Dublin: Carysfort Press, 2008), pp. 245–77

Thompson, Helen, *The Current Debate about the Irish Literary Canon* (Lampeter, UK and Lewiston, NY: Edwin Mellen Press, 2006)

Upton, Dell, *Architecture in the United States* (Oxford: Oxford University Press, 1998)

Valente, Joseph, 'The Myth of Sovereignty: Gender in the Literature of Irish Nationalism', *ELH*, vol. 61, no. 1 (1994), pp. 189–210

Valiulis, Maryann Gialanella and Mary O'Dowd (eds), *Women and Irish History* (Dublin: Wolfhound Press, 1997)

Vasari, Giorgio, *Lives of the Artists*, trans. Julia Conway Bondanella and Peter Bondanella (Oxford: Oxford University Press, 2007)

Villar-Argáiz, Pilar, '"The Text of It": A Conversation with Eavan Boland', *New Hibernia Review*, vol. 10, no. 2 (2006), pp. 52–67

Walshe, Éibhear (ed.), *Sex, Nation and Dissent* (Cork: Cork University Press, 1997)

Ward, Margaret, *Unmanageable Revolutionaries: Women and Irish Nationalism* (London: Pluto Press, 1983)

Ward, Margaret, *The Missing Sex: Putting Women into Irish History* (Dublin: Attic Press, 1991)

Warner, Marina, *Alone of All her Sex: The Myth and Cult of the Virgin Mary* (New York: Knopf, 1976)

Webster, Fiona, 'The Politics of Sex and Gender', *Hypatia*, vol. 15, no. 1 (2000), pp. 1–22

Williams, Leslie, '"The stone recalls its quarry": An Interview with Eiléan Ní Chuilleanáin', in Susan Shaw Sailer (ed.), *Representing Ireland: Gender, Class, Nationality* (Gainesville, FL: University Press of Florida, 1997), pp. 29–44

Wills, Clair, 'Nearer by Keeping Still', *New York Times Book Review*, vol. 25, no. 3 (1987), p. 1435

Wills, Clair, *Improprieties: Politics and Sexuality in Modern Irish Poetry* (Oxford: Oxford University Press, 1994)

Yeats, W.B. *W.B. Yeats: Collected Poems*, ed. Augustine Martin (London: Arena, 1990)

Zamorano Llena, Carmen, '(Re)membering the Disembodied Verse: Constructs of Identity in Irish Women's Poetry', in Merete Falck Borch and Anna Rutherford (eds), *Bodies and Voices: The Force Field of Representation and Discourse in Colonial and Postcolonial Studies* (Amsterdam and New York: Rodopi, 2008), pp. 349–62

Index